REALTORS' LIABILITY

Real Estate for Professional Practitioners

DAVID CLURMAN, Editor

CONDOMINIUMS AND COOPERATIVES
    by David Clurman and Eda L. Hebard

THE BUSINESS CONDOMINIUM
    by David Clurman

HOW TO PROFITABLY BUY AND SELL LAND
    by Rene A. Henry, Jr.

REAL ESTATE LIMITED PARTNERSHIPS
    by Theodore S. Lynn, Harry F. Goldberg,
    and Daniel S. Abrams

THE REAL ESTATE INVESTOR AND THE FEDERAL
INCOME TAX
    by Gaylon E. Greer

REALTORS' LIABILITY
    by Mark Lee Levine

REALTORS' LIABILITY

MARK LEE LEVINE
University of Denver
College of Business Administration

A RONALD PRESS PUBLICATION

JOHN WILEY & SONS

New York · Chichester · Brisbane · Toronto

52711

Library of Congress Cataloging in Publication Data:

Levine, Mark Lee.
   Realtors' liability.

   (Real estate for professional practitioners)
   Bibliography: p.
   Includes index.
   1. Real estate agents--Malpractice--United States.
2. Real estate business--Law and legislation--United
States. I. Title.
KF2042.R4L48   346'.73'033   79-4133
ISBN 0-471-05208-6

Series Preface

Since the end of World War II, tremendous changes have taken place in the business and residential real estate fields throughout the world. This has been evidenced not only by architectural changes, exemplified by the modern shopping center, but also in the many innovative financing responses that have enabled development of new structures and complexes, such as multiuse buildings. It can be expected that real estate development will speed in new directions at an ever increasing pace to match the oncoming needs of our time. With this perspective, the Real Estate for Professional Practitioners series has been developed in response to professional needs.

As real estate professional activities have become divided into specialties, because of intensive demand for expertise at all stages, so has there developed an increasing need for extensive training and continual education for persons directly involved or dealing in business ventures requiring detailed knowledge of realty procedures.

Perhaps no field of business endeavor is more in need of a series of professional books than real estate. Working in the practical world of business and residential construction and space utilization, or at advanced levels of college training covering these areas, one is constantly aware that too little of existing creative thinking has been transcribed into viable books. Many of the books that have been written do not thoroughly enough encompass both the practical and theoretical aspects of complex subjects. Too often the drive for immediate answers has led to the overlooking of fundamental purposes and technical know-how that might lead to much more favorable results for the persons seeking knowledge.

This series will be made up of books thoroughly and expertly expounding existing procedures in the many fields of real estate, but searching as well for innovative solutions to current and future problems. These books are intended to offer a compendium of each author's wide experience and knowledge to aid the seasoned professional.

The series is addressed to professionals in all walks of realty endeavor. These include business investors and developers, urban affairs specialists, attorneys, accountants, and the many others whose work involves real estate creativity and investment. Just as importantly, the series will present to advanced students in many realty fields the opportunity to review professional thinking that will help to stimulate their own thoughts on modern trends in housing and business construction.

We believe these goals can be achieved by the outstanding group of authors who will create the books in the series.

DAVID CLURMAN

Preface

Realtors Liability emphasizes the areas of exposure for practicing real estate professionals who, whether operating on large or small scale, must be aware of the increasing exposure they face. Not only is there general exposure through normal sales, but also in the related topics of tax, securities, statements, general business advice, and investment counseling.

The material provides a general introduction to each area and presents case histories and court decisions. You should analyze each problem and develop possible solutions for the issues.

Readers should also consider the areas that might provide insulation or protection to the practitioner. Solutions or alternatives to avoid or lessen your exposure is a primary goal.

This book takes a discussion approach to common questions of potential liability that face the practitioner in the real estate field. There is no attempt to make it a resarch-treatise. The number of treatises in this area is ample. There are many real estate law texts available. This is *not* one. This material highlights current cases and issues that give rise to liability. We can learn from the cases to attempt to lessen our exposure.

The text covers many areas of liability. It discusses such topics as the evolution of responsibility in general and regulating and policing the field. From the legal standpoint, it also touches on the developments in the field of litigation techniques, preparing for litigation, discovery, and other items in the litigation process.

Once again, the purpose of this material is to examine, in discussion format, and provide a forum for review of the current liability pitfalls facing the real estate practitioner.

Denver, Colorado　　　　　　　　　　　　　　　　MARK LEE LEVINE
March 1979

Acknowledgments

I acknowledge the support and impetus given by my law firm, Levine and Pitler, P.C., the research efforts of Gary Levine, Mark Rubin, and Jeff Wagner; the assistance and materials supplied by many professors, my colleagues at the University of Denver, many of the members of the National Association of Realtors (NAR) including their state and local boards, and various institutes under NAR, for example the Real Estate Securities and Syndication Institute, the Realtors National Marketing Institute, the Institute of Real Estate Management, and students: Mark, Steve, Walt, Seth, and Tom.

I also thank those who have participated, without being specifically named. The *Professional Liability Reporter,* on whose board I serve in an advisory capacity, has also been helpful in supplying various recent cases. For transcript support, other documentation, and mechanical work, I acknowledge the very kind support of my wife, Ellen, and our devoted secretaries which includes, but certainly is not limited to, the strong and extra efforts by Diane, Gino, Elaine, and Lynn.

To those I have not named specifically, I acknowledge that this work would not have been produced without their support in collecting the myriad cases that were forthcoming in this area. I strongly encourage and respect the input from readers in relation to this material so that we might expand the coverage and current cases that will continuously spring forth as this area ripens. Finally, I acknowledge the assistance of Kent Jay Levine, attorney, professor, broker, and brother. Kent aided in the collection of many of the cases herein.

M.L.L.

Contents

CHAPTER 4

CLOSINGS AND CONDITION OF THE PROPERTY

CHAPTER 5

OTHER LICENSES: INSURANCE, SECURITIES, OTHERS

CHAPTER 6

GOVERNMENTAL CONTROLS, DISCRIMINATION, INTERSTATE LAND SALES, F.H.A.

CHAPTER 7

UNAUTHORIZED PRACTICE OF LAW

CHAPTER 16

PREVENTIVE MEDICINE UPDATING YOUR KNOWLEDGE, STEPS TO PROTECT THE REALTOR   248

BIBLIOGRAPHY   251

APPENDIX   253

INDEX   263

REALTORS' LIABILITY

CHAPTER 1

Common Theories of Liability

This material covers the various areas of exposure that exist for the practicing Realtor. This is an expanding and developing area, in which there are often more questions than answers.

The material is to assist you in developing procedures you can follow to avoid or minimize exposure in these areas.

State law plays an important part in many of the court decisions included in the material. You should, therefore, be aware of particular problems in your state.

Many cases are included in the material which you can use as background and reference if you are unable to study them thoroughly at this time. The outcome of a case is based not only on questions of law but also on *key facts*. Most of the cases can be decided on the basis of the *facts* presented. Usually only a complete review and analysis of the case enables you to make this distinction.

Therefore, readers should be aware that the cases you are given have been edited by the author to restrict the issues to those related to the Realtor. (Asterisks * * * indicate omitted material.) Cases may often be reversed on appeal, new statutes may be passed, and other events may change the results of a case given herein. Consult your attorney. Do not rely on simply the cases herein.

TYPES OF EXPOSURE: CIVIL AND CRIMINAL

Fraud—Actual and Constructive. It is much more difficult to prove fraud than negligence. Fraud has the element of intent, or the holding out of a given material fact with the intent to have someone else reasonably rely on that fact. You must show that the injured plaintiff reasonably relied on the improper misrepresentation or fraudulent position, and that the plaintiff was injured as a result of that reasonable reliance.

Many cases overlap in the fraud and negligence fields. Rather than distinguish cases between fraud and/or negligence, the cases have been placed in the negligence section. You should note that many cases which raise negligence issues also raise a fraud allegation. Because of the heavier burden of proof in fraud, most successful plaintiffs find the Court awarding relief based on their position of the negligence action as opposed to fraud.

For more information on fraud as opposed to negligence see *Business and The Law,* by Mark Lee Levine, assisted by Kent Jay Levine, West Publishing Company (1976).

Negligence—An Explanation. Proving negligence is much easier than proving fraud. Negligence is not absolute. That is, the plaintiff must show that the defendant was negligent. Negligence generally means an act or omission which constitutes a failure to exercise reasonable care. The question is, what is reasonable care under the circumstances? Generally, the court defines a reasonable standard of care as "that which a reasonably prudent man would have exercised under similar circumstances."

Although the definition is of little help out of context, within standards assigned by the court, the standards of due care of a reasonably prudent man are assumed. Therefore, a party would be "negligent" if he failed to exercise this standard of due care.

To prove negligence, the plaintiff must establish the act or omission to act reasonably by the defendant. However, the defendant must be under a *duty* to exercise due care to the given plaintiff. This is important. Many cases have taken the position that there is no duty on the defendant to the plaintiff. For example, if the defendant, the Realtor, prepares statements for the client, and subsequently a third party, the plaintiff, relies on those statements when purchasing realty or in dealing with the client, does the defendant owe a duty *to that third party?* Historically, cases might indicate there is no connection between the defendant and the plaintiff regarding the financial statements. However, there has been a breakdown of the privity requirement (*i.e.,* some tie or relationship). The court today is inclined to hold that the Realtor should reasonably recognize that a third party may rely on the statements. Therefore, a direct connection or privity relationship is *not* necessary.

In addition to showing that an act or omission by the defendant and that there was a duty owing, the court requires the plaintiff to show that the defendant *breached* that duty. This again raises the question of what obligations the defendant undertook. There must be showing of what is reasonable—what would be the standard of care—and therefore a showing that the defendant acted less than reasonably and breached his duty.

The breach must be the (*proximate*) *cause* of the damage (injury) in question. Another way of saying this is: If the defendant can show that the plaintiff would have been damaged, even if the acts of the defendant had not been undertaken, the plaintiff's cause of action may fail. Keep in mind that the plaintiff has the burden to show proximate cause, a chain of events that shows the connection from the defendant's failure to perform his duty and the injury to the plaintiff as a result of that failure.

There is also the never-ending question of showing the *actual damage* (*e.g.*, dollars lost) suffered by the plaintiff as a result of the breach. (This may not be a major problem in accounting cases: the defendant might be liable for the investment lost by the plaintiff if the plaintiff can show the other elements mentioned.)

Negligence is a tort action (*i.e.*, a civil wrong, not arising from a contract action). Therefore, the contractual requirements for proving a breach of contract are technically not present. Obviously, a plaintiff may *also* argue that there was a breach of contract, if applicable, in addition to fraud or negligence.

Therefore, if the defendant is a Realtor, the standard of care for the "reasonable man" would be the standard of care for a reasonably prudent Realtor. Here it is important to review ethical standards and limitations, duties imposed by generally accepted principles in the industry, federal and state ethical considerations, and interpretative positions by cases.

To whom is the duty of due care owing? The court has decided a number of cases in this area which include a concept of "scope or zone of danger." That is, if it is reasonably anticipated that a third party may be damaged because he is reasonably in the "zone of danger," liability may be imposed. Therefore, if the Realtor prepares statements and the statements reasonably might be used by third parties, (*i.e.*, potential purchasers), it is argued that the plaintiff, the third party relying on those statements, is in the zone of danger.

Even if negligence is shown, there are arguments to contend that no liability is imposed on the Realtor. The Realtor may argue that there is *contributory negligence* by the plaintiff (plaintiff *too*, was careless) and therefore he, the plaintiff, is not entitled to damages. The plaintiff also must show he acted reasonably or that the damage would have occurred notwithstanding the actions of the plaintiff.

Some states, avoiding a complete barring of the action by a plaintiff who is guilty of contributory negligence, employ the doctrine of comparative negligence. In these jurisdictions, the jury or the court weighs the comparative or *relative* amounts of negligence committed by the plaintiff and the defendant. The *net* effect reduces the plaintiff's recovery by an amount equal to the negligence of the plaintiff relative to that of the defendant. Therefore, in simplified form, if it was shown that the defendant was negligent but the plaintiff also contributed to the negligence, a jury may hold that the plaintiff was 20 percent negligent. Then, of the damages determined, the plaintiff should be awarded only 80 percent of the total amount, as opposed to 100 percent. Obviously, it is difficult to determine this percentage. However, this is a better treatment than an all-or-nothing position as utilized in many jurisdictions.

The following cases illustrate various circumstances in which negligence might be argued. These include cases dealing with disclosure, nondisclosure, defective conditions, and other acts argued to constitute negligence by the Realtor, and those where a third party relies on the Realtor.

PRIVITY AND THE COMMON LAW

There has been an historical requirement of privity between the parties involved in order to assert that responsibility is owing by the Realtor to a third party. The question that has arisen in many of the cases, is whether privity or some relationship must exist between the Realtor and some injured third party, for example, the party who relied on statements furnished by the Realtor.

Some courts have been hesitant to extend the Realtor's responsibility to some third parties. This position was announced by Justice Cardoza in the Ultramares case, 174 NE 441 (1934), dealing with CPAs. However, as discussed in the case, liability was imposed where there was gross negligence which was *equated to be fraud*. The standard of Ultramares has been relaxed, if not eliminated, by subsequent decisions, as the cases indicate. The net effect is the "privity requirement" is all but eliminated by subsequent decisions which enforce a general scope of reasonableness or scope of foreseeability wherein the Realtor should recognize that his actions may well be relied on by some third party and therefore liability should be extended in those circumstances. For more on this subject, see Prosser, "Misrepresentation and Third Persons," 19 Vand. L. Rev. 231 (1966).

CHAPTER 2

Negligence, Misrepresentation, and Fraud

NEGLIGENCE

Zwick owned a ranch in Minnesota. He listed it for sale with the broker, United. Subsequently potential buyers, Gregg and Bartz, inquired about the property. An offer was made, and it was further agreed that, as an expression of good faith, the buyers would temporarily convey title to a trailer park. This was to be, in effect, an earnest deposit, and the trailer park was allegedly valued at approximately $175,000.00. Subsequent information revealed by the broker determined that the value of the property as earnest money was substantially less. It turns out that the potential purchasers had very little assets. There were a number of other activities relative to showing the credit of the purchasers.

Without going into the details of the potential case, what exposure might a real estate broker have with regard to the ability of a purchaser to consummate the transaction? For the details of the potential breach, see *Zwick v. United Farm Agency,* a 1976 Supreme Court of Wyoming case.

Dwight ZWICK (Defendant, Cross-claimant and Third-party Plaintiff below), and Zwick Ranch, Inc., a Minnesota Corportation (Third-party Plaintiff by Joinder below), Appellants,

v.

UNITED FARM AGENCY, INC., a Minnesota Corporation * * * * * * Appellee.

Supreme Court of Wyoming.

* * * 1976.

* * *

ROSE, Justice.

FACTS

Appellants-third-party plaintiffs, Dwight Zwick and Zwick Ranch, Inc., filed their amended complaint in the District Court in and for Campbell County, Wyoming, on the 26th day of September, 1974, against United Farm Agency, Inc., appellee-third-party defendant, a real estate broker, in which Zwick and Zwick Ranch, Inc., claimed damages for negligence and misrepresentation of facts. While numerous parties were involved in the suit below, only Zwick and United are interested in this appeal.

Zwick owned a ranch in Minnesota and in February, 1966, listed it for sale with real estate broker, United, at its Erskine, Minnesota office operated by Jerry and Hazel Bernard. On Friday, April 15, 1966, potential buyers Gregg and Bartz made telephone contact with United about Zwick's ranch and came to Erskine the next day, Saturday, April 16th, to inspect it. On the last mentioned day Gregg and Bartz were introduced to Zwick and expressed an interest in acquiring the property for a corporation which was identified as Acoma West, Inc.

On Sunday, the 17th of April, the Bernards called V. R. Gillingham, the district manager of United, to aid in consummating the transaction, whereupon Gillingham came to Erskine that afternoon and the deal was finalized through execution of a "Deposit Receipt and Agreement for Sale" showing Acoma West, Inc., to be the purchaser—Dwight Zwick the seller— and the purchase price to be $600,000.00. No payment was made on April 17, but $175,000.00 was to be paid on the purchase price on June 15, 1966, it being agreed the transaction would be closed on that date, or sooner if title was found to be satisfactory.

It was further agreed:

"As expression of good faith, the buyers shall temporarily convey title to a certain trailer park located in Gillette, Wyoming into trust, to be deeded back upon completion of the terms of the contract."

The trailer park referred to was the "Westward Ho" located at Gillette, Wyoming and owned by Gregg, who was to convey it to Zwick in return for Acoma stock. Bartz was to furnish the $175,000.00 down payment and the Westward Ho deed was to be held in trust by United, to be released to Zwick if the deal was not consummated but returned to the grantor if it was.

Gregg testified that upon signing the agreement on April 17, 1966, he executed a warranty deed to Acoma for the Westward Ho property, depositing it in the custody of Beal, attorney for Acoma. This instrument was never recorded and was subsequently returned to the possession of Gregg, who, in December, 1966, caused to be recorded a deed conveying the Westward Ho to Nellie B. Gregg, with Gregg shown therein as the grantor. On April 29, 1966, Bernards of United received a deed from Acoma to United for Westward Ho, dated April 20, 1966, which was recorded in Campbell County on June 9, 1966. At the time when the Acoma deed was executed, delivered and recorded, Acoma did not have record title to the property since the aforementioned deed from Gregg to Acoma was never recorded and was returned to Gregg, the grantor.

United, through Bernards, wrote Zwick on April 30, 1966, informing him that United had received the Westward Ho deed, showing Acoma as grantor and United as grantee and acknowledging that Bernard understood the agreement to have been that the conveyance was to have transferred Westward Ho from Gregg to Zwick, with United holding the deed in trust subject to the applicable terms of the Deposit Receipt and Agreement of Sale. The Bernards, in the same letter, said they planned to call the Gillette bank holding the mortgage on Westward Ho and inquire about the title.

The evidence showed the call revealed the Westward Ho appraised value to be $38,000.00, with a first mortgage in the amount of $12,000.00 and a second mortgage in the amount of $1,000.00. The bank represented to Bernards that Gregg was basically honest. This information was timely conveyed to Zwick.

United ordered a Dun and Bradstreet report on Gregg, Bartz and Acoma. The response, dated April 27, 1966, and other reports obtained about this time were generally negative, which information was, upon receipt, immediately conveyed to Zwick in May, 1966. Soon afterward Bartz vanished, inquiry revealing him to be totally without assets; in May of 1966 Gregg advised that Acoma could not perform its obligations.

In June of 1966, Gregg became associated with one Billy Joe Griffith, and together they attempted to renegotiate the purchase of Zwick's ranch. A written offer was made which included a tendered deed to the Westward Ho property. At this time United was holding the Acoma deed to Westward Ho in trust for Zwick, but Gregg's original unrecorded deed of Westward Ho to Acoma had, by then, been returned to him. Zwick did not, however, execute a contract with Gregg and Griffith for the sale and purchase of the ranch property and, in January, 1967, Zwick sold the ranch to others. Zwick and Gregg thereupon asked United for a conveyance of the Westward Ho property and in 1968 United did execute a quitclaim deed which purported to quit claim any interest it may have had in the Westward Ho to Zwick. This deed was recorded in Campbell County January 31, 1968.

ISSUES ON APPEAL

The issue framed by appellants' brief is:

Did United Farm Agency breach its fiduciary duty to its principals, Dwight Zwick and Zwick Ranch, Inc. for which damages should be awarded?

* * *

HOLDING

We hold that there was no negligence and no breach of United's alleged fiduciary duty to Zwick and therefore affirm the Trial Court. * * *

In pursuit of its fiduciary-trust theory, appellants Zwick charge United with these kinds of breaches:

The broker did not determine the buyer's ability to pay.

The broker misrepresented the value of the Westward Ho Motel and misrepresented whether it was encumbered.

The broker's agent prepared the contract and acting as a lawyer failed to furnish the principal with adequate legal protection.

The broker failed to disclose the failure of the contract between Acoma and Zwick and to timely disclose the fact of default.

The broker failed to divest itself of the trust asset—the deed to Westward Ho—at a time when such divestiture would have been of value.

The relationship extant between United and Zwick at all times material here was that of broker and principal. A broker is an agent of his principal, which relationship we have defined as one of representation by one for another in contractual negotiations or transactions akin thereto.

Essentially, the duties and obligations owed by a broker to his employer are the same as those owed by any agent to his principal. It is the broker's duty to exercise ordinary care under the circumstances. A broker is obligated to make full, fair and prompt disclosure to his principal of all the facts within his knowledge which are or might be material to the purpose of the agency. The broker is bound to the highest degree of good faith. In fact he usually acts as a fiduciary. We have observed that, while a broker as a trustee must act in good faith, the trustee's good faith obligation to his cestui que trust may be greater than that a broker owes to his principal, absence a trust relationship. Included within these duties and obligations is the duty to transmit offers to the principal, as well as the duty to disclose the purchaser's financial condition if the broker has this knowledge.

The broker is not, however, liable for alleged duties not performed which are not within the contemplation of the contract, and he has no obligation to his principal by reason of the nonperformance of the contract by the other party. He is not liable for a mere mistake in judgment which does not result from a failure to know or do that which a person of ordinary prudence under similar circumstances would know or do.

With these concepts as our backdrop, we resolve the contentions of this appeal as follows:

The Trial Court found by its judgment, which was general in nature, that United timely disclosed to its principal, Zwick, all facts it had with respect to ownership and title to the trailer court, the manner by which it would be conveyed and held in trust, its encumbrance, and its value. As soon as reasonably possible, inquiry and disclosure were made and given relative to the financial condition of Acoma, Gregg and Bartz. While the facts were in controversy concerning these disclosures and inquires, the Trial Court made a general finding in favor of United and it must therefore be presumed that all controverted issues of fact were resolved in favor of the appellee. * * *

Not only was Zwick on notice that there had been no investigation of the buyers before the signing of the contract, but the law permits the broker to assume that a prospective buyer is both truthful and candid unless he has notice or knowledge to the contrary. Zwick elected to sign the sales agreement with full knowledge that a thorough investigation had not been made. This decision cannot now be translated as United's negligence.

In the absence of proof of damages, the acceptance of a worthless deed as a good faith earnest tender does not constitute grounds for Zwick's recovery, especially where United revealed all it knew about the transactions to Zwick and at no time acted in bad faith or beyond the scope of authority. Where a purchaser was financially irresponsible and a real estate agent accepted a worthless note as an earnest tender, the Minnesota Supreme Court held that, absent a damage showing, the vendor could not recover the amount of the earnest money from the agent even if the agent had been negligent or had acted in bad faith. Zwick's claim for recovery from United is even weaker.

No damages flowed from United's failure to earlier convey Westward Ho to Zwick. This is so because neither United nor Acoma had title to Westward Ho after Acoma redelivered the unrecorded deed to Gregg and in which deed Gregg as grantor had conveyed the Westward Ho properties to Acoma instead of Zwick as the agreement called for.

Whether or not a broker who draws a contract under conditions where he can be thought about as practicing law and thus held to an attorney's strict standards of excellence need not be specifically discussed because the record in this appeal does not show that Zwick was misled by the contract, that he did not understand it, or that he was left unprotected by it in any manner concerning which United had any obligation to protect him. Zwick's damages did not flow from the manner in which the contract was drafted.

For the reasons stated herein and under the authorities cited, the Trial Court is affirmed.

Although the case of Mattieligh raises the issue of commission, it is worthwhile to note the language of the court where the commission can certainly be denied if "the negligence, ignorance, stupidity, incompetence or fraud of a real estate broker causes the rescission of a sale negotiated by him. . . :"

MATTIELIGH v. POE
Supreme Court of Washington, 1960.
356 P.2d 328

* * *

FOSTER, Judge.

Plaintiff below appeals from a judgment of dismissal. Appellant sued to recover a real estate broker's commission paid to respondent Poe. At the conclusion of appellant's evidence, the court orally granted respondent's motion to dismiss "on the ground that the evidence produced by the plaintiff was not sufficient to sustain his cause of action," and the judgment recites that plaintiff's case was dismissed because of the insufficiency of his evidence. * * *

So circumstanced, the appellant's evidence must be considered in the light most favorable to him; that is to say, his evidence must be accepted at its face value. He is entitled to every reasonable inference to be drawn therefrom. * * *

Appellant is an elderly foreign-born farmer, for many years employed as a garbage collector. He is unschooled, and has a very limited ability to read, write or speak the English language.

Respondent is a licensed real estate broker.

The appellant does not claim fraud; indeed, he specifically disclaims it. The appellant, in effect, charges malpractice by the respondent broker in the practice of his profession. * * *

The appellant's proof was that the contract prepared by respondent was at variance in many particulars with his instructions. When a broker undertakes to practice law, he is liable for negligence. It is immaterial whether the broker's attempt to prepare a contract, such as had been authorized by his client, failed because of his ignorance, stupidity, incompetence, negligence or fraud. * * *

Upon discovery of such variance in the contract, appellant sued for a modification to conform with the terms to which he had agreed. The result was an agreed rescission of the sale. * * *

If a real estate broker fails to exercise reasonable care and skill, he is liable to his client for the damages resulting from such failure. * * *

If the negligence, ignorance, stupidity, incompetence or fraud of a real estate broker causes the rescission of a sale negotiated by him, one of the items of the principal's damage is the commission paid. * * *

The appellant made a prima facie case against his broker, the respondent. Consequently, respondent's challenge to the sufficiency of appellant's evidence should have been denied, and the complaint should not have been dismissed.

The judgment is reversed and a new trial granted.

MISREPRESENTATION AND FRAUD

Recently the plaintiff in question purchased the Autrey Plaza Building from Johnston. Subsequently, latent defects that existed in the heating and cooling system from the time of its construction were discovered by the plaintiff. Defendants had previously managed the building which was owned by Johnston. The defendants had knowledge of a continuing problem with the heating and air-conditioning system of the building. The defendants did not communicate this defect to the plaintiff. Defendants represented to the plaintiff that there was no problem or inadequacy in the heating and air-conditioning system at the time of purchase.

The issue in the particular case is whether the defendants would be responsible for the expenses incurred by the plaintiff in correcting the deficiencies in the heating and cooling system of the building, which deficiencies amounted to $37,249.

What would the potential exposure to the real estate company be, even though the seller also knew of the defects in question. What would have been the obvious solution to this problem so far as the real estate company was concerned?

---

89 N.M. 145
Ed NEFF, Trustee, Plaintiff-Appellee-Cross-Appellant,
v.
BUD LEWIS COMPANY, Bud Lewis, and Loren Gibson,
defendants-Appellants, Cross-Appellees,
* * *

Court of Appeals of New Mexico
March 9, 1976.
Rehearing denied March 18, 1976.

* * *

OPINION

SUTIN, Judge.

Plaintiff sued defendants, real estate broker and salesmen, claiming damages for misrepresentation of material facts, and for defendants' failure to disclose facts, regarding defects in the heating and cooling system of a building purchased by plaintiff. Defendant Bud Lewis Company counterclaimed against plaintiff for brokerage and lease commissions.

Defendants appeal from an adverse judgment in favor of plaintiff, and plaintiff appeals from an adverse judgment in favor of Bud Lewis Company.

A.   Findings of Fact and Judgments

The Trial Court found:

On August 1, 1970, plaintiff purchased the Autrey Plaza Building from Johnston * * * A fiduciary relationship existed between plaintiff and defendants. Latent defects existed in the heating and cooling system from the time of construction of the building. Prior to plaintiff's purchase, defendants had managed the building for Johnston and had knowledge of continuing problems with the heating and air conditioning system of the building. They failed to communicate them to the plaintiff and concealed the facts when inquiry was made by plaintiff. Defendants represented to plaintiff that there was no problem or inadequacy in the heating and air conditioning system at the time of purchase and that all problems had been resolved. The lower Court held that plaintiff relied on defendants' representations and was damaged.

Plaintiff was required to expend the sum of $37,249.80 to correct the deficiencies in the heating and cooling system of the building.

Plaintiff owes defendant $3,070.08 plus interest from August 1, 1972, at 6%, for a real estate commission. Plaintiff owed defendants $7,246.44 for a lease commission as of April 1, 1975, and further payments that come due and payable under the terms of a lease commission agreement. The Trial Court found that defendant Bud Lewis Company was entitled to an offset of the two commissions against plaintiff's judgment.

Judgment was entered for plaintiff in the sum of $25,732.89 plus costs and interest at 6% per annum from April 1, 1975, until paid.

B.   Plaintiff's Case

1.   Evidence in support of Court's findings on plaintiff's case.

Prior to the purchase of the Autrey Plaza Building by plaintiff, Bud Lewis managed the building for Johnston. He had recommended to Johnston that about $10,000.00 be expended to repair the heating and cooling system and this was done. It was a revamp of the first and second floor system. This problem was inherent in the construction of the building. After this expenditure, Johnston continued to have problems with the heating and cooling system. Three other additional expenditures were incurred. Defendants were also acquainted with numerous complaints by tenants of the building. However, defendants assured plaintiff that the condition of the building was excellent, that it was well constructed and functioning well, and that the heating and cooling system had been checked; that there was no problem with the inadequacy of the system and that all problems had been resolved.

The building was purchased August 1, 1970. Thereafter, Bud Lewis Company managed the building for plaintiff. In December, 1971, the Bud

Lewis Company told plaintiff of numerous complaints. At a conference plaintiff was told, for the first time, that the whole heating system was defective.

Plaintiff engaged Bridgers and Paxton Consulting Engineers to make a study of the problem and report. After the study and report were presented, the construction firm of Corzine and Rapp performed the work.

2. Defendants failed to disclose all material facts.

First, defendants contend that they did not fail to disclose to plaintiff any material facts. We disagree. There was a conflict in the evidence.

Defendants rely primarily upon a letter dated June 10, 1970, from Johnson Service Company to defendant Gibson. This letter was attached to the exchange contract of the same date between plaintiff and Johnston under which contract plaintiff agreed to acquire the Autrey Plaza Building, and was reviewed by plaintiff and his attorney. It briefly explained some of the problems the Johnson Service Company had with the Aarkla-Servel heating and cooling units which served this building.

The Trial Court considered this evidence in arriving at its decision. The Court also found that this letter did not disclose all material facts within the knowledge of defendants, facts upon which plaintiff relied. Despite the problems set out in the Johnson letter of June 10, 1970, defendants represented that, at the time plaintiff purchased the property, all of the problems had been resolved.

The Trial Court's belief, based on substantial evidence presented below, that defendants failed to disclose all the material facts within their knowledge, foreclosed defendants' position on appeal. "A broker is a fiduciary, holding a position of great trust and confidence, and is required to exercise the utmost good faith toward his principal throughout the entire transaction. . . . (A) real estate broker is under a legal obligation to make a full, fair and prompt disclosure to his employer of all facts within his knowledge which are or may be material, or which might affect his principal's rights and interest or influence his action relative to the disposition of the property." * * *

Defendants failed to comply with this rule. They failed to disclose all material facts.

3. Plaintiff relied on defendants' statements.

Second, defendants contend that plaintiff did not rely on the statements of defendants, but made an independent investigation prior to purchase. Defendants rely on the testimony of their own witnesses to establish this independent investigation. Our duty is to view the evidence most favorable to plaintiff. In doing so, we affirm the Trial Court on the point that plaintiff relied upon the statements of defendants.

4. Contributory negligence of plaintiff is not an issue.

Third, in its conclusion of law No. 14, the Court recited that its decision was based upon the "negligent omission and breach of duty on the part of defendants to make full disclosure to plaintiff of inadequacies in the heating and cooling system of the Autrey Plaza Building." Defendants contend that if the appellants were guilty of negligence, plaintiff was guilty of contributory negligence which was a proximate cause of plaintiff's damage. We disagree.

* * *

Justifiable reliance by plaintiff is the issue, and we must agree with the Trial Court that plaintiff had a right to rely on the defendants' respresentations that the Autrey Plaza Building was in excellent condition and that all problems with the heating and cooling system had been resolved.

We hold that contributory negligence is not a defense. The doctrine of negligent misrepresentation did not afford the defendants a defense of contributory negligence.

5.   Damages were proved by the evidence.

Fourth, defendants contend that no damage has been proven by the evidence. This point is without merit.

Plaintiff's judgment is affirmed.

C.   Defendant Bud Lewis Company's Counterclaim.

1.   Defendant Bud Lewis Company was not entitled to payment of commission on real estate transaction.

On July 30, 1970, Bud Lewis Company and plaintiff entered into an agreement for the payment of a commission to this defendant for the consummation of the transaction between plaintiff and Johnston. The amount of the commission was $5,116.80, payable in semi-annual installments of $511.68 at 6% interest. Plaintiff paid four installments of principal and interest up to and including August 1, 1972.

* * *

Bud Lewis Company profited by plaintiff's prior payments on the commission, which plaintiff did not seek to recover. Under the constructive trust doctrine, it would be unjust enrichment for defendant to be allowed an additional profit of principal and interest in the sum of $3,545.93 awarded Bud Lewis Company by the Trial Court. This part of the judgment for defendant Bud Lewis Company is reversed.

2.   Defendant Bud Lewis Company was entitled to commission on lease agreements.

Johnston and plaintiff entered into an agreement called "Assignment and Assumption." Johnston assigned lease to plaintiff subject to the commission agreements in which Bud Lewis Company was broker. The commission agreements provided Bud Lewis Company with a real estate lease commission for the consummation of leases for tenants obtained in the Autrey Plaza Building, and an additional commission for any renewals or extensions of the leases. The terms of each lease varied.

Bud Lewis Company commissions, earned for leases obtained, did not fall within the constructive trust doctrine. Judgment is affirmed for Bud Lewis Company in the sum of $7,264.44 as of April 1, 1975, and for further payments that come due and payable under the terms of the lease agreements.

D. Conclusion

Judgment for plaintiff in the sum of $37,249.80 is affirmed. The offset for Bud Lewis Company is the sum of $3,545.93 and interest is reversed. The offset for Bud Lewis in the sum of $7,264.44 and further payments due and payable is affirmed.

It is so ordered.

What is the exposure to a real estate broker who represents that a given property can be utilized for apartment purposes when in fact a variance has not been obtained and the property is only subject to single-family use? This issue is raised in the Nelson case, where it is argued that a purchaser acquired the property with the intent to use it for an apartment use. This type of use was implied by the broker, but subsequently the multiple use for an apartment building was denied.

Would the real estate broker have additional exposure in the sense of losing his real estate license or for representing the facts indicated?

NELSON v. REAL ESTATE COMMISSION
Court of Special Appeals of Maryland, 1977.
370 A.2d 608

* * *

GILBERT, Chief Judge.

Having been unsuccessful in defending himself on charges brought before the Real Estate Commission for the State of Maryland and in the subsequent appeal to the Circuit Court * * * Morris E. Nelson now by way of motion challenges for the first time the jurisdiction of the Commission and the court. * * *

We shall now set the scene from which this controversy arose.

John Meridith Tayler, an English and Canadian lawyer, on June 6, 1971, read an advertisement in the Washington Post. The ad read as follows:

"Apt.—4 units in heart of Riverdale. Older type. Excel. potential. Assume $21,000 loan. Asking $29,500. Owner leaving area. Prin. call 772-0033."

Mr. Tayler responded to the ad by telephoning the listed number and spoke with the appellant, Nelson, who identified himself as a real estate broker. Nelson provided Tayler with particulars concerning the property.

Tayler met with Nelson and inspected the apartments which were located at 4409 Queensbury Road, Riverdale, Maryland. Tayler testified before the Commission that Nelson, in reply to a question by Tayler, stated that the property was licensed for apartment usage. Nelson produced a temporary certificate from the Prince George's County Department of Inspections and Permits. Nelson informed Tayler that a permanent certificate would be forthcoming when certain necessary repairs to the property were completed. Tayler verified the information received from Nelson with an unnamed individual employee of the Department of Inspections and Permits. Tayler then entered into a contract to purchase the property. At the time Nelson signed the contract as "contract owner," title to the property was in one Rogeis, who apparently was a straw party.

Immediately prior to settlement, which occurred within a few days of the execution of the contract of sale, Tayler requested Nelson to give written assurance that a license would be issued when the necessary repairs to the property were completed. Nelson penned upon the reverse side of the contract of sale, "Notwithstanding anything in the contract, subject property described herein is sold as a bona fide apartment house." Both Nelson and Tayler subscribed their respective names under the sentence that Nelson had written. Tayler proceeded to settlement and executed a deed of trust note in the amount of $8,750 in favor of Nelson. The record is not clear as to whether Tayler assumed the outstanding $21,000 obligation then existing upon the property.

Sometime later, Tayler received a letter from the appropriate authorities requesting that he apply for an apartment house license. The letter was prompted by a complaint filed by a neighbor or tenant. * * * In investigating the complaint, the Department learned of the transfer of the ownership of 4409 Queensbury Road. Tayler applied for the license, but it was denied on the ground that the property was in a single family residential zoning area. Efforts by Tayler to show a non-conforming use to obtain rezoning failed. We do observe that Tayler, in his application for a use permit, sought five (5) apartments. Being unable to utilize the property for four apartments, Tayler lost the property at foreclosure. He filed a complaint with the Real Estate Commission against Nelson. * * *

The Commission found that Nelson had willfully misrepresented the property that he sold to Tayler, and it, on December 26, 1975, revoked Nelson's license, ordered his salesmen's licenses surrendered, cancelled his real estate listings, and directed Nelson to ". . . cease and desist from the practice of real estate. . . ."

As we have indicated, Nelson now challenges the jurisdiction of the Commission in the first instance. Nelson contends that the Commission records, as introduced into evidence at the hearing, disclose that Nelson was not a licensed broker during the period "November 1, 1970 to November 1, 1971," the time frame "within which the alleged misconduct occurred." Ergo, Nelson reasons, inasmuch as he was not licensed at that time, he and any acts committed by him with respect to Tayler were outside the ambit of the Commission's jurisdiction.

Nelson also contends that he was selling his own property and not acting as a broker. * * *

We think Nelson's argument must fail because Md.Ann. Code * * * provides in pertinent part that the Commission may investigate ". . . the actions of any real estate broker or real estate salesman, or *any person* who shall assume to act in either such capacity within this State. . . ." (Emphasis supplied.) The statute specifically confers jurisdiction upon the Commission to investigate not only real estate brokers and salesmen but also those who "assume to act" as brokers or salesmen. In the case sub-judice, the uncontradicted testimony was that Nelson held himself out to Tayler as a real estate broker, thus thrusting himself clearly within the Commission's jurisdiction.

* * * We think it would be seriocomic to construe § 224(a) so as to allow the Real Estate Commission to call to task those brokers who violated the Commission's precepts while acting as brokers and at the same time carve from the Commission's jurisdiction the very same violations, committed by the identical broker, in a nonbroker capacity. In the former instance, the broker might be branded as unethical but in the latter, even though the broker committed the same violation, he would retain, officially, his good character. * * *

I

The proceedings before the Commission had as its objective the protection of the public from "sharp" practices of real estate brokers. Just as members of the bar are subject to disciplinary proceedings for professional misconduct, even though not strictly related to the practice of law, so are real estate brokers.

* * *

We are unable to perceive any difference between protecting the public from unscrupulous practices by an attorney and the same type of practice by a real estate broker.

* * *

Finally, Nelson asserts that the evidence before the Commission did not support a finding of "willful misrepresentation." Based on the evidence submitted to it, the Commission held the following, which we quote with minor editing:

> "In order to sustain a charge under Section 224 (b), the State must prove two facts:
> 1. Any statements the licensee made to the complainant were false, and
> 2. At the time the licensee made such statements, he knew them to be false.

. . . (As to the) first fact, the State produced a newspaper advertisement for the property in question. The ad was listed under 'Investment Property' and stated 'APTA.—4 units.' The State also produced the contract of sale, on the back of which . . . (Nelson) wrote that the property was a 'bona fide apartment house.' From the testimony of . . . Mr. Taylor (sic), the Commission finds that . . . (Nelson) never mentioned to him that there was any type of zoning problem. In fact, . . . (Nelson) told Mr. Taylor (sic) that he—Taylor (sic)— could have obtained the requisite license by making certain repairs.

Nowhere , however, does it appear that . . . (Nelson) made any flat statement to the effect that there were no zoning problems.

. . . (T)he question the Commission must first determine is whether these statements and writings of . . . (Nelson) are false representations. The Commission finds that the ad, the statement on the back of the contract, and . . . (Nelson's) statement about the availability of a license clearly implied that there were no zoning problems affecting the usage of the structure as a four-unit apartment building. Because of this implication which the Commission finds so clear, in the absence of any disclaimer by . . . (Nelson), the Commission concludes that . . . (Nelson's) ad, writing on the contract, and statement about the license are false by implying the existance (sic) of no problem when in fact there was clearly a substantial problem.

. . . As to the second fact—knowledge of . . . (Nelson) at the time— the State presented an affidavit of . . . (Nelson), which affidavit was dated March 4, 1975. Paragraphs 5 and 8 thereof indicate that, at the time the contract was signed, . . . (Nelson) knew that there was a problem with the zoning of the property and that, in 1970, a license had been denied because of it.

. . . This is confirmed by . . . (Nelson's) letter of October 8, 1975.

. . . The affidavit of Doug M. Smiley dated March 29, 1975 also confirms that . . . (Nelson) knew at the time of contract that the property did not have the requisite zoning for a four-unit apartment house.

. . . (Nelson) claims that the 1970 zoning decision was erroneous or a clerical error and that the apartments were a legal, non-conforming use. . . . (Nelson) bases this upon his allegation that a Use and Occupancy permit #5160U was issued in 1961. The County's records are . . . unclear, but fail to substantiate that a permit was indeed issued in 1961. The obvious zoning violation and the fact that there is no record of a previous application for a non-conforming use indicate that the permit was never issued."

* * * We believe there was ample evidence for the Commission to find, as it did, that Nelson willfully misrepresented the zoning situation to Tayler and knew at the time that he was so doing. Judge Mathias, in our view, properly upheld the findings of the Commission.

MOTION FOR ORDER AS TO JURISDICTION DENIED. ORDER
AFFIRMED.

RICE v. HILTY
Colorado Court of Appeals, 1976.
559 P.2d 725
Certiorari Denied Feb. 7, 1977.

* * *

KELLY, Judge.

The defendants, Robert and Ruby Hilty, appeal from the judgment of
the trial court awarding damages to plaintiffs, George and Barbara Rice,
for the defendants' fraud in the sale of a motel. The Hiltys argue that the
representation relied upon by the plaintiffs was not actionable, and further, that no competent evidence of damages was presented. The Rices
cross-appeal the amount of damages. We affirm the judgment as to the
Hiltys' liability, and remand the case for further proceedings on the
amount of recovery to which the plaintiffs are entitled.

* * * The Rices' complaint alleged that they relied upon the Hiltys'
representation that the annual gross income of the motel was over $50,000
per year. The Hiltys contend, however, that the plaintiffs merely relied
upon "assurances" by Mr. Hilty that the motel was making adequate
money for the Hiltys, and would make adequate money for the Rices. The
trial court found, among other things, that the Hiltys did make the representation to the Rices concerning the amount of annual gross income of
the motel, that the representation was false and that the Rices relied upon
that misrepresentation. The evidence, when viewed as a whole, supports
these findings, and they are, therefore, binding on review. * * *

The Hiltys further contend that the trial court erroneously failed to apply the benefit-of-the-bargain rule of damages applicable in fraud cases,
and that, because no evidence consistent with that rule was presented, the
Rices were not entitled to any recovery. While we agree that the benefit-of-
the-bargain rule is ordinarily appropriate in fraud cases, see *Otis & Co.* v.
Grimes, 97 Colo. 219, 48 P.2d 788, (1935), there are additional factors in
this case making different principles of recovery applicable.

As the trial court noted in its findings, under the parties' agreement,
the motel was not conveyed to the Rices. Rather, the parties had signed a
contract for sale under which the Hiltys were to deliver to the Rices a
deed to the property when the unpaid balance of a promissory note given
in partial payment for the motel had been reduced to a specific amount.
The trial court also found that, sometime during the pendency of the action, the Rices had surrendered possession of the motel to the Hiltys, who
then resold the property by exchange. This finding is uncontroverted. It is
thus apparent that rescission of the contract was effected by the actions of
the parties. * * *

The trial court apparently considering the effect of this rescission by the parties, ruled that the correct measure of damages was the actual loss suffered by the defrauded plaintiffs, and awarded them the $15,000 they had paid at the time of the execution of the contract, and the $4,000 credit given to them for property which they had conveyed to the Hiltys. Although the trial court found that the plaintiffs had paid a total of $32,908 in payments on the promissory note, the court declined to award plaintiffs any of those sums because of the insufficiency of the evidence of the plaintiffs' net income from the property during the period of their possession.

* * * Although the Rices originally sought damages in an action at law, equitable relief is not precluded where a change in circumstances alters the posture of the case and renders the original relief sought inappropriate.

* * *

Equity may fashion a remedy to effect justice suitable to the circumstances of the case. * * *

The trial court, being aware that plaintiffs neither owned the property nor had possession of it, recognized the inappropriateness of an award for damages under the benefit-of-the-bargain rule. However, neither of the parties at trial presented evidence relevant to a determination of the amount to be awarded as a result of the rescission. Thus, further proceedings are necessary so that the parties may present appropriate evidence to enable the trial court to order the proper amount of restitution. * * *

In suits involving rescission, the parties must be placed in status quo. * * * Since the Rices have already surrendered possession of the motel to the Hiltys, the Hiltys must now return whatever consideration they received under the contract. Therefore, in addition to the $19,000 awarded by the trial court, the Rices are entitled to a return of their payments, each payment from the date thereof. * * *

For the purpose of determining the other equities between the parties resulting from the rescission, the factors to be considered may include, but are not limited to, the amount of net profit or loss realized by plaintiffs during their period of operation of the motel, the amount of any capital improvements made by them that were of benefit to the motel property, the reasonable rental value of that portion of the property utilized by plaintiffs for their own personal use, and the reasonable value of their services in managing the motel.

* * *

The judgment as to the liability issues is affirmed. The judgment as to the award of damages is reversed, and the cause is remanded for further evidentiary proceedings to determine the amount of recovery to which the plaintiffs are entitled, and for findings of fact, conclusions of law, and entry of judgment thereon.

* * *

PETERSON v. AUVEL
Supreme Court of Oregon, 1976.
552 P.2d 538

* * *

McALLISTER, Justice.

The plaintiffs, Robert C. Peterson and Diane J. Peterson, brought this action for damages for fraudulent representations made by defendants during the purchase of real property by plaintiffs from Florence Johnston. The defendants Calvin Auvel and Russell Wilson were real estate brokers employed by the defendant Milton Erickson, dba Milt Erickson Realty, who acted for the seller Johnston in the transaction.

The plaintiffs appeal from an order dismissing their action after the trial court sustained defendants' demurrer to plaintiffs' third amended complaint and plaintiffs were unable to plead further.

Since this case was decided by a demurrer to plaintiffs' complaint, we are limited to consideration of the facts alleged in the complaint as hereinafter set out.

The complaint alleges that on or about June 1, 1973 plaintiffs, for a valid consideration, entered into an earnest money agreement with Florence Johnston to purchase for $21,200 approximately 1940 acres of real property in Clackamas County.

That defendant Milton Erickson was engaged in business as a real estate broker and that defendants Auvel and Wilson were employed by Erickson and at all pertinent times were acting in the scope of their employment.

That on or about July 12, 1973, Auvel and Wilson stated to plaintiff Robert C. Peterson "that Florence Johnston was unwilling to sell the property described in the earnest money agreement * * * at the price agreed upon" and that "the Plaintiffs would not be able to enforce the earnest money agreement in a court, and that they would spend three years trying unsuccessfully if they insisted on enforcing the earnest money agreement," which had been signed by their client Florence Johnston.

That Auvel and Wilson knew that their representations "were not correct and were made to induce Plaintiffs to sign a new earnest money agreement to purchase the property at a higher price."

That plaintiffs reasonably relied on Auvel's and Wilson's representations "by releasing Florence Johnston from any responsibility under the agreement" and that "on or about July 12, 1973 Plaintiffs entered into a new earnest money agreement with Florence Johnston * * * to purchase the same real property * * * for $25,000.00."

That as a result of Auvel's and Wilson's alleged misrepresentations that plaintiffs "were damaged in the amount of $3,800.000, plus additional interest payments in the amount of $2,850.00."

Plaintiffs also alleged that defendants' acts were intentional and malicious and that plaintiffs are entitled to puntitive damages.

Plaintiffs assign as error the sustaining of the demurrer to plaintiffs' complaint.

The necessary elements of an action for deceit have been stated in Prosser, Law of Torts (4th ed 1971). * * *

"1. A false representation made by the defendant. In the ordinary case, this representation must be one of fact.

"2. Knowledge or belief on the part of the defendant that the representation is false—or, what is regarded as equivalent, that he has not a sufficient basis of information to make it. This element often is given the technical name of 'scienter.'

"3. An intention to induce the plaintiff to act or to refrain from action in reliance upon the misrepresentation.

"4. Justifiable reliance upon the representation on the part of the plaintiff, in taking action or refraining from it.

"5. Damage to the plaintiff, resulting from such reliance." See, also, Restatement of Torts, § 525.

The defendants contend that plaintiffs' complaint was defective because (a) the misrepresentations alleged were not representations of fact, and (b) because plaintiffs did not allege their right to rely on the alleged misrepresentations. * * *

We think that neither of defendants' contentions is valid and that plaintiffs' complaint states a cause of action. Although the complaint does not specifically allege that plaintiffs had a right to rely on the misrepresentations we think the right to rely clearly appears from the alleged relationship of the parties and defendants' status as real estate brokers. We quote from Restatement of Torts, § 545, Comment on Subsection (2):

"* * * It is, however, not necessary that the person making the fraudulent misrepresentation of law be a lawyer; it is enough that he is dealing in a capacity which entitles the recipient to believe that he has a superior ability to reach an accurate opinion. Thus, the ordinary layman dealing with a real estate or insurance agent may be justified in relying upon the latter to know enough in regard to real estate and insurance law to give a reliable opinion upon the simpler problems arising therein. * * *"

Under the circumstances, we think that plaintiffs' allegation that they "reasonably relied" on the defendants' representations is sufficient.

We further hold that defendants' representations were representations of fact rather than expressions of opinion. Although it is often said that an action will not lie for expressions of opinion or misstatements of law as distinguished from those of fact, as said by Prosser:

"The present tendency is strongly in favor of eliminating the distinction between law and fact as 'useless duffle of an older and more arbitrary day,' and recognizing that a statement as to the law, like a statement as to anything else, may be intended and understood either as one of fact or one of opinion only, according to the circumstances of the case. Most courts still render lip service to the older rule, but they have been inclined whenever possible to find statements of fact 'implied' in representations as to the law." Prosser, op, cit. supra at 725, § 109. * * *

The defendants pointed to the plaintiffs' own knowledge and experience in beer retailing. The court held, 176 Or. at 185, 156 P.2d 571, that it was for the jury to decide whether "it would have been folly" for the plaintiffs to rely on the defendants' misrepresentation and therefore whether or not it was justifiable reliance.

Holland v. *Lentz,* 239 Or. 332, 345, 397 P.2d 787 (1964), recognized that statements of opinion may be actionable where the parties are not on equal knowledge or means of knowledge. * * *

When representations by the defendant may be fact or opinion, according to the circumstances, a pleading may not be held insufficient on the ground that the representations are not factual. * * * In such case, the question of whether the representation was one of fact or of opinion is for the trier of fact to decide upon proof at trial. * * *

Because the defendants in this case were real estate brokers their statements of opinion as to the legal consequences of the earnest money agreement which were knowingly false and made with the intent to induce the plaintiffs to agree to a larger sales price were actionable as fraudulent representations. It is at least a question for the jury whether the reliance by the plaintiffs on the representations was justified.

The court erred in sustaining the demurrer to plaintiffs' complaint. The case is remanded with instructions to overrule the demurrer and for further proceedings not inconsistent with this opinion.

In the case of *Edwards* v. *Sergi,* 30 P.2d 541 (1934) the court stated very clearly the importance of statements made by sellers as to the size of the property. Factually, the case is older, but it illustrates the importance of representations made to induce third parties to buy. In 1927 the plaintiff had purchased from the defendants 160 acres of land in Napa County. Approximately 3½ years later, the plaintiff brought an action against the defendant for damages for a mistake alleging that the 19-acre tract of timber had been represented by the defendant to constitute part of 160-acre tract, where in fact it was not so contained. If the particular 19 acres of wooded land had been part of the larger tract, it would have been of greater value. The court held for the plaintiff and awarded damages.

The court stated that it may have been that the appellant, defendant, was sincere in his belief when selling the property that the wooded land was embraced within the boundary of the larger tract. But the court stated that even if "one honestly believes his statements as to character of land to be true, he is not justified in making them in order to induce a purchaser to enter into a contract where they are in fact untrue."

Once again, this older case, in some reform herein, illustrates the importance of accurate statements and the exposure for an inaccurate statement. The broker should take this to heart when representing parties and conveying information.

ANDERSON v. APPLEBURY
Supreme Court of Montana, 1977.
567 P.2d 951

* * *

HARRISON, Justice.

This is an action wherein plaintiffs Carl F. and Joyce A. Anderson, husband and wife, by their amended complaint sought damages, statutory penalties and attorney fees against defendants Andrew T. Lund and Anvil R. Summers and their sureties under the provisions of the Montana Real Estate License Act. This action arose out of the purchase by plaintiffs of a motel from defendants James S. and Ruth M. Applebury. * * *

In the fall of 1971, plaintiffs contacted Anvil R. Summers, a real estate salesman employed by Western States, Inc. of Hamilton, Montana, to locate a business in Hamilton available for purchase. Two businesses were shown and rejected. Summers indicated the Sportsman Motel might be for sale. Andrew T. Lund, a real estate broker d/b/a Western States, Inc., contacted James and Ruth Applebury, then owners of the Sportsman Motel, concerning a possible sale. The Appleburys subsequently informed him of their desire to sell. They indicated their selling price and stated the motel stood on land leased from the Burlington Northern Railway Co. Summers informed the Andersons of the availability of the motel for purchase.

Plaintiffs were shown the motel, its supplies and the surrounding property by James Applebury, in the company of Lund and Summers. At no time did Lund or Summers make representations regarding the location of the building or related structures upon the leased premises, the condition of the motel, the potential profitability of the business, or the availability of title insurance. Plaintiffs later conducted a second brief inspection of the premises.

On November 8, 1971, plaintiffs agreed to purchase the Sportsman Motel, admittedly relying in substance upon their inspections of the

premises and the small amount of information given them by James Applebury regarding the property. Lund and Summers represented both parties
in drafting the resultant "Contract for Sale of Property" executed on December 20, 1971. * * *

Plaintiffs took possession of the motel in January, 1972. Various problems with the physical structure of the building surfaced immediately, and
the motel was promptly listed for sale. In 1974 plaintiffs were informed
by the Montana Department of Highways that a portion of their motel
parking lot, sign, and canopy encroached upon a highway right-of-way.
Plaintiffs on July 3, 1975, filed their initial complaint against the Appleburys and Lund. Summers was added as a defendant by the amended
complaint, filed on October 23, 1975. Plaintiffs alleged various violations
of the Montana Real Estate License Act by Lund and Summers. * * *
The alleged violations essentially involve elements of fraud and misrepresentation in the inducement of the contract to purchase the motel. * * *

The specific acts alleged to have been committed by Lund and Summers include:

"(1) Intentionally misleading, untruthful, or inaccurate advertising,
whether printed or by radio, display or other nature, which advertising in any material particular or in any material way misrepresents
any property, terms, values, policies or services of the business conducted;
"(2) Making any false promises of a character likely to influence,
persuade or induce;
"(3) Pursuing a continued and flagrant course of misrepresentation,
or making false promises through agents or salesmen, or any medium
of advertising, or otherwise;

"* * *

It is well settled that a prima facie case of fraud is not established unless plaintiff proves the making of a material misrepresentation, and reliance upon the truth of such misrepresentation. * * *

In the instant case the question is the making of material misrepresentations and reliance thereon by plaintiffs. However, the record indicates the
parties are in complete agreement, in all material respects, that virtually no
representations were made by Lund and Summers regarding the motel or
the property upon which it is situated. The deposition testimony of plaintiff
Joyce A. Anderson is replete with statements supporting that conclusion.
In her August 11, 1975 depositions, she testified:

"Q. In other words, at that point you and your husband felt that you
had all the information that you needed to make up your minds to
buy? A. We had all the information that we—we had gotten, and we
couldn't get, like I said, a financial statement of any sort. We simply
relied on the honesty and integrity of these people and on their word.

"Q. You were *relying* on the statement that Mr. Applebury made that you could make a good living there? A. Absolutely." (Emphasis added.)

In her November 22, 1975 deposition, she testified:

"Q. Then I would be correct in summing all these up that inasfar as your contacts with Mr. Summers is concerned, that at no time did he make any statement to you or your husband in your presence concerning any of the aspects of the motel? A. I would say that you were correct in saying that.

"Q. And when I say any of the aspects, I'm referring specifically to the grounds of the Complaint that you have set forth in your Amended Complaint, is that correct? A. Yes, Sir.

* * *

"Q. Do you have any present recollection that Mr. Lund told you anything about that lease other than the fact that the lease was in existence at that time? A. No, I believe we got the figures from Mr. Applebury when we were talking in the lobby after he had shown us the motel.

"Q. So that with respect to the lease, then we start out with the fact that Mr. Lund had *told you* that there was a lease and that the Sportsman was located on the Burlington leased property? A. I believe this is correct." (Emphasis added.)

* * * It is plain that there is no genuine issue of material fact disclosed in the record, particularly in the depositions of the parties, which relates to the alleged fraud. Clearly, plaintiffs offer nothing in contraposition to defendants' proof no material misrepresentations were made and none relied upon. We hold, there being no genuine issue of material fact as to whether fraudulent representations were made or relied upon, defendants Lund and Summers were entitled to judgment on this point as a matter of law. * * *

Also, there is a second ground which supports the district court in its order granting summary judgment. * * *

All of the acts giving rise to plaintiffs' cause of action occurred in late 1971 and early 1972. The above period of limitation had run by early 1974, regardless of plaintiffs' knowledge or lack of knowledge of the existence of their claims.

* * * Likewise plaintiffs' claim, in regard to the encroachment, is barred by the running of the statute. * * *

The district court was correct in granting summary judgment to defendants, Lund and Summers. * *

Third Parties:
Representations to Third Parties

REALTORS' LIABILITY TO THIRD-PARTY PURCHASERS

Ben and Betty recently inquired through a licensed real estate broker in Idaho as to certain real property which was on the market. The salesman allowed for a showing of the property which was listed with Tifft Agency. Thereafter, Ben and Betty, enthused about the property, wrote their earnest money deposit and signed the agreement to purchase for $30,000.

The Tifft Agency mailed the offer by Ben and Betty to the owner. Before the owner received their offer, the salesman for Tifft called the owner and informed owner that he and two other parties were mailing an offer of $30,000 for the same property, with allegedly better terms.

Upon hearing these facts, the owner accepted the offer from the Tifft group. Later, after receiving a phone call from the potential purchasers, Ben and Betty, the Tifft salesman returned the earnest money deposit to Ben and Betty and told them their offer was rejected.

Subsequently the potential purchasers, Ben and Betty, learned that the Tifft group purchased the property. They were furious and have now sued the Tifft group to have the court hold that the property should really be theirs, and that they should be entitled to pay the purchase price to the Tifft group.

What would your decision be as to the duty of the Tifft group to a buyer? That is, do the Tiffts owe a duty to the buyers, and if so, what would be the remedy? See the following case of *Funk* v. *Tifft,* 515 F. 2d 23 (9th Cir. 1975). See also an interesting discussion of this matter in Case Note, "Real Estate Brokers' Duties to Prospective Purchasers-*Funk* v. *Tifft,*" *Brigham Young University Law Review* 513 (1976).

FUNK v. TIFFT
United States Court of Appeals,
Ninth Circuit, 1975.
As Amended on Denial of Rehearing
May 28, 1975.
515 F.2d 23

* * *

OPINION

LUMBARD, Circuit Judge:

Plaintiffs Benjamin and Betty Lou Funk appeal from a judgment of the District Court of Idaho entered on November 10, 1972, by J. Blaine Anderson, J., dismissing their complaint. The principal issue presented by this diversity of citizenship case is whether a licensed real estate broker in Idaho owes a fiduciary duty to a prospective buyer not to purchase a tract of land for himself while his prospective buyer's offer to buy that land is outstanding. This district court found that there had been no breach of duty and refused to impose a constructive trust in favor of plaintiffs. We reverse.

In 1968, defendant Ward Tifft was a licensed real estate broker doing business as the Tifft Agency in Sandpoint, Idaho. On August 22, 1968, the plaintiffs, Benjamin and Betty Lou Funk, who were residents of California, came into the Tifft Agency and asked to see some property. Salesman Ron Fillion showed them the Godfrey property, which is the subject matter of this suit. The following day the Funks made out a check for $100 to the Tifft Agency as an earnest money deposit and signed an agreement to purchase the property for $30,000, with $1,000 to be paid upon acceptance of the offer followed by payments of $100 per month for fifteen months, followed by a lump sum payment of $5,000 and payments of $150 per month thereafter.

On August 26th, Tifft mailed the Funk offer to Mrs. Carlock, the daughter of the owner. Mrs. Carlock, who lived in Florida, had a power of attorney from her father which authorized her to act with respect to the property. Two days later and before Mrs. Carlock received the Funk offer, Tifft called Mrs. Carlock and advised her that he, Fillion and a Mr. Kahn were mailing her an offer for $30,000, with $6,000 down and payments of $300 per month.

A month later, in response to a telephone call from the Funks, Tifft returned their $100 and informed them that their offer had been rejected. He did not tell them that he, Fillion, and Kahn had purchased the property.

Kahn, Fillion, and Tifft formed the Pendor-Idaho Corporation on October 23, 1968. Kahn received 51% of the stock, and Tifft and Fillion split the remaining 49%. Tifft was a director and president of the corporation. The deed to the Godfrey property was granted to the corporation.

When the Funks returned to Idaho in 1970, they learned who had purchased the property, and they sued to have Pendor-Idaho declared a constructive trustee and to obtain other relief. The district court found for the defendants and asked their counsel to prepare findings of fact and conclusions of law.

While it is agreed that Idaho law governs, the Idaho Supreme Court has never ruled on the duty that a realtor owes a prospective buyer. Consequently we must distill from the decisions of other jurisdictions the principles which we believe the Idaho courts would apply.

Most modern cases dealing with the relationship of a broker and a buyer impose a duty of fairness and honesty on the broker. One of the leading cases, *Quinn* v. *Phipps,* 93 Fla. 805, 113 So. 419 (1927), held that when a person undertakes to act as an intermediary between the seller and a prospective buyer of a parcel of land, he becomes a constructive trustee for the benefit of the prospective buyer if he purchases the land from the seller for himself without advising the prospective buyer of his actions. * * * These cases are consistent with the testimony of two Idaho real estate brokers who stated at trial that a realtor who acts as an intermediary between a seller and a prospective buyer has a duty not to compete secretly with and outbid the prospective buyer when that buyer has made an offer on a piece of property and signed an earnest money purchase agreement. The trial judge found that Tifft did not breach his duty to the Funks when he outbid them without their knowledge. * * * However, the legal conclusions of the district court are not binding upon us.* * * We think that it is clear on the fact outlined above that Tifft did breach the fiduciary duties he owed the Funks. When a real estate broker acts as an intermediary between a seller and a prospective buyer, he is under a duty to deal fairly and honestly with the prospective buyer. That duty is breached when the real estate agent outbids the prospective buyer without notice to him before the seller has acted on his offer. Our holding obviously benefits the prospective buyer, but it is important to note that the seller is also better served by this rule. If the real estate agent sends his own offer to a seller without notifying the prospective buyer, the seller is deprived of the possibility that the prospective buyer might better the agent's offer. * * *

The district court refused to impose liability on the defendants because it felt that Kahn, not Tifft, was the principal offeror in the second offer and because it found no "malice or legal wrongdoing" involved in Tifft's actions. We do not agree. Tifft was director and a 24.5% stockholder of the corporation that bought the land. The lack of malice is irrelevant; there is sufficient "legal wrongdoing" in Tifft's breach of his fiduciary duty. * * * Suffice it to say that Tifft's involvement tainted the actions of his fellow stockholder and those of the corporation. * * * Idaho has long recognized the constructive trust as the appropriate remedy when a fiduciary violates his duties and takes property for his own use. * * * Here the Funks established the essential elements required for imposition of a constructive trust—the existence of a fiduciary relationship, its breach, and the wrongful acquisition of the land by the breacher. * * * The court will also have to take into consideration any capital improvements made to the property by Pendor-Idaho. See generally *Ryan* v. *Plath,* 18 Wash. 2d 839, 140 P.2d 968 (1943). When it fashions its final order, the court should give the parties and the seller opportunity to be heard should that be necessary. * * *

Reversed and remanded.

DUTIES OF SELLING AGENT TO PROSPECTIVE PURCHASER

Problem. The plaintiff, a prospective purchaser, argues that he was warned by the salesman in question that "If you are going to do anything, you had better do it pretty quick, because I have a buyer for this potential home." That is, the real estate agent represented that there was another purchaser who was ready to buy the house and therefore this prospective purchaser should offer very quickly.

What responsibility, if any, does the real estate agent have to a prospective purchaser? What if the prospective purchaser, fearful of losing the transaction, offered more than he would have otherwise offered had the statement not been made, as indicated above?

The Lamplighters Realty case examines this proposition out of the Courts of Oklahoma in 1976.

Larry W. BEAVERS, Appellant,

v/

LAMPLIGHTERS REALTY, INC.,

Appellee.

No. 48700.

Court of Appeals of Oklahoma,

division 2

* * * 1976.

Rehearing Denied * * *

certiorari Denied * * * 1976.

* * *

* * *

BRIGHTMIRE, Judge.

Plaintiff, the prospective purchaser of an Oklahoma City home, was warned by the realty salesman that "If you are going to do anything, you had better do it pretty quick, because I've got a buyer for it . . . the original builder and he is coming in . . . with a check . . . within the hour." This, alleges plaintiff, was a lie which induced him to agree to pay more for the house than he otherwise would have had to had he known the truth.

These facts defendant Lamplighters Realty, Inc. admitted to be true for the purpose of demurring to plaintiff Beavers' evidence—a plea sustained by the trial judge followed by the rendition of judgment for defendant. From an order rejecting plaintiff's motion for a new trial he appeals assigning one reversible error—that defendant's demurrer to his evidence should have been overruled. We agree it should have been and reverse.

I

It was sometime in January 1974 plaintiff saw a Lamplighters' for sale sign in front of an attractive Spanish-style house at 4912 Larissa Lane. He liked the storybook looks of the abode, called the telephone number printed on the sign, and eventually was shown the house by agent Norma Ray. Shortly thereafter, on February 11, 1974, plaintiff's offer of $34,500 for the dwelling was rejected. Plaintiff still wanted the place, however. He let a day or two pass and again called Lamplighters. This time a "Mr. Taylor came on the phone" and asked if plaintiff was still interested in the home. "Yes," said plaintiff, "but doggone it . . . they were asking too much."

"If you are going to do anything, you had better do it pretty quick, because I've got a buyer for it," said the realtor.

"You do?" responded plaintiff.

"Yes," said Taylor, "it (is) the original builder and he is coming in."

"Paul Good?" asked plaintiff.

"Yes," answered Taylor, adding that Good was coming in with a check right away.

"How much is it?" plaintiff asked concerning the check.

"Thirty-seven thousand dollars" was the answer.

"Well, he's bought it."

"No," retorted Taylor, "(i)f you want to put in a bid, he's going to be here within the hour. I just talked to him."

The high pressure tactic worked. Said plaintiff, "I (don't) know whether 'panicked' (is) the (right) word or not, but I figured . . . that (if) the original builder would pay thirty-seven thousand for the home, that maybe . . . it absolutely should be worth that much to me . . . and I just increased it (the fictitious offer) two hundred and fifty dollars. And the next thing I know I bought myself a home" for $37,250, by executing a contract dated February 15, 1974.

It was a while before plaintiff found out he had been a victim of a gross deception. One day, after he had moved into the house—and found, incidentally, that the agent Ray had made false representations about the condition of the house, requiring him to expend about $6,000 for repairs—he chanced to meet builder Paul Good at a neighbor's home, got to talking to him about plaintiff's house and came upon some interesting facts. Good said he had earlier looked at the house "but it was out of the ball park as far as he was concerned" and that he "would have given in the . . . lower thirties."

"Well," said plaintiff, "I'd offered thirty-four five to start."

"That should have bought it," said Good.

"Didn't you offer thirty-seven thousand?" plaintiff asked Good.

"No," he answered.

Upon discovering this, plaintiff took the matter up with his lawyer and instituted this action seeking compensatory damages for his detriment in the amount of $2,750 and punitive damages of $50,000.

Besides plaintiff's own testimony there was that of builder Good, who confirmed that he and his wife had looked at the house while it was on the market. Good said he found the dwelling to be in bad shape needing around $9,000 in repairs and had discussed the possibility of purchasing the property with agent Ray for $35,000, but he never made a formal offer to purchase it. Good testified he never discussed the house with Jim Taylor, though he had told Norma Ray he thought $37,000 "was a little high due to the fact there was so much work to be done to the house."

* * *

II

Plaintiff argues, with merit, that he proved all essential elements of fraud, namely, that Taylor made representations of material facts he knew were false to induce plaintiff to alter his position, which plaintiff damagingly did. Defendant on the other hand proposes that (1) the representations complained of are not actionable because they "are so commonly made by those having property to sell in order to enhance its value . . ." and (2) plaintiff has proved no resulting "damages."

The first contention was quite forcefully destroyed over a half century ago by a high-minded Court in *Chisum* v. *Huggins,* * * * (1916). There, recovery on a note was denied because it was the fruit of a real estate sale induced by fraud of seller's agents in making false statements as to the "future prospects" of the land, its "actual value, and general environments. . . ." While Chisum is factually distinguishable, its importance to us here is that the Court premised its decision on the rationale of the yet earlier case of *Prescott* v. *Brown,* * * * (1911), which featured a remarkably lucid no-nonsense opinion executing a powerful assault on one of the less admirable hand-me-downs of our Anglo-Saxon common law heritage—the doctrine of caveat emptor, a doctrine that exalts deceit, condemns fair dealing, and scorns the credulous.

The time had come, observed the Prescott author, for the Court to recognize that the rule of caveat emptor is not founded on a high standard of morality and to outlaw use of this ally of dishonesty as a shield to protect gains of the "blue sky shark" achieved by his deliberate frauds and cheats.

* * *

A prospective buyer has a right to rely on the veracity of the seller (or his agent) without investigation. The risk of harm in this state lies with the wrongdoer rather than his victim. And as noted in Prescott, this right of reliance must be protected even if the representations be "so extravagant that sensible, cautious people would not have believed them. . . . It is as much an actionable fraud willfully to deceive a credulous person with an improbable falsehood as it is to deceive a cautious and sagacious person with a plausible one. The law draws no line between the two falsehoods. It only asks . . . Was the lie spoken with intent to deceive and defraud, and was the false statement believed, and money paid on this faith that it was true? These questions are for the jury."

In the instant case the evidence so far adduced establishes that realtor Taylor, upon becoming aware of plaintiff's desire for the Spanish villa, undertook to bring about a rather rapid resolution of the price problem by using, as it were, a dynamite sales technique to blast an immediate positive response out of plaintiff. The deliberate lie did indeed achieve the intended and expected effect and induced plaintiff to purchase the property for a figure higher than he would have to pay absent the fraud.

III

Defendant's second proposition—that plaintiff proved no damage as a result of the falsehood—is likewise without merit. Its theory is that in electing to affirm the contract and seek damages, plaintiff's recovery is limited to "the difference between the actual value of the property at the time it was purchased and the value it was represented to be," and here, there was no proof to show the actual value of the house at the time of purchase.

This notion of the applicable law is not quite right. * * *

As we mentioned earlier, the representations here did not go to the issue of value, but to the issue of price—to the question of whether plaintiff was tricked into paying more for the property than he would have otherwise had to. To recover, therefore, plaintiff need not show what the value was of the dwelling he bought. He need only produce evidence from which the jury can find that he probably could have bought the house for less than the $37,250 he paid. As the record now stands, demurrants admit that the seller would have taken $37,000—a fact inferable from defendant's fabricated representation about the imminent Good sale. Assuming, without saying one way or the other, that no other detriment has been shown evidence there is of at least $250 actual damage—enough to perfect plaintiff's cause of action for an intentional and malicious fraud, and enough to provide a foundation for an award of punitive damages. Moreover, having shown he sustained some detriment as a result of the fraud, plaintiff's action does not fail merely because he cannot prove an exact amount of damages. * * * In such a situation, plaintiff is entitled to at least nominal damage. * * * And a nominal damage award is likewise sufficient to support punitive (punishment) damages. * * *

The judgment below is reversed and the cause is remanded for a new trial.

     * * *

Once again the question is raised about the responsibility of a broker to a third party, where the third party relies on certain factual information relayed to the third party by the broker. Assume that the broker acquired certain factual information about rentals from the seller and that the broker conveyed this information to the third party. If this information was incorrect, what responsibility or liability might exist for the broker?

One might easily argue that this problem could be solved by the broker's confirming all the data relayed by the seller to the broker and in turn to a third-party purchaser. Real estate salespeople should confirm the data given to them by their seller. Once again, this issue is examined in the following case of *Jansen* v. *Herman,* a Minnesota decision.

COMMISSIONS WHICH MIGHT BE EARNED AFTER THE EXPIRATION OF A LISTING

There are many cases that affect the rights and responsibilities of a seller and broker with regard to commissions.

Do you feel a commission would be owing in a circumstance where a broker listed a property, the listing expired, but the broker and the seller mutually agreed, orally, that if the broker produced a purchaser, the seller would pay a commission? It should be added that the transaction was never consummated by the seller with the prospective purchaser, introduced to the seller by the broker. The transaction failed as a result of disagreement on various terms.

This case is not that unusual, but it illustrates many of the commission problems, the potential defects with oral agreements for commission, and many other related issues. This issue is examined in the Jansen case, out of the Supreme Court of Minnesota in 1975. For more on the commission issue, see Mark Lee Levine and Kent Jay Levine, *Real Estate Law* (1977).

Jan L. JANSEN, Plaintiff,

v.

Allen H. HERMAN, defendant and cross-defendant, Respondent,
Edward M. Carlin, et al., defendants and cross-claimants, Appellants.

230 N.W. 2d. 460 (1975)

Supreme Court of Minnesota.

* * *

PER CURIAM.

This action was originally commenced to rescind a purchase agreement involving a Minneapolis apartment complex. That issue was settled out of Court. The litigation now on appeal involves a dispute between two defendants, one of whom claims a commission for services rendered as a real estate broker in connection with the property.

Edward M. Carlin is a licensed real estate broker doing business as Edwards Realty, a division of C & Z Investments, Inc. Allen Herman was at all pertinent times the sole owner of the Williamsburg Estates apartment complex located in Minneapolis.

In May 1970 and August 1971 Carlin and Herman entered into short-term exclusive listing agreements. No sale or contract to sell was produced during the terms of these agreements. Neither of the written listing agreements was ever extended in writing, and no other written listing agreements relating to Williamsburg Estates were entered into by the parties.

Although Carlin continued his efforts to sell Williamsburg Estates after the expiration of the listing agreements, there was a conflict in the testimony as to the basis upon which these efforts were made. Carlin testified that he and Herman never actually came to any agreement relating to his commission, but that Herman knew of and acquiesced in his continued efforts to sell Williamsburg Estates. Herman, on the other hand, testified that, after the expiration of the second listing agreement, he told Carlin that "he was working as a volunteer, that he was not going to tie my property up any further, and he was on his own." Herman also testified that it was agreed that Carlin would earn a $50,000 fee if and when a transaction actually closed.

During the fall of 1971, Carlin introduced Herman to Jan L. Jansen, plaintiff in this action, and Herman and Jansen commenced negotiations regarding Williamsburg Estates. On May 1, 1972, Jansen and Herman entered into a purchase agreement which set the date of closing the sale for June 1, 1972.

Sometime between May 1 and June 1, 1972, after the purchase agreement had been signed, Carlin and Herman executed a document (exhibit E) which, in relevant part, provided:

"THAT, WHEREAS, ALLEN M. HERMAN AND LOIS HERMAN, husband and wife, and indebted to Edward's Realty, a Division of C & Z Investments, Inc., as and for commission earned in the sum of Fifty Thousand ($50,000.00) Dollars for the sale of certain property owned by said ALLEN M. HERMAN AND ——— HERMAN, and

* * *

"NOW, THEREFORE, IT IS UNDERSTOOD AND AGREED BY THESE PRESENTS: That ALLEN M. HERMAN AND ——— HERMAN, husband and wife hereinafter called Assignors, for and in consideration of the monies due to said Edward's Realty and as security for the same, do hereby sell, assign, and transfer unto said Edward's Realty, a Division of C & Z Investments, Inc., its successors and assigns, the total sum of Fifty Thousand ($50,000.00) Dollars from the monies now due and owing and which may hereafter be or become due and owing to the Assignors hereunder, pursuant to the terms and conditions of that certain Contract for Deed dated the 1st day of June, 1972, made by ALLEN M. HERMAN AND ——— HERMAN, husband and wife, as Vendors, to JAN L. JANSEN AND GRETCHEN J. JANSEN, husband and wife, as Vendees, by the terms of which the Vendees have agreed to pay for certain property described in said Contract for Deed the total sum of One Million Eight Hundred Thousand ($1,800,000.00) Dollars."

Referring to this agreement, Herman testified:

"It was mutually agreed by both of us that had no sale taken place, that he wasn't entitled to any commission for said services, and he wouldn't be entitled to any consideration under exhibit E * * *."

No closing ever occurred, and no contract for deed was entered into. In October 1972, Jansen notified Herman that he was rescinding the purchase agreement because of claimed inaccuracies contained in a schedule of annual rentals and in a schedule of the fixed expenses for Williamsburg Estates for 1970, delivered to Jansen during the negotiations.

Thereafter, Jansen brought this action against both Herman and Carlin, alleging fraud and misrepresentation with regard to the income and expenses for Williamsburg Estates. Carlin denied the allegations and cross-claimed against Herman for his real estate commission. The parties agreed to settle the issues raised by Jansen's complaint and entered into a stipulation of partial dismissal and a mutual release which provided for the return of Jansen's earnest money, preserving only Carlin's claim for a commission.

The Trial Court concluded that the agreement contained in exhibit E was to become effective only upon the closing of the sale. Since the closing never occurred, its terms were held not to be binding, and judgment was ordered in favor of Herman. Carlin appeals from the denial of his motion for a new trial.

1. Carlin bases his claim for a commission on the contract known as exhibit E, an instrument purporting to establish Herman's liability to Carlin in the amount of $50,000. On the basis of parol evidence, Herman asserts, and the Trial Court agreed, that the written contract was conditioned upon the actual closing of the sale. Carlin contends, however, that the parol evidence was not properly admissible at trial.

The law is clear that oral evidence of discussions, negotiations, or understandings is not admissible to vary or contradict the terms of a clear, unambiguous, and integrated written contract. * * *

In every instance where the parol evidence rule is sought to be applied, however, a threshold question must be asked: Is the contract valid and operative? If the contract was to be binding only upon performance of an agreed-upon condition precedent, then the contract goes into force only upon the performance of that condition. Thus, parol evidence may be admissible to show that, notwithstanding the existence of a written contract, it was the intention of the parties that the contract should not become operative except upon the happening of some future event. * * *

In Minnesota we have repeatedly held that parol evidence is admissible to show that, notwithstanding the delivery of an instrument, the intention of the parties was that it should not become operative as a binding contract except upon the happening of a future contingent event. * * * Thus, parol evidence was clearly admissible to show the existence of a condition precedent to the contract set out in exhibit E.

2. Carlin next asserts, notwithstanding the admissibility of the contrary parol evidence, that the agreement between Herman and him was not subject to a condition precedent. Rather, Carlin argues, exhibit E speaks only of a "commission earned in the sum of $50,000." Herman, however, testified that it was agreed that Carlin would earn his $50,000 commission if and only if the transaction actually closed.

Based on this conflicting evidence, the Trial Court concluded that the parties had agreed that the commission agreement would be effective only upon the closing of the sale. The closing was a condition precedent to the validity of the contract. * * *

There is sufficient evidence to support the Trial Court's finding. Herman's testimony on the issue is substantiated by exhibit E. It states that a $50,000 commission was earned "for the sale" of Herman's property, and it also refers to an existing contract for deed, when in fact there was no contract for deed. This language, too, gives support to the Trial Court's conclusion that this contract was to go into effect only upon the closing of the sale.

We therefore affirm the finding of the Trial Court that the document known as exhibit E never became effective because a condition precedent (the closing) never occurred. Thus, Carlin is foreclosed from claiming his commission based on that agreement alone.

3. Even if Carlin and Herman had agreed that Carlin's commission was contingent upon the closing of the sale, yet another question must be asked. The law is clearly established that if Herman is solely to blame for the failure of the closing, Carlin may nonetheless recover.

In *Olson* v. *Penkert,* * * * we stated:

"We think the rule is well established that, if the efforts of the broker are rendered a failure by the fault of the employer, the broker does not lose his commission. This rule is based upon the familiar principle that no one can avail himself of the nonperformance of a condition precedent who has himself occasioned its nonperformance."

* * *

Carlin asserts that the closing failed to occur solely because of Herman's misrepresentations to Jansen. The law is settled that Carlin bore the burden of proof of demonstrating such a fact. * * * The record shows that Carlin did not do so.

Affirmed.

Recently the plaintiff in *Becker* v. *Capwell* filed an action for what he alleges are secret profits. The defendant is the plaintiff's real estate broker or at least "prior broker."

Factually, the defendant purchased the property in question in 1969 and is referred to as the Lancaster property. The defendant, again, is a real estate broker. The plaintiff, a doctor, eventually purchased the Lancaster property from an employee of the defendant, broker. There was no disclosure to the doctor that the property in question was actually owned by the broker.

Do you believe the broker has exposure under the circumstances indicated, even though the property was sold by an employee of the broker? If so, what do you consider will be the damages to the doctor in the sense of his recovery?

How could the broker and employee of the broker have avoided the problem in question? These questions are answered in the following case of *Becker* v. *Capwell,* a decision out of Oregon.

BECKER v. CAPWELL
Supreme Court of Oregon, 1974.
527 P.2d 120

* * *

HOWELL, Justice.

Plaintiff filed this action at law to recover alleged "secret profits" from the defendant, who was plaintiff's agent and a real estate broker. The trial court granted defendant's motion for a judgment of involuntary nonsuit, and plaintiff appeals.

On June 3, 1969, the defendant purchased certain property known as the Lancaster property. * * * Defendant was an experienced real estate broker who worked as a consultant for clients on an ongoing basis. His services consisted of the purchase, sale and exchange of investment real property on behalf of his clients.

The plaintiff, a medical doctor with no prior land investment experience, became acquainted with an employee of the defendant who explained the defendant's services. On or about September 15, 1969, the plaintiff was introduced to the defendant. Shortly thereafter the plaintiff and the defendant entered into an agreement whereby the defendant would advise the plaintiff concerning investment real property.

Th defendant's employee told the plaintiff that the Lancaster property was for sale and made a favorable analysis of it. Defendant did not disclose that the property was owned by the defendant, or the price which the defendant had paid for the property in June 1969. The plaintiff purchased the property in early October 1969.

Plaintiff contends that his measure of damages is the "secret profit" made by the defendant—the difference between the amount defendant originally paid for the property and the price at which defendant sold the property to plaintiff. The defendant contends that the proper measure of damages is the difference between the price paid by plaintiff to defendant and the actual value of the property. The plaintiff introduced no evidence of the actual value, and for this reason the trial court granted the motion for a judgment of involuntary nonsuit.

The precise question is: What is the measure of damages when an agent acquires property prior to the creation of the agency relationship and subsequently sells that property to his principal without disclosure of his adverse interest?

* * * It is clear that an agency relationship was created between the plaintiff and the defendant. It is also clear that, by his actions concerning the Lancaster property, the defendant breached his duty to the plaintiff:

"* * * (A) real estate broker stands in a fiduciary relationship with his customer or client and is thus bound to protect his clients' interests. He must, therefore, make a full, fair and understandable explanation to the client before having him sign any contracts, particularly when those contracts are with the broker himself. * * *"

* * *

In support of his contention that he is entitled to recover the difference between the original price paid by the defendant and the sale price to plaintiff, plaintiff cites 2 Restatement supra, at 203, § 388:

"Unless otherwise agreed, an agent who makes a profit in connection with transactions conducted by him on behalf of the principal is under a duty to give such profit to the principal."

We agree with this principle. However, the comments to § 388 indicate that the section applies to profits or gratuities received by the agent while acting for his principal. Here we are dealing with real property purchased by the agent before any agency relationship was established with the principal.

When an agent sells his property to his principal without full disclosure of the material facts, the remedies available to the principal depend upon the facts of the case.

* * The equitable remedy of rescission is available whenever there is a breach of the agent's fiduciary duty by a failure to disclosure material facts. 2 Restatement, supra at 208, 209, § 390, presents the example chasing the agent's land but other material facts remain undisclosed:

> "P employs A to purchase a suitable manufacturing site for him. A owns one which is suitable and sells it to P at the fair price of $25,000, telling P all the relevant facts except that, a short time previously, he purchased the land for $15,000. The transaction can be rescinded by P." (Comment a, illustration 2.)

If the principal elects to pursue a legal remedy against his agent, the proper * * * measure of damages also depends upon the facts of the case.

* * *

* * * If an agent purchases property for a purpose other than to resell it to his principal and subsequently does resell it to * * * his principal, the principal may elect to rescind the contract or to recover any difference between the actual value of the property and the sale price to the principal. * * *

> "The remedy of the principal in such a case is usually the repudiation of the transaction. He cannot, it is held, recover, as a profit made by the agent, the difference between the amount at which the agent sold to him and the price which the agent may have paid for the property before the agency was created, though he may recover the difference between the price paid by the principal and the fair value."

* * * The instant case falls within the latter category. The defendant purchased the property before the agency was created and with no intention of selling it to plaintiff because he did not meet plaintiff until three months later. Because of defendant's failure to disclose the material facts of his ownership, the plaintiff was entitled to rescind the transaction or bring an action at law for damages. In the latter event, in order to recover damages the plaintiff would have to show a difference in value between the price he paid for the property and its actual value at the time he purchased it from defendant. * * * He failed to do so.

* * *

Affirmed.

BROKER'S LIABILITY TO PROSPECTIVE PURCHASER FOR REFUND OF DEPOSIT

There are a great number of cases covering the potential exposure of a real estate broker for deposit money. Many of these are collected at one point in 38 American Law Reports (A.L.R.) annotated 2d (1382). In this particular area the scope of the annotation examines real estate transactions in which the broker receives the deposit or earnest money. If the transaction is not completed, of course, the broker is generally required to return the deposit to the purchaser, assuming no breach by the purchaser. However, there are many questions that arise in this area, such as the broker's right to a commission under those circumstances, the agreements with regard to refund where the title is defective, and the general exposure of a broker under these circumstances. Reference to this annotation is suggested. See also an additional A.L.R. annotation in 9 A.L.R. 2d 495, discussing "relative rights and liabilities of vendor and his broker to down payment or earnest money forfeited by vendee for default under real estate contract."

GILBEY v. COOPER
310 N.E.2d 268

* * *

TOBIN, Judge.
* * * The Complaint asks for actual and punitive damages relative to the sale by the Coopers to the Gilbeys, through the auspices of the Robert Capel Agency, by and through their Agent, Bruce Capel, on March 15, 1969, of the piece of real estate known as 770 Benton Road, Perry Township, Columbiana County, Ohio, and being Lots Number 1285 and 1286, part of plat No. Four, Salem Heights, Allotment, Vol. Seven Page 55, of Columbiana County Plat Records and being the same property conveyed to the Coopers by Frank Sepic in Vol. 893, Deed Records of Columbiana County, Ohio.

The Complaint states that the plaintiffs bought the land as described but were never informed by the defendants or their agent, that part of the property was being taken by the state of Ohio for road purposes and never told by the defendants that there was a temporary easement for work purposes taken by the state of Ohio, and therefore, asks for actual damages in the amount of five thousand dollars ($5,000), and punitive damages in the same amount. The defendants' answer denies the essential allegations of the Complaint and also alleges there were stakes marking the boundary of the premises referred to in the Complaint at the time of the negotiations.

The court finds the following to be in the facts:

One: Bruce Capel was at all times an agent of the Robert Capel Real Estate Agency and at all times represented them in this negotiation. Also, that he was the agent, for the Coopers in the negotiations between the Coopers and Gilbeys.

Two: The following are the dates of importance in this case: The center line of the new road was made a matter of record on August 9, 1968. That a temporary and permanent easement was taken by the state on January 23, 1969, and signed by the Coopers, for which they were compensated some $3750 on January 15, 1969, but that said easement was never recorded in the Columbiana County, Ohio, records until March 18, 1969.

Three: That a listing was made by the Capel Agency to sell the property for $10,500 and a listing agreement was made with the Capel Agency on March 8, 1969.

Four: That a purchase agreement was signed by the Gilbeys to purchase said property on March 15, 1969, which the court finds to be a binding agreement to buy the property therein described subject at all road and street easements. That a deed was given on April 4, 1969, recorded on April 9, 1969. The court also finds the matter was financed through the Home Savings and Loan of Salem, Ohio, who obtained an abstract on the same for mortgage purposes but at no time did they offer to show, nor was it shown, to the Gilbeys. That the abstract does show the easement, but at the time the Gilbeys entered into the purchase agreement, to-wit: March 15, 1969, a binding agreement, this matter was not of record. The court also finds that there were some stakes in the ground. Mr. Baird, state surveyor, states that said stakes of the easement were not placed before August, 1969, and on the temporary easement, June 29, 1970.

The court also finds from the evidence, that the Gilbeys were shown the property by Bruce Capel in the presence of the Coopers. That they asked how far the line ran and were shown the line where the road was then and assessed by Mr. Bruce Capel that the by-pass would not touch their land, without any reference to the fact that the by-pass was coming in and was going to take some of the property and without any reference whatsoever to the temporary easement.

The court further finds that the Gilbeys did not actually become aware of the same until work began on the road in which their front yard was cut across as per the easement agreement by the state of Ohio.

The court has listened to the arguments of counsel and read their briefs. The court finds from the facts, that there was no way at the time the binding purchase agreement was entered into, for the Gilbeys to know there was an easement that had been given for part of the property, together with a temporary easement, since it was not recorded until March 18, 1969, or three days later than the binding agreement signed to purchase the property.

It was true that they could have found out by calling New Philadelphia, Ohio, where the center line was but these people are laymen, not engineers, and that would not have told them very much, if anything at all, nor does the court think they were compelled to do so. The court finds from the facts that the said Bruce Capel pointed out, in the presence of the Coopers, and from whom he had full authority, where the limits of the property were, and this was beyond the easement taken and made no reference to the easement. That he made statements to them that they had to go down and sign right away because there were other people waiting for it. In the court's mind, Mr. Bruce Capel put undue pressure on these people and very hurriedly sold them, before it frankly became known that part of the property had already been taken for easement purposes, and part of the property was going to be used, or the inconveniences of being used, for temporary work easements.

The court believes that both the Coopers and most assuredly Bruce Capel, as the agent, owed a duty of complete disclosure of all facts in the sale of this house, about anything that could not visibly be seen.

* * * Therefore, Bruce Capel, as the agent, and the Coopers as the sellers, who were there, owed the Gilbeys absolute duty to disclose to them that an easement had been taken which was twenty (20) feet wide at one end and twenty-seven (27) feet wide at the southeast end, making a wedge-shaped property 140 feet across the property, twenty-seven feet wide at one end of the triangle and twenty-one feet at the northwest side of the property.

In addition to that, he owed a duty to tell them there would be a temporary easement. That their place would be torn up until the road was finished, over a considerable period of time, whenever the state decided to come in and do this.

The court finds this was not done and therefore, finds it was a fraud upon the Gilbeys for not doing so, since the court finds it was an absolute duty on the part of the both the real estate agent and the sellers, to make this disclosure.

* * * Therefore, the court finds that the parties were guilty of wilful misrepresentation to include that of the real estate agent, Bruce Capel, and since he was also the Agent, acknowledged so of the Robert Capel Agency, therefore the misrepresentation becomes that of his superiors.

* * * Coming now to the matter of damages: The Court finds that the value of the land taken as land and the inconvenience damaged the Gilbeys in the amount of Seventeen Hundred Fifty Dollars ($1750) and punitive damages are assessed in the amount of Seven Hundred Fifty Dollars ($750). All damages are to be divided equally between the Coopers and the Capels, to-wit: One Thousand Two Hundred Fifty Dollars ($1250) against the Coopers and One Thousand Two Hundred Fifty Dollars ($1250) against the Capels. * * *

DUTY TO THIRD PARTIES

Recently a real estate broker listed a house for sale and showed the same to a prospective purchaser, Mr. Dicker. The house was inspected for termites and, without the knowledge of Mr. Dicker, termites were discovered. This fact was never relayed by the owners or the real estate broker, both of whom knew the termites existed, to the prospective purchaser. Subsequently the prospective purchaser acquired the house, closed the transaction, and discovered termites.

The question relates to the exposure to the real estate broker of the existence of termites, the duty of the broker to the third-party purchaser, and the right of the purchaser to obtain punitive or punishment damages. What do you consider is the exposure of the real estate broker in this case, and how could he have avoided the problem, other than disclosing this fact to the purchaser and possibly eliminating the sale? These questions are answered in *Dicker* v. *Smith,* a Supreme Court decision out of Kansas (1974).

DICKER v. SMITH
Supreme Court of Kansas, 1974.
523 P.2d 371

* * *

FOTH, Commissioner:

This is an action for actual and punitive damages for fraud in the sale of a home in Wichita. The plaintiff, Michael H. Dicker, alleged that the defendants fraudulently represented the house to be free from termites when he bought it. The defendants, Benjamin and Yvonne Smith are the owner-sellers, and the defendant Edwin R. Clarke is the real estate broker who handled the sale.

At the conclusion of plaintiff's case the trial court sustained a motion by the realtor, Clarke, for a directed verdict on the issue of punitive damages as to him. Plaintiff's later efforts to have this issue reinstated were fruitless, and as to Clarke the case was submitted to the jury on the issue of actual damages only. The jury returned a verdict against him for $795, the full amount of actual damages paid for, representing the cost of treating the house for termites and repairing the damage they had done. Clarke appealed from this judgment, but has abandoned his appeal in this court.

As to the defendant sellers, the Smiths, the case went to the jury on both actual and punitive damages. The jury returned a verdict against them for $2,750 in punitive damages only—as to them no actual damages were awarded. They did not appeal from this judgment. Rather, they filed a motion for relief from the judgment under K.S.A. 60-260(b)(4) on the theory that it was void because not supported by a judgment for actual damages. The trial court overruled their motion and they have appealed from that order.

The main appeal in this case is by the plaintiff, Dicker. He contends that it was error for the trial court, first, to take away from the jury his claim for punitive damages against Clarke, and second, to accept the verdict against the Smiths for punitive damages only. Although at least nominally the successful party below, he seeks a new trial as to all defendants. Resolution of the issues raised requires a brief examination of the transactions among the parties.

In February, 1971, Dicker was house-hunting in anticipation of his impending marriage. A Clarke employee showed him the Smith house, and when he showed interest conveyed him into the presence of Clarke himself. Dicker explained that he would have to finance the purchase through a no-down-payment Veterans Administration loan, and Clarke volunteered to assist him in obtaining such a loan. One V.A. requirement, Clarke explained, was a certificate showing that the house was free of active termites. A proposed sales contract was drawn by Clarke and executed by Dicker, containing a covenant that the sellers Smith would furnish the necessary termite certificate.

The next day, February 18, 1971, Clarke presented the offer to his clients, the Smiths. They signed, with a slight price modification subsequently assented to by Dicker, and the sale was "on."

As soon as the Smiths signed the contract Clarke arranged to have the house inspected for termites by Hawks Inter-State Exterminators, a pest control firm Clarke frequently employed for such inspections. The inspection was made the same day. The inspector, one Herbert Stepp, found active termites and, he testified, so advised Mrs. Smith. He also called Clarke to advise him of the findings, and forwarded a written report to Clarke.

Clarke, in turn, called the Smiths and informed them of the report. There was some discussion as to whether the Smiths were bound to employ Hawks and it was agreed that the Smiths could call in another firm.

Smith in due course had another inspection made by United Pest Control, on March 14, 1971. He did not tell United of the Hawks inspection or findings. United reported "no termites," and certified their finding to Clarke, who used their certificate to satisfy the Veterans Administration.

Five days later, on March 19, 1971, the sale was closed. Neither Clarke nor the Smiths ever mentioned the first inspection by Hawks Inter-State, or that active termites had been found in the house.

Dicker and his new bride didn't actually move in until late August, following a session of summer school in Michigan. It was the following April that Mrs. Dicker first noticed and cleaned off a mud blob on an exposed ceiling beam. When it reappeared a week later she pointed it out to her husband, who noticed some small insects in the area. After capturing a few specimens Dicker sought a termite inspection.

As luck would have it he called Hawks Inter-State, who sent out the trusty Mr. Stepp. Stepp remembered the house and, as he told Dicker, he found termites just where he had found them a little more than a year before. Although his proposal to treat the house had been declined by the Smiths, Stepp was surprised at finding termites still there, and that the house had not been treated. Dicker, needless to say, was even more surprised. This suit followed.

* * * We turn first to the claim against Clarke. When the trial court took the issue of punitive damages away from the jury, it commented "fraud is hard to prove" and that as to Clarke it had "heard no testimony of any fraud or misrepresentation." Yet Dicker's claim against Clarke was based solely on a theory of fraudulent concealment. While all the instructions are not in the record on appeal, it appears the jury was thoroughly instructed on that theory. A specific instruction was given on a broker's duty to inquire so as to avoid misrepresentation. No other basis of liability was asserted against Clarke, and we can perceive no other basis in the record. If, as the trial court apparently believed, there was no evidence of fraud on Clarke's part it would appear that he should have been out of the case entirely. If, on the other hand, there was evidence of fraud then Dicker was entitled to have the jury consider the question of punitive damages. * * *

We think there was evidence from which the jury could have inferred a fraudulent intent on Clarke's part. Dicker testified to a conversation with Clarke within a week of the closing date of March 19, 1971. At that time the first Hawks inspection had long since been made, Clarke had been advised of the presence of termites both orally and in writing, and he had discussed the problem of treatment with Smith. But when Dicker asked for a progress report, "Mr. Clarke advised him that everything was going through okay and the only thing pending was the termite inspection on the house and that would be taken care of."

The jury could easily infer from this response, together with Clarke's later silence at the closing, a deliberate intent on Clarke's part to conceal the existence and contents of the Hawks report. He didn't speak of a termite treatment, but of a termite inspection as the only cause of delay. While Clarke explained his failure to disclose by claiming to rely on the Smiths to have the house treated, he admitted that they never told him they had done so. His motives and intent presented a jury question.

As to the Smiths, the claim was of affirmative fraud as well as fraudulent concealment. Dicker and Smith, while not social friends, were colleagues in the fine arts department of Wichita State University. On one occasion between the contract signing and closing they had a chance encounter on campus. At that time, according to Dicker, Smith assured him that "the deal was real good," that the termite inspection was complete and that Smith had discouraged the inspector from drilling unnecessary holes in the concrete porches because "everything in the house was in great shape," that "the wood was beautiful," and "there wasn't a termite anywhere near the place."

Both Dicker and the Smiths agree that the judgment against the Smiths for punitive damages only is improper. The difference is that the Smiths claim the judgment is void, while Dicker says it is merely erroneous. * * * The Smiths cite no cases which hold such a judgment is void, and we are aware of none. The cases they do cite stand for the well accepted proposition that "before exemplary or punitive damages may be awarded, there must be actual damages and a right of recovery therefor established." * * *

We think the trial court was correct insofar as it thus found that the judgment was not void. The rationale of the rule requiring actual damages before punitive damages may be awarded is that we do not punish conduct, no matter how malicious or reprehensible, which in fact causes no injury. That rationale has no application here. The jury, by its verdict, found the Smiths guilty of fraud. It also, by its verdict against Clarke, found that Dicker had been actually damaged. Just why it returned the verdicts it did is a matter of conjecture—perhaps it wished to ensure that each of the guilty parties paid a share of the judgment, and with punitive damages ruled out as to Clarke this was its way of making an apportionment. * * * In any event, the award of punitive damages was bottomed on a finding and award of actual damages. * * * The judgment was clearly not void. * * * The question remains whether the trial court should have accepted the verdicts as they were returned or whether, as Dicker urges, it should have granted a new trial. The jury implicitly found both Clarke and the Smiths guilty of fraudulent misrepresentations, and it found that Dicker suffered actual damages. It could not consistently make such findings and still fail to return a verdict for actual damages against the Smiths. It is apparent that the jury either misunderstood the instructions, or it disregarded them in an attempt to fashion its own concept of justice. * * *

The proper remedy is a new trial, which is what the plaintiff Dicker sought below and is seeking here.

Accordingly the judgment is reversed as to all defendants and the case is remanded for a new trial on all issues in accordance with the views expressed herein.

Approved by the Court.

UHLICH v. MEDALLION REALTY, INC.
Court of Appeals of Louisiana, 1976.
334 So.2d 788

* * *

REDMANN, Judge.

This case depends heavily on its multifaceted facts. Our trial brother's evaluation of those facts is apparently not different from ours. But he ruled, in effect, that a real estate broker has no legal obligation to would-be purchasers for whom he agreed to look for a vacant lot abutting a levee in a specified location, not even when representing to them that he has found such a lot for them. What occurred was that, after agreeing to look for such a lot for plaintiffs, the agent found one and obtained an agreement to sell it for $11,300 (roughly the then market value) to a longtime friend who dabbled in real estate. The agent then immediately persuaded plaintiffs to pay $14,800 for it. The agent did not reveal (but misrepresented, testify plaintiffs and a disinterested third party) the circumstances. Plaintiffs learned at their act of sale (making plaintiff husband look "distraught," the notary thrice testified) that their vendor had acquired the lot that very day. Believing themselves victimized, they sued the agent and his employer for the difference between the $11,300 and $14,800 prices, for incidental expenses, and for damages for mental anguish.

The trial judge dismissed the suit, reasoning that plaintiffs "have a rather strict burden of proving fraud . . ." and failed to carry that burden. Plaintiffs appeal. We reverse.

Facts

Plaintiff husband and wife in 1971 wanted a vacant lot abutting Lake Pontchartrain's levee. The wife first found such lots on a map on the then-undeveloped Palm Vista subdivision at Kenner. She found herself unable to reach the lots by automobile; "the (drainage) canal (was) as far as I could go." Looking then in newspaper classified advertisements, she found and responded by telephone to defendant Medallion informed her that those lots were not levee lots, but he said he would look for a levee lot for her, although they were "scarce." On October 30, 1971, plaintiff met with Laplace at Medallion to reassert their willingness and ability to buy a levee lot, and to ask Laplace and Medallion to find a lot for them.

Between March and November 1971 there were sales of nine levee lots in Palm Vista. All lots were undeveloped, 75 feet front by 142 to 148 feet deep, and all in our lot's square. Laplace himself was the real estate agent on seven of these nine earlier sales. Two lots of Laplace's seven are not precisely priceable because sold as part of a group including five non-levee lots. The individual level lots Laplace sold included four at $10,000 each (on March 22, May 4, July 1 and August 20) and one at $10,800—the last sale being October 22, 1971, eight days before plaintiffs went to Medallion's office to confer with Laplace. There were also two sales in this period on which Laplace was apparently not an agent: on May 5 one lot sold for $11,500 and on November 4 one sold for $7,000.

On November 5, Laplace persuaded plaintiffs to offer $14,800 for their lot—a lot which Laplace's friend Vincent Danna bought through Laplace at the same time, from a seller represented by a broker with 47 years of experience (though no other experience in this small subdivision), for only $11,300. * * * Thus, on November 3 when he advised plaintiffs he had found a lot for them at $14,800, and on November 5 when he advised plaintiffs to sign the $14,800 offer, Laplace knew both that he had found the lot, available from a broker-represented owner, for only $11,300 ($10,000 net), and also that he, Laplace had handled four other sales at $10,000 in the previous few months and one sale at $10,800 just two weeks earlier.

(As a further indicator of the lots' market value and of the Laplace-Danna relationship, we note that on November 17 or 19 Laplace as agent procured an agreement to sell to Danna yet another levee lot in the same square for $11,000. That lot was also sold through Laplace, for $14,900, about a week later, to a Tennessee resident: the same Tennesseean whom Laplace mentioned to plaintiffs in October as another would-be purchaser for whom Laplace was looking for a levee lot.) * * *

Interpreting the facts most favorably towards Laplace, one might conclude that Laplace had (as he and Danna testified) also been looking for Palm Vista levee lots for long-time friend Danna; * * * that, naturally enough, he preferred his friend and either prospect by offering the lot first to Danna, who accepted, intending the lot for his own purposes; that Danna, on being informed he might make a quick profit, agreed to sell. * * * Even so, Laplace must be held to have breached his obligations towards plaintiff, and the breach to have damaged plaintiffs. * * *

The fundamental Louisiana law is that a broker is the agent of both parties: "The broker or intermediary is he who is employed to negotiate a matter between two parties, and who, for that reason, is considered as the manadatary of both." C.C. 3016. "The obligations of a broker are similar to those of an ordinary mandatary, with this difference, that his engagement is double, and requires that he should observe the same fidelity towards all parties, and not favor one more than another," C.C. 3017. "Brokers are . . . , as other agents, answerable for fraud or faults," C.C. 3018.

We first observe that a real estate agent's agreement to "look for" a reasonably defined lot for a prospective purchaser is not a selfless gratuity. The agent works for a commission on any ultimate purchase, and the prospective purchaser who enlists the agent's professional aid impliedly promises that the agent shall be paid his usual commission if the agent finds a suitable lot which the purchaser buys. (That the custom is for the seller to pay the commission does not alter either the agent's working for commission or the "employing" purchaser's implied obligation that commission shall be paid. The custom of splitting commission when each of buyer and seller has his own agent concedes the truism that the buyer is as indispensable to the sale as is the seller.)

Thus it is error to conclude that the prospective purchaser's conditional obligation to the agent is no obligation and that therefore (for lack of cause, C.C. 1893) the agent has no obligation to the purchaser. The agent's obligation to "look" is difficult to quantify (and therefore to enforce): but it is an obligation. Our bargain was more than "if you find a lot, I will see that you are paid a commission." Our agent was asked and agreed to look for a lot. Plaintiffs had themselves been looking, knew looking was necessary, and decided upon dealing with a professional so that he would look for them; and defendants agreed to look. * * *

More important, in reporting successful completion of his mission to look, Laplace had the obligation of good faith, * * * and fidelity towards plaintiffs, * * * which required him to advise them that, while he had indeed found the lot, he had obtained an agreement to purchase it in favor of Danna for a price approximately the same as that several similar lots had brought in recent months, and that it was Danna, the new purchaser, who was willing to sell the lot to plaintiffs, at a profit. In our judgment, a reasonably informed reasonable buyer would not have agreed to pay the extra $3,500 Danna was asking. And, had Danna kept that lot, it is more probable than not that plaintiff—instead of Danna again—would have bought the next lot that Laplace found, at only $11,000. * * *

Laplace's failure to perform with good faith and fidelity thus deprived plaintiffs of the opportunity to await another lot—a lot that would have cost them only $11,000. We conclude, however, that plaintiffs' damage is not their cost over that $11,000 next sale, but their cost over market price. The best evidence of market is the $11,300 sale to Danna * * * in which seller and buyer were represented by independent real estate agents. Plaintiffs' damage was thus $3,500. * * *

Plaintiffs' demand for the incidental expenses of sale is rejected. Those costs would have been incurred in any event: they were not caused by any breach of contract. * * *

Plaintiffs' demand for damages for mental anguish is also rejected, as not allowable for breach of contract (other than contract for "the gratification of some intellectual enjoyment"). * * *

INFORMATION GIVEN TO THIRD PARTIES

Many suits are the result of information given in writing by the broker to prospective purchasers. This may be what is often referred to "as the listing sheet," charts, graphs, or other information. In the Bails case which follows, the Supreme Court of Montana reviewed the exposure for a party who presented a brochure that contained certain representations which were arguably incorrect.

In addition to the brochure in question, one of the other issues argued is whether the real estate broker and seller are responsible with regard to a representation that the ranch in question would "produce $80,000 in income." This issue is whether a representation as to income on the property is an opinion in general and therefore not actionable or whether it is a representation of a fact and therefore, if the fact is incorrect, may result in an action against the party making the representation. Again, this matter is reviewed in a summary fashion in the Bails case, which follows.

BAILS v. WHEELER
Supreme Court of Montana, 1977.
559 P.2d 1180

* * *

HASWELL, Justice.

This is an action for damages by the purchaser of a ranch against two real estate agents based on alleged fraudulent representations whereby he was induced to enter into the purchase contract. The district * * * court of Gallatin County entered summary judgment for defendants. Plaintiff purchaser appeals.

* * * A synopsis of the transaction forming the basis of this suit appears in our opinion in *Bails* v. *Gar,* Mont. 558 P.2d 458, 33 St. Rep. 1256. That case was a suit by the purchaser of the ranch against the seller based on alleged false representations inducing the purchaser to enter into the contract; the instant case is a suit by the purchaser against the two real estate agents based upon substantially the same representations. We vacate the summary judgment here for the same reasons we vacated it in *Bails* v. *Gar,* supra, viz. that there are genuine issues of material fact precluding summary judgment.

The alleged false representations in the instant suit are that the ranch contains 5,200 deeded acres; that it would raise and sustain 400 animal units; that there were 300 acres of hay land which produced 900 tons of hay per year; that there were 60 acres of crop which produced 21 bushels of grain per acre; and that the property would produce an income of at least $80,000 per year.

A so-called "brochure" appears to contain the principal representations on which the instant case is based, and the real source of factual issues. It is both identified as "Exhibit A" attached to the complaint which contains the first four representations complained of, and at one point it is referred to by a defense attorney as the "mision brochure". There is much confusion surrounding it.

Bails says he received a "brochure," apparently from Richardson, describing the ranch and containing most of the misrepresentations complained of. Although he does not identify "Exhibit A" as the document he received, he says it is very similar to it. Richardson says he received the "brochure" from Wheeler and simply relayed it to Bails. Wheeler argues

Richardson must have changed it because Bails does not identify the one Wheeler sent as the one he received.

These conflicting contentions concerning the "brochure" together with our discussion in *Bails* v. *Gar,* supra, indicate issues of fact precluding summary judgment.

* * * As to the fifth representation, defendants argue the representation the ranch would produce $80,000 income is an opinion and not actionable as fraud. This representation apparently came out of a discussion among the parties while Bails was being shown the ranch. Bails says Richardson stated the ranch would produce $100,000 income and Wheeler reduced that figure to $80,000. Bails says he believed these men to be honest and trusted them.

All parties cite the following rule as controlling:

> "* * * If the party expressing the opinion possesses superior knowledge, such as would reasonably justify the conclusion that his opinion carries with it the implied assertion that he knows the facts which justify it, his statement is actionable if he knows that he does not honestly entertain the opinion because it is contrary to the facts." *Como Orchard Land Co.* v. *Markham,* 54 Mont, 438, 443, 171 P.274, 275.

The opinion of the Court in Como continues:

> "So, likewise, an opinion may be so blended with facts that it amounts to a statement of facts."

We hold the income representation may be actionable within either of the above rules depending on determination of issues of fact. Indications are the real estate brokers had superior knowledge of ranching and one of them had superior knowledge of the particular ranch in question. A cash flow estimate had been prepared that year indicating a much lower income.

For the foregoing reasons, the summary judgment is vacated and the cause remanded to the district court, Gallatin County, for further proceedings consistent with this opinion.

CHAPTER 4

Closings and Condition of the Property

CLOSINGS

The case of Lester raises the issue of responsibility of a broker for purchasers who are out of town and are relying on the real estate broker to make sure that the property closes properly and also that all liens are paid. What extra duties or responsibilities do you think might exist where your purchasers are out of state?

LESTER v. MARSHALL
Supreme Court of Colorado, 1960.
352 P.2d 786

* * *

DOYLYE, Justice.

William and Louise Marshall, plaintiffs below and herein referred to as plaintiffs, purchased a home at 3200 South Delaware Street, Englewood, Colorado on August 3, 1955. Plaintiffs paid the full purchase price of $18,500 in cash on the occasion of the closing. At this time there was an outstanding first deed of trust to the Industrial Federal Savings and Loan Association amounting to $11,152.43. Plaintiffs delivered to Mr. Richard Hurd, the broker who had the listing, a cashier's check payable to them and endorsed in blank. Hurd made the disbursements called for on the closing statement, including the payment to the seller, the payoff of the second mortgage and other expenses, but failed to pay off the indebtedness to the Industrial Federal Savings and Loan Association. This amount he converted to his own use. Plaintiffs did not learn of this conversion until some three months had passed. They then brought an action and named Hurd, R. J. Lester and Ellen K. Wilson as defendants. Lester and Wilson, real estate broker and saleslady respectively, had represented plaintiffs in the transaction. Trial was to the court and during the course of it, Hurd confessed judgment and is not a party in this Court. At the trial's conclusion judgment was entered against the defendants, Lester and Wilson, in the sum of $12,625.21. They seek review by writ of error.

There is little dispute in the evidence. Dr. Marshall is a minister who had resided at Rawlins, Wyoming prior to the transaction hereafter described. He had visited Denver during 1954, during which time he became acquainted with the defendant, Mrs. Wilson, a licensed real estate saleslady employed by R. J. Lester, a real estate broker. Upon deciding to move to the Denver area in July, 1955, the Marshalls employed Mrs. Wilson to locate a house for them. Mrs. Wilson showed plaintiffs several houses, none of which were satisfactory to them. Then, on July 27, 1955, plaintiffs called Mrs. Wilson and told her that they had located a house and asked her to show it to them. This is the house described above which was then listed with the defendant Hurd.

After being shown the house, the Marshalls and Mrs. Wilson went to the Lester real estate office and proceeded to fill in a form receipt and option contract for the purpose of making an offer to the defendant Hurd. The Marshalls gave Lester a check for $900 to be transmitted with the contract to Hurd. Mrs. Wilson had told the Marshalls that she and Lester were in a listing exchange arrangement with Hurd. The offer providing for a sale price of $18,000 was transmitted to Hurd. Telephone negotiations followed between Mrs. Wilson, acting for plaintiffs, and Hurd, acting for the sellers. As a result of these negotiations, the sellers, who had demanded $19,500, agreed to sell for $18,500, subject to modifications all of which were inked into the contract. Plaintiffs agreed to buy for this amount.

It is noteworthy that the Marshalls were insistent that they obtain possession on August 3, 1955, and that the property should be free and clear of encumbrances. They inquired of Mrs. Wilson as to how the existing encumbrances were to be paid off. She, in turn, according to her testimony, told them that this was all handled by the broker at the time of the closing. Her statements to the plaintiffs were of such a nature as to reassure plaintiffs that this was a matter of routine.

After the contract was completed and signed, plaintiffs returned to Rawlins, telling Mrs. Wilson that they would not be back to Denver until the date of the closing. She in turn assured plaintiffs that she would take care of everything.

On August 3, 1955, the closing took place at the office of defendant Hurd. A settlement sheet presented by the broker, Hurd, disclosed in detail various items of receipts and disbursements, including the out-standing obligation to the Industrial Federal Savings and Loan Association in excess of $11,100. Plaintiffs accepted delivery of a warranty deed which purported to convey the premises free and clear of all liens and encumbrances. The plaintiff, Dr. Marshall, then endorsed his cashier's check in blank and delivered it to Hurd.

Again, after the closing, the plaintiffs expressed some apprehension to Mrs. Wilson and she again assured them that they had nothing to worry about and that she would take care of everything. The testimony establishes further that neither Mrs. Wilson nor Lester advised the plaintiffs to retain an attorney or to have the title examined. Mrs. Wilson did testify, however, that on her own initiative she had requested a title opinion from Hurd's lawyer. No such opinion was ever provided.

Some weeks after the closing, plaintiffs called the Lester office and complained that the deed (which Hurd was supposed to have recorded) had not been received. Lester then called Hurd, who stated that through an oversight the deed had not been recorded. Lester did not inquire as to whether the deeds of trust had been released. The information that the Industrial Federal deed of trust had not been paid off did not come to light until some time later in the fall of 1955. The existence of the unpaid note came to plaintiff's attention after Hurd failed to make the November payment. Thereafter they kept the loan in good standing and subsequently commenced the present action.

The trial court found that the defendants Wilson and Lester were buyers' agents; that they were aware of the plaintiffs' desire to pay cash and had undertaken the employment with this in mind; that Mrs. Wilson had given the plaintiffs assurance that she would see to it that their wishes were carried out fully. The court concluded that the two agents had by their representation and conduct lulled the plaintiffs into a false sense of security as a result of which the plaintiffs failed to take steps which they would otherwise have taken in order to protect themselves, and as a consequence the loss was suffered. The court also reasoned that apart from the express terms of the agency, the real estate broker was obligated, under the circumstances such as those disclosed, to protect his client against the kind of hazard here present, and concluded that this duty could have been discharged and the loss avoided if the defendants had instructed the plaintiffs to draw checks jointly to the owner and the holders of the first and second deeds of trust or had they themselves held the funds in escrow, or if they had instructed plaintiffs to specially endorse the cashier's check to Lester and Hurd as joint endorsees.

Defendants argue that there was neither contractual nor tort obligation toward the plaintiffs following the closing; that their duties were discharged once the deed was delivered and that the risk of the conversion was one to which the plaintiffs subjected themselves when they delivered the bearer check to Hurd.

Defendants further argue that the evidence fails to support a judgment against Lester either directly or vicariously and, thirdly, that Mrs. Wilson and Lester were agents of the plaintiffs; that their relationship to the plaintiffs at the time in question was a gratuitous one which imposed no legal obligations.

The determinative question is whether the defendants were legally obligated to take preventive measures to protect plaintiffs from loss, or having failed to do so, whether they were required to ascertain whether the encumbrance was actually paid off. * * *

There are two theories upon which the liability of defendants here is predicated. The first of these is based upon the failure of defendants to carry out an express undertaking which the plaintiffs had relied on them to carry out, as a result of which the plaintiffs suffered a loss. The second is failure to perform a duty implied in relationship of real estate broker and client. * * * The trial court was of the opinion that both of these duties were present and that the evidence was sufficient to establish violations.

Our conclusion that the evidence was sufficient to support the trial court's finding that there was an express undertaking by the defendants on which the plaintiffs relied to their damage renders unnecessary a consideration of the legal duties implicit in the relationship of broker to client.

We deem it significant that the plaintiffs resided out of Denver and that they were thus dependent on the services of the defendants. Defendants, in turn, were agreeable to plaintiffs' leaving the arrangements to them since they did not recommend employment of counsel to examine the title and to render services at the time of the closing. The assurances given to the plaintiffs that everything would be taken care of prior to the closing; that they would get a title free of encumbrances; that the disbursements were made routinely; and that everything would be cared for after the closing, resulted in a quieting of any apprehension plaintiffs may have had, and a reliance on the defendants to perform whatever duties were requisite. * * *

Affirmed.

EXPOSURE FOR CONDITION
OF THE PROPERTY

Checklist When Inspecting a Home. Because there are so many areas where real estate brokers may have exposure with regard to the sale of homes, especially where there are problems with the homes, it is interesting to note the following checklist of items to consider when inspecting a house published in *Realtor's Review* in November of 1977. This is a worthwhile checklist for a real estate broker, inasmuch as the broker may be considered negligent in failing to advise a purchaser on certain items. This does not mean that the purchaser is protected by the broker; the broker has an obligation to advise of all defects, since some defects are more apparent than others. Once again, this checklist is an important tool for a purchaser and for the real estate broker.

CHECKLIST FOR SELLING A SAFE HOME

Home safety is like good health: When it's there, you don't think about it, but once jeopardized, it can change a person's whole world. In the excitement and pressure of real estate transactions, it's easy for the buyer and the seller to let factors such as price, location, and size edge out actual safety considerations. But economy, beauty, and convenience all take a fast second place to safety when haphazardness and cases of poor design, jerry-built remodeling, or lazy upkeep can imperil human well-being.

REALTORS® and REALTOR ASSOCIATE®s don't pretend to be safety engineers, but they are constantly aware of the fact that a house must be safe to be salable. Here we discuss several steps you can take to help clients sell, and prospects buy, a home in which people can feel safe— that is, according to Webster, "secure from threat of danger, harm, or loss."

How Safe Is the Home? Figures from the National Safety Council's 1977 edition of *Accident Facts* show 24,000 deaths and 3,700,000 disabling injuries resulting from accidents in the home in 1976. Including wage loss, medical expense, health insurance administration, and fire losses, the cost of these fatalities and injuries climbed to $6.3 billion for that year alone. Falls ranked as the leading cause of death, followed by fires and burns. Among the other fatality-producing accidents were gas and vapor poisoning (principally from carbon monoxide) and electric shock. Dangers from the intrusions of burglars is another safety threat: The National Sheriffs' Association reports that more than 3,000,000 burglaries are committed each year in the United States, and many of them do include personal attacks.

These alarming statistics underline the need for everyone to place more emphasis on home safety. Real estate salespeople are in a prime position to help prescribe what might be called preventive medicine for future accidents. Whenever you check out a new listing, you can watch for danger spots to be remedied as well as safety features to be highlighted. When recommending to buyers or sellers a home inspection by an impartial but qualified professional (see, "How the Home Protection Program Works," *REALTORS® Review,* March, 1977, page 25), you can stress the safety aspects of this assessment of the property's mechanical and structural components. In addition, you can pass on extra safety tips for homeowners to follow long after the sales transaction is completed. On page 24, we've included a practical checklist, "Tips to Sharpen Three Safety Senses: Yours, the Buyer's, the Seller's," to be shared with established as well as prospective clients and customers.

Safety and the Real Estate Salesperson. No real estate salesperson wants to spring on a client a long list of improvements to be made before marketing a new listing. But by Articles 7 and 9 of the Code of Ethics, not only are you pledged to promote and protect the interests of your client, you also are obliged to treat fairly all parties to the transaction and to discover adverse factors that a reasonably competent and diligent investigation would disclose.

Many safety hazards are easy to spot when you first visit a property to study its general condition and market value. Did you stumble over a loose brick in the sidewalk? Chances are that a prospect will, too, so point out the hazard to your client. Are the basement stairs dimly lit and minus a handrail? Sellers should consider remedying problems such as these before someone—perhaps a good prospect—falls and gets hurt.

"Faulty stairways are a big bugaboo with me," says Rich Howse, a REALTOR® and assistant vice-president of Hardin Stockton Company, in Kansas City, Kansas. What reaction does he get to citing a danger? "In many cases, people have been living in their homes a long time and just haven't noticed that something has become a hazard. In other cases, you'll get sellers who've noticed but who say, 'Oh, that thing's been working like that for 15 years—it's bound to last at least another 15.' "

Whether any repair is made by the seller or by the new owner varies with each situation and frequently becomes a matter of negotiation between the two. Jeri Block, a Realtor with Pine Valley Realty, in Wilmington, North Carolina, finds that sellers are anxious to know about everything you think is wrong with the property. "But sometimes they aren't anxious to do much about it until a sales contract is ready to be signed. 'I'll fix this when I get a buyer,' they say, but sometimes they're not going to get a contract until it's fixed, and you have to point that out."

In beach and waterfront communities, such as Block's Wilmington, piers and outdoor decks are often part of the property. The moist and sometimes salty air is wearing on them, and rotten wood is common, says Block. A crumbling pier or a deck with loose planks is certainly a hazard someone should correct.

No home, new or old, is guaranteed not to burn down, and many new homes today come equipped with smoke detectors. "I've become especially aware of their importance," says Block. She looks for them in every new home, and recommends that all homeowners have one, whether they're moving in or moving out.

While every home should be basically sound and safe, buyers do have individual safety considerations that salespeople can help them be more aware of. For example, parents with small children should be alert to stairway design: Toddlers are less likely to fall through or get their heads caught between tightly spaced stairway balusters than if these rail spindles were sparsely placed. Another example: The sunken living room that might hold glamorous appeal for the couple with no children, might be entirely ruled out by a family that includes elderly members who could have trouble stepping into or out of it.

Tips to Sharpen Three Safety Senses: Yours, the Buyer's, the Seller's. It is a human trait to assume you are safe in your own home. But the thousands of deaths and millions of injuries that result from falls, fires, shocks, and other accidents inside or around the home attest to the actual risks encountered there. Every homeowner should actively take precautions for safety. The following features are some of the most important.

Escaping or Avoiding Fires, Burns, Electric Shocks
- Each room has door or window access to the outside.
- Bedroom and stairway doors are solid, not louvered.
- Closet doors and those between rooms have doorknobs on both sides.
- Basements, especially if recreational, have ceilings of fire-resistive materials such as dry-wall or plaster.
- Adequate storage space cuts down on the clutter and disorder that can cause fires (and falls).
- Window wells, wooden stairs, and areas under porches are kept clear of dry leaves.
- Water-heating equipment has a temperature and/or pressure-relief valve that can readily be tested by the homeowner.
- Discharge for pressure and temperature-relief valves is piped toward and near to the floor.
- Chimneys are in good repair at bottom and top, and combustible structure parts are not tight against them; chimneys should be at least 2 feet above the highest point of the house if not more than 10 feet from any vertical projection.
- Prefab or factory-assembled chimneys and vents should bear the label of a nationally recognized testing agency, such as Underwriters Laboratories.
- Fireplace hearth extends a minimum of 16 inches into room.
- Fireplaces have dampers.
- Radiator covers protect against contact burns.
- House has smoke detector.
- Wiring is adequate to accommodate the appliance load.

- There are circuit breakers or fuses to protect against overload.
- Fuses or circuit breakers are labeled to identify outlets and fixtures they protect.
- All electrical equipment bears the label of a nationally recognized testing laboratory.
- Octopus or jerry-built wiring is avoided.
- No frayed cords or cracked plugs are used, and no extension cords are run under carpets or through doors.
- Outlets are of the three-hole, grounding type, or at least are grounded so that adapters may be used.
- Electrical sockets have covers to prevent children from poking objects into them.
- Homeowner knows proper fuse ratings for electric circuits.
- Homeowner knows location of the main electric switch, how to turn it off, and pulls it before changing a fuse.
- Cause of blown fuse is determined before fuse is replaced.

Safety Outside the House
- No garden tools are lying around, especially upturned rakes and shovels.
- Hedges, trees, and shrubs do not obscure driveway views.
- Large trees are healthy and well maintained, with no dead limbs.
- Electric and lift-up garage doors are regularly inspected.
- Porches and steps are sound and protected by sturdy railings.
- Driveway and all exterior walkways are well lighted.
- Sidewalks, exposed porches, and driveway have rough finish to prevent slipperiness when wet and are graded to a slight slope away from the house to eliminate puddles of water or spots of ice.
- Indoor-outdoor carpeting, slippery when wet, is protected from rain.
- Walks and driveways are kept in repair, not broken.
- Children's backyard playground equipment is maintained in safe condition.
- Sliding glass doors to outside are glazed with safety glass.
- Garage has adequate ventilation.

Utility Areas
- Washer and dryer are properly grounded.
- Homeowner knows location of main gas and water valves and how to close them; gas and water lines are distinctly tagged.
- Homeowner knows how to light the pilot light on furnace and water heater.
- Furnace room is adequately ventilated.
- Fuel-consuming heating devices are vented to the outside, either directly or through a chimney, and have draft hoods or dampers appropriate to the fuel being used.

• Vent pipes are tightly connected to chimneys, not rusted through, not sagging.
• Fuel lines do not extend into areas where they may be easily damaged or ruptured.
• Fuel shutoffs are identified.
• Liquid fuel containers are labeled by a nationally recognized testing agency.
• Workshop is well ventilated and well lighted, power-tool guards are kept in place, and tool switches are locked or disconnected when not in use.
• Adequate storage keeps tools out of reach of small children.

Stairway and Hall Safety
• Every stairway has at least one handrail, preferably two, at a comfortable, convenient height from the stair treads.
• Riser heights on each stairway are uniform and not greater than eight inches; treads are at least nine inches deep.
• Stairway treads, nosing, and carpeting are in sound condition.
• Stairways have good daylight and/or artificial light.
• Light switches are located at top and bottom of main stairs and at both ends of long hallways.
• Doors do not swing out over stair steps.

Kitchen and Bathroom Safety
• Gas equipment has pilot lights and automatic cutoff in event of flame failure.
• Appliances have American Gas Association or Underwriters Laboratories labels.
• Adequate lighting and sufficient grounded outlets are provided for all work surfaces.
• Kitchen exhaust system discharges directly or through ducts to the outside and not into the attic or other unused spaces.
• Bath and shower doors are glazed with safety glass or plastic.
• Bathtubs have nearly flat, nonslip or textured bottoms.
• Firm, unbreakable grab bars—not towel bars used as substitutes—are installed in tub and shower enclosures.
• Electric fixtures and switches are not within reach of tub or shower enclosure.
• Bathroom floor has nonslip finish.

Safety in Other Family Areas
• Floors are not splintered and all floor coverings are in good condition and firmly anchored.
• Scatter rugs have nonskid backing.
• All exits and traffic areas are clear of tripping hazards.
• Screens are used in front of all fireplaces.

- Doors open against walls and do not interfere with foot traffic or other doors.
- Exterior doors and doors leading from garage or basement into house have jimmy-proof deadlocks.
- Windows have key-operated sash or latch locks.
- Landscaping near the house—trees and shrubs—does not provide burglar hideouts nor access to the home's second story.
- Garage door is kept closed and locked.

Safety and the Home Inspector. Your roving eye for safety ends where the deeper probe of qualified, professional inspectors begins. Their evaluation of the home's soundness; of the condition of its heating, plumbing, and electric systems; and of the reliability of its structure serves not only as a measure of salability and a projection of maintenance costs. It also lets the future inhabitants know how free they can reasonably expect to feel from such dangers as fires or shock caused by faulty wiring, gas poisoning from a cracked heat-exchange system, or burns caused by an exploding hot water heater.

Inspection costs are based on the market value, age, and location of a property. They vary across the country, but seem to hover around $100. "It's inexpensive insurance for the buyer," says Rich Howse. Encouraging sellers to let a professional inspector come in, as well as suggesting that buyers engage an inspection service, can save everyone future headaches. "We've been told by many real estate people that we've saved far more sales than we've ever caused to collapse," says Doreen Kolesar, office manager of Home Inspection Consultants of Colorado, in Wheat Ridge, a suburb of Denver. This company provides a complete and unbiased report of the home's condition, suggests the most practical means of correcting any defects, and provides an estimate of the cost of each repair. Like other inspection services we talked with, these consultants avoid a conflict of interests: They do not make any repairs, nor do they recommend the name of any repair company or person.

Some of the safety problems encountered by engineers at the Colorado firm include: improper ventilation in rooms with gas furnaces; downspouts that discharge water onto sidewalks where it can freeze and cause falls; the flammable combination of worn wires and old, tinder-like plaster; and, also a fire hazard, newspapers or sawdust used as attic insulation in some very old houses.

"Buyers have a right to know what they are getting into, what to expect in the way of hazard and repair," says J. S. James, an architectural engineer and owner of American Building Inspection Service, in Chicago. Part of his service includes answering the prospective buyer's questions regarding a particular home—"How do I start this furnace safely? Where's the main electric switch? How do I shut off the water line?"

The average inspection takes about two hours and requires no fancy equipment—usually just a strong searchlight, a level, a ladder, and a pencil and clipboard. Many services require inspectors to be registered engineers, while others may employ former contractors or former city inspectors. "Background and experience are important," said J. S. James. "We have to know what to look for, what signs show something is wrong."

Additional safety-related construction features professional inspectors can evaluate are included in the accompanying checklist, compiled with the help of *Family Safety* Magazine, the National Safety Council, and the National Sheriffs' Association. The checklist also offers many more guidelines for safety that you, as salespeople, may want to share with home buyers and homeowners.

(Reprinted from the November 1977 issue of *Realtors® Review,* a publication of the National Association of Realtors®.)

GUARANTEEING THE PROPERTY YOU MARKET

In response to the potential exposure of Realtors for property that they market, I previously wrote an article entitled, "So You Don't Think You Guarantee the Property You Market!" This article introduces many of the potential problems for Realtors when marketing property.

The article, entitled "So You Don't Think You Guarantee the Property You Market!" follows:

Most real estate salespeople would say they don't. Real estate companies tend to operate under a marketing concept, not a construction or engineering approach. When marketing property, salespeople may point out structural advantages and disadvantages, saying, for example, that this is a brick house, and brick is more durable than wood. But recently, many real estate companies have been approached with programs to guarantee the condition of the property they are marketing. These programs have received support due to lawsuits filed against some real estate people because of defects discovered in a house after it was marketed by the company.

This chapter discusses the real estate salesperson's exposure to liability when marketing property. Do salespeople guarantee the property they are marketing?

The Problem: to Sell. Obviously, the salesperson wants to sell the property on the seller's terms: to sell it fast and at the right price.

Hence the sales pitch. Some real estate people exhibit a form of behavior known as "puffing." Statements are often made such as, "This is the most beautiful house on the block," "This is the best built house on the block," and "This is the most functional house on the block." These are examples of puffing. There is a distinction between *puffing* and legitimate *representations of fact or opinion of an expert.* From a legal standpoint, the representation of fact and the representation of opinion by an expert are thought to result in a position which may be relied on by the buyer.

A statement by the real estate salesperson that "the roof is in good condition, the furnace is operating and has no problems, there are no soil problems, there are no termites or other infestations in the house, the house has not suffered from water damage, there are no structural problems," or any other representations of fact or opinion by an expert (the real estate person, for instance) can result in exposure if the facts are inaccurate.

The real estate salesperson has usually been thought of as an expert only in the field of *marketing* and related functions. The salesperson does not usually represent himself or herself as an expert in construction, engineering, or general physical condition of a property. (An exception to this is if the real estate person is also the builder.)

Recently, real estate salespeople have been sued because of a defective roof, furnace, structural condition, and soil position, all of which were discovered by the buyer after the sale was closed. In most of these cases the real estate salesperson had not been representing fact or expert opinion. The defect was discovered in most of the suits after the sale closes. The real estate salesperson is often sued because of the defective condition and because of his failure to disclose the condition to the purchaser.

If the real estate salesperson did not know of the defect, new questions are raised. If the real estate salesperson knew of the defective condition, the law may require the salesperson to point them out to a prospective buyer. However, the developing concept of the law addresses the idea that the real estate salesperson should have general knowledge of the structural condition and soil defects, (etc.) of the property he is marketing.

To take the position the real estate salesperson *should have known* and pointed out the conditions, the purchaser or plaintiff must assert that the real estate salesperson was represented as being a professional (expert) *as to such items, e.g.,* the structure.

Real estate people should be familiar with certain problems in given areas. For example, many houses are bound to have problems because they are in slide zones, water zones, flood zones, and weak soil areas.

Other questions of potential liability and conflict of interest for the real estate salesperson are: Does the real estate salesperson violate any fiduciary duties owed to his principal when disclosing certain facts to a prospective purchaser? Should a real estate salesperson disclose to a prospective purchaser that other houses in this area have had water damage? Must the real estate salesperson explain this to a prospective purchaser when the house in question has not had any water damage? If the real estate salesperson fails to disclose this information and the house is damaged by water seepage after the purchase, is there liability on the agent? And if the agent does disclose this information, has a duty of good faith to his principal been violated because the negative factors have perhaps discouraged the sale of the property or brought the price down?

More cases will give answers to these questions. Presently, the indication seems to be that it is the agent's duty to disclose property conditions.

The opposing position seems to argue the marketing concept. That is, the real estate salesperson is a market expert: he is not trained to know the structural conditions of property. This is allegedly left to engineers and others involved in the structural quality of property. Also, it is argued that the seller or purchaser are free to use any experts they want to examine the property. Thus, a purchaser could easily condition the purchase upon an inspection of the property by an engineer. But should the agent advise a purchaser to have the property inspected? Some states require an agent to do this and to recommend an attorney be present at the closing to review the documents. It is conceivable that real estate inspections may be required by law in the future. Until that point, real estate people can expect a wave of litigation which will engulf their boat, too.

Implications of the Problem. A major implication of the potential increased liability exposure to Realtors is the cost to cover the exposure. Such costs may be in the form of insurance, fees for inspections, and attempted exculpatory language in contracts (which may not be enforceable).

Professional liability insurance (errors and omissions, E & O) for real estate firms has greatly increased recently.

Many firms are implementing inspection programs or strongly suggesting that purchasers have properties inspected. Other firms are implementing programs in which certain conditions of property are guaranteed for a one-year period.

Someone must pay for the increase in costly liability insurance. The agent's clients are the most likely source of funding.

How to Avoid the Problem. Assuming for the moment that the law develops in the manner suggested and that the Realtor's liability exposure continues to increase, there are various ways the problem might be counteracted.

First, salespeople need to be informed that they should be careful in making statements about the condition of property. A mere statement that the roof is in good condition could result in potential liability. Most real estate suits go against the broker because of his fiduciary responsibilities.

The potential use of inspections can be profitable. However, unless a reasonable basis is created for this program, the costs might be prohibitive. Many firms are joining to hire an inspector. Each firm bears the cost of the inspector's fees in proportion to the number of inspections done.

It would be helpful to provide exculpatory clauses in the contract in which the purchaser is warned that the company is not guaranteeing or in any way representing the physical condition of the property, and that such condition must be reviewed by an expert in the area. But any false or materially misleading statements by the salesperson can result in liability.

There is also the possibility of legislation to protect salespeople. Realtors generally have a strong legislative force to initiate legislation. A recovery fund may be created to aid purchasers damaged by conditions beyond their knowledge at the time of purchase.

How Do Other Professions Avoid the Problem? Other professionals use many of the above suggestions. Doctors and attorneys use professional liability insurance for protection in the areas of negligence. If the real estate firm is faced with a real need for protection, insurance may provide some coverage. But the cost of premiums will likely be borne indirectly by the buyer and the seller. Insurance may not be the full answer. Potential gaps and high rates may eliminate it as an alternative or reduce its feasibility.

Owner's Exposure to Liability. Not only is the salesperson potentially liable for the condition of a property, but the owner can also be liable. If aware of a defect in the property, the owner could be liable. Also, the owner can be liable on the theory of agency law.

(Reprinted with permission from Mark Lee Levine, *Real Estate Fundamentals* (West 1976).

CONDITION OF THE PROPERTY

Under the facts, Mr. and Mrs. Spargnapani bought a house from Sarsfield, through the brokerage office of Wright. After taking possession of the property they discovered that the heating plant was defective. There is testimony that the broker-salesperson had represented that the heating system was in good condition and that the oil burner was practically new. Under these facts, would the real estate company be responsible and would the agent also be responsible? This case again is answered in Spargnapani, a 1954 decision out of the District of Columbia.

SPARGNAPANI v. WRIGHT
District of Columbia, 1954.
110 A.2d 82

* * *

CAYTON, Chief Judge.

Mr. and Mrs. Spargnapani bought a house from Sarsfield through the brokerage office of Wright. After taking possession they discovered that the heating plant was defective and unusable, and after unsuccessful demands for payment of repair costs sued the seller and the broker. Plaintiffs' testimony was that the broker's saleswoman had represented that the heating system was in good condition, that the oil burner was practically new and that so long as they kept oil in the tank they would have plenty of heat. The negotiations commenced in July or August, and the contract of sale was executed August 22, 1953. Their testimony (discussed in greater detail later) was that sometime in mid-October rusty water started leaking from the boiler and this leak was traced to a crack some four inches long in the top section of the boiler. There was evidence that the former owner, a Mrs. Hutchinson, * * * had the crack concealed by a black patch, and then had the entire boiler painted over with black paint which gave it a shiny, new appearance.

The broker's saleswoman testified that she made no representation to the Spargnapanis as to the age or working condition of the heating system, but admitted that she told them the house could be heated for a little over a hundred dollars a year, and that the walls and ceilings were insulated—this being the information she had gotten from Mrs. Hutchinson. She also admitted that she was trying to impress on them that the house could be heated very reasonably. She said she then had no knowledge of any defect in the heating system. The trial judge decided the case in favor of defendants, and plaintiffs bring this appeal. * * *

The first finding was that "defendants had no knowledge of the defect in the boiler." Conceding this finding to be accurate, it cannot be held decisive of the major issue, for the inescapable fact is that there was a bad defect in the boiler which had been artfully concealed. If the broker innocently represented that the heating plant was in workable condition and was mistaken in that representation, or made the representation without knowing whether it was true or false, the injured party may recover in an action for fraud. * * *

The same general principle applies to the judge's second finding that, "(2) defendants practiced no deception upon the plaintiffs with respect to the heating system, either by affirmative statements or by withholding knowledge of any concealed defects." We may assume that the broker was guilty of no deliberate deception and had no actual knowledge of the concealed defect. * * *

The trial court also found: "(3) the plaintiffs were cognizant of the fact that they were purchasing an old house, and did not rely on the statements of the defendant as to the condition of the property; (4) plaintiffs twice inspected the house, once in the company of their own remodeling and redecorating agent." It is true that plaintiffs knew they were buying an old house, but we are unaware of any rule of law which says that one who buys an old house must expect to get a worthless heating system, particularly in the face of the representation discussed above. And the uncontradicted evidence was that the man who went with them was asked for advice only as to termite protection and redecorating, * * * and that they never discussed the heating plant with him. The finding that the purchasers did not rely on the broker's statements is contrary to the direct and uncontradicted evidence, such reliance being voiced in such plain expressions as, "I didn't doubt it," "I believed it," and "we took her word for it." The finding was erroneous. * * *

The trial judge found, "(5) plaintiffs were put on notice by the recent paint job to examine the boiler for any defects which might have been covered by the paint. This finding was based on an erroneous concept of law. * * * These purchasers testified that the saleswoman gave them specific assurances that the heating system was very good and that they only needed to keep oil in the tank to obtain heat. Her own testimony was that she did not make those particular statements; but as we have seen she admitted telling them that the annual heating cost would be little more than one hundred dollars. Whichever version was accepted by the trial judge, there was no basis in law or logic for ruling that the purchasers were required to investigate and make tests to determine what was under the shiny black paint on the boiler. It is hardly reasonable to expect one buying a house in August, when a heating plant is shut off for the season, to subject it to tests calculated to determine how well it will work when winter comes. * * *

For the same reasons we decline to rule, as appellees would have us do and as the trial court did, that caveat emptor applies. We agree with the trial court that, "The mere sale of a defective article does not establish fraud on the part of the seller." * * * But we have more than that naked hypothesis here. We have an article with a concealed defect, which was at the very least (adopting defendants' version) represented to be in functioning condition when it was in fact completely inoperable and had to be replaced. This pretense of knowledge on the part of the seller's agent, this vital though innocent misrepresentation, being in the eyes of the law a fraud, left no room for the application of caveat emptor. * * *

We do not agree with appellees that because there were factual disputes at the trial there is nothing for us to review here. It is, of course, not surprising that plaintiffs told a stronger and more detailed story of misrepresentations, and that defendants' version was less damaging to themselves. But damaging it was, as we have already explained in considerable detail: damaging enough to constitute actionable fraud. Moreover, there is recent and unassailable authority that "(a) finding is clearly erroneous when 'although there is evidence to support it, the reviewing court on the entire evidence is left with a definite and firm conviction that a mistake has been committed.'" *McAllister v. United States*, 75 S.Ct. 6, 8. * * * We note also that the Supreme Court has denied certiorari in a case in which the second circuit ruled that where the evidence is partly oral and the balance is written, or deals with undisputed facts, then the appeals court may ignore the trial judge's finding and substitute its own, if the written evidence or some undisputed fact renders the credibility of the oral testimony extremely doubtful. * * *

In the case before us there was a letter, written by the broker, stating that his office had been told by the former owner that the heating plant was in good condition; and this letter was in contradiction of the testimony that the saleswoman told these purchasers nothing about the subject because she knew nothing about it. But we have not based our decision on that written admission or on contradictions between writings and verbal testimony.

Nevertheless, the cases just cited fortify us in our conclusion that in any view of the evidence as a whole, the answer is not doubtful and the broker Wright and his principal Sarsfield must be held answerable in damages to these plaintiffs.

* * * There is a dispute between the parties as to the proper measure of damages. Defendants seem to contend that compensation should be on the basis of the difference between the price paid for the house itself and its depreciated market value resulting from the discovered defect. That is a test frequently employed, and one we have in some circumstances approved. * * * But it is not the only or inevitable test. We think it would be just as wise and proper in this case to take the direct and simple approach, and award damages on the basis of the actual cost of replacing the defective boiler, with suitable recognition of the age of the boiler and of the further useful life it would have had if it had not cracked. * * * If the parties cannot agree on an amount which would meet these tests, then damages are to be assessed by the trial court on the basis of the evidence already adduced, or by taking further testimony on the subject.

Reversed, with instructions to award judgment to plaintiffs against both defendants.

BROKER'S RESPONSIBILITY WHEN LEASING PROPERTY

The question in the Wright case raises the issue as to whether a real estate broker is responsible to an owner of the house when the real estate broker leased the property but did not make proper credit investigations of tenants before he executed the lease and did not have the utility account transferred. Further, there was a breach: the broker did not keep the owners fully informed as to lack of payment of rents and other requirements imposed on the tenant. There is also the question of punitive damages.

Do you feel a real estate broker would be responsible if he failed to undertake a proper credit check of prospective tenants? How far must the real estate broker go and would he be liable for punitive-punishment damages? Again, the Wright case attempts to answer some of these questions.

WRIGHT v. EVERETT
Supreme Court of Appeals of Virginia, 1956.
90 S.E.2d 855

* * *

HUDGINS, Chief Justice.

Harris W. Everett and Patricia A. Everett, his wife, instituted this action against W. B. Wright, a real estate broker, claiming compensatory and punitive damages for his failure to exercise proper care in the management of their furnished home which they had authorized him to lease. The jury returned a verdict for plaintiffs in the sum of $325.17, compensatory damages, and $3,000, punitive damages, upon which the trial court entered judgment. This writ of error was awarded W. B. Wright, the defendant, to review that judgment.

The decisive question presented is whether the evidence is sufficient to sustain a verdict for exemplary or punitive damages.

The evidence from the plaintiffs' point of view may be summarized as follows:

Plaintiffs owned a furnished home in Arlington County, Virginia, that they desired to rent for four months while they were on a business trip to Nassau, Bahamas. On being assured by Leonard R. Honnold, an agent of W. B. Wright, that he always checked "the credit rating and references" of prospective tenants before leasing property entrusted to his care, they engaged him to lease the property for four months beginning December, 1952. Pursuant to this engagement and through the efforts of Honnold, the home as furnished was leased to Warden C. Stillwell and Joanne Stillwell, his wife, from December 5, 1952, to April 5, 1953, at a rental of $225 per month. At the time the Stillwells signed the lease Honnold required them to give him $150 as security for the payment of any breakage or damage to the house or furniture during their occupancy. In addition, Honnold agreed that he would have the account of all utilities, including water, electricity, gas and telephone, transferred from the names of the owners to the names of the lessees, and to collect the rent, deduct the broker's commissions and deposit the remainder in a local bank to the credit of Harris W. Everett.

While Honnold and Stillwell were inspecting the premises it developed that Stillwell and Everett had attended the same college. They became very friendly and later, before the lease was executed, the plaintiffs invited Stillwell to have dinner with them, at which time Mrs. Everett told Stillwell that they would be glad to lease him the property. This fact was communicated to the agent, who thereupon prepared a lease, and on the night of December 5th took it to the Everetts' home. There he found that the plaintiffs had given their consent for the Stillwells to move and in fact Stillwell signed the lease and the plaintiffs were willing to sign, but at Honnold's suggestion they permitted him to retain the lease until he could obtain Mrs. Stillwell's signature. This was done and he mailed the lease to Nassau to be executed by plaintiffs.

Honnold, on being assured by Stillwell that he would promptly pay the accounts of all utilities, violated his agreement with plaintiffs and did not have the accounts transferred from the names of plaintiffs to those of the lessees. Consequently, all such bills were charged to plaintiffs, including a telephone bill for $424.95 incurred by the lessees.

On January 24, 1953, Mrs. Everett wrote Honnold that no part of the rent had been paid and suggested that thereafter checks for the rent be sent directly to her. She closed the letter with the statement that she expected to hear from the agent "on the next mail." The broker made no reply to this letter, but did continue his efforts to collect the rent from the lessees. The first check given for rent had been returned by the bank on which it was drawn marked "Insufficient Funds." The agent made several attempts to talk to Stillwell about the past due rent, but was informed that he was in Mexico. On January 14, 1953, the lessees gave him another check for two months' rent and past due utility bills. This check was likewise dishonored although at the repeated request of the lessees it was redeposited for collection several times. The broker did not inform plaintiffs of his futile attempts to collect the rent until February 10, 1953, on which date he gave an account of his activities in the following letter:

"When we gave possession to Mr. Stillwell, he deposited with us $150.00 in cash and gave us a check for the first month's rental of $225.00. We deposited this check in the bank, but it was returned to us marked 'Insufficient Funds.' We could not replace this check until around the middle of January for the reason that Mr. Stillwell travels and is out of the city a great portion of the time. When he did return, he gave us a check for $502.00, which was to pay for two (2) months' rental and certain utility bills. When he gave us this check we returned the check that he had given us originally for the first month's rent. This check was issued payable to W. B. Wright on a California Bank and made by Kyril Ralston.

"We deposited this check and within a reasonable time it was returned to us with a notation 'Refer to Maker.' Mr. Honnold of our Virginia office contacted Mr. Ralston, the maker of the check, who instructed him to redeposit the check, which we did. We had begun to get worried about this check and when it was deposited the second time we asked for a special report by telegram. When the report came back after depositing it the second time, the notation was 'Refer to Maker' and 'Unauthorized Signature.'

"We contacted Mrs. Stillwell who informed us that her husband was in Mexico City, Mexico, but that Mr. Ralston would take care of the matter. We contacted Mr. Ralston for the third time, as we had become very suspicious of this transaction. In the meanwhile, we received a telegram from Mr. Stillwell in Mexico City, a copy of which we are enclosing, and upon the instructions in the telegram we have again re-deposited this chek.

"We do not want to worry you about this transaction but we think it better that you know the facts as they are transpiring. We have also contacted our attorneys for instructions, which we are following, regardless of the instructions from the tenant and Mr. Ralston. Also, we are trying to obtain information about them from the Credit Bureau of Washington, a mercantile agency which has offices all over the country.

"We will keep you informed as to what is taking place."

It will be noted that the broker in this letter did not inform his principal of the fact that the accounts of utilities had not been transferred from the names of the owners to the names of the lessees.

The plaintiffs did not reply to this letter until March 11, 1953, when Harris W. Everett wrote the broker expressing strong indignation at the failure of the Stillwells to pay the rent and offering to let them stay in the house until April 15, 1953, on the payment of $200 extra. He further stated that he did not know how the broker was handling the non-payment of rent, but would like to hear and that his part of all the collections for rent be deposited in the local bank and duplicate deposit slips be sent to him by air mail.

Under date of March 12, 1953, Mrs. Everett wrote the broker that she had received a letter from Mrs. Stillwell stating that she was taking good care of the house, furniture and garden. She thanked the broker for his letter of February 10th informing them of the situation. She authorized the broker to take such steps as he thought best to collect the rents and repeated that plaintiffs needed the money.

On March 18, 1953, a few days after receiving this letter, the broker caused a distress warrant to be issued, but before the sheriff could levy the warrant the Stillwells moved out leaving in the house only a combination radio, phonograph and television set, upon which the distress warrant was levied. However, this article seemed to be of little value. Thereafter, the broker caused all utilities except water to be disconnected.

On April 2, 1953, the broker wrote plaintiffs informing them of his inability to collect the rent and that the Stillwells had vacated the premises but had left the house in "immaculate condition." With the letter were enclosed bills for utilities amounting to several hundred dollars.

On April 14, 1953, the Everetts returned to Arlington and found the utilities disconnected. They were unable to spend the night at home as they had expected to do. On the next day, April 15, 1953, they had an interview with W. B. Wright and his agent, Honnold, during which time the Everetts were informed for the first time that the utility accounts had not been transferred to the names of the lessees and that accumulated utility bills totaled $681.41. W. B. Wright offered to pay and did pay a sufficient amount of the electric and gas bills to have them connected, but he declined to pay any part of the telephone bill. This action followed with the result above stated.

Defendant admitted in oral argument that he was liable to plaintiffs for compensatory damages, but denied that the facts in the case justified the court in submitting the question of punitive damages to the jury.

Plaintiffs' contention is thus stated in their brief: "The law in Virginia is clear that gross negligence or circumstance which add up to aggravation will properly found (sustain) an award of exemplary or punitive damages."

There are some expressions in the Virginia cases cited by plaintiffs which tend to support this contention, but in each case the evidence tends to prove that defendant had acted wantonly, oppressively, with such malice or recklessness as implied a spirit of mischief or criminal indifference to his obligation. We have been cited no case and have found none in Virginia in which recovery of exemplary or punitive damages was allowed on proof of gross negligence without proof of one or more of the elements stated. * * *

The theory upon which exemplary, punitive, or vindictive damages, sometimes called "smart money," are allowed is not so much as compensation for the plaintiff's loss as to warn others, and to punish the wrongdoer if he has acted wantonly, oppressively, recklessly, or with such malice as implies a spirit of mischief, or criminal indifference to civil obligations. * * *

The general rule is that exemplary or punitive damages (with certain exceptions not here pertinent) are not allowed for breach of contract. * * *

The evidence proves that the defendant did not make the proper credit investigation of the lessees before he caused the lease to be executed; that he did not have the utility accounts transferred as he promised to do; he did not keep plaintiffs fully informed as to the situation as he should have done. However, the evidence for plaintiffs is insufficient to prove any element of bad motive, or fraud, or that defendant acted in a manner so wanton or oppressive, or with such recklessness as implied a spirit of mischief or criminal indifference to the rights of plaintiffs. Therefore, defendant is liable to plaintiffs for compensatory damages only; i.e., compensation for all the pecuniary loss and inconvenience which are the natural and proximate result of his failure to fulfill the obligations assumed by him as a real estate agent. Upon this state of facts the trial court committed reversible error in giving any instruction allowing recovery of exemplary or punitive damages. * * *

Reversed and remanded.

CHAPTER 5

Other Licenses:
Insurance, Securities, Others

REALTORS' LIABILITY IN THE SALE OF NEW HOMES AND INSURANCE

There is a substantial body of case law affecting the liability of builders with regard to new homes. Realtors, when participating in this area, possibly acting as a builder, and/or Realtor in the sense of sales only, can also be affected.

Another area of exposure for the Realtor is with regard to the condition of homes. That is, if a purchaser acquires the house and subsequently discovers a faulty washing machine, a defective furnace, an inability to operate a solar heating system, or some other defect, the question is whether the Realtor has any exposure under these circumstances. (It is entirely possible an owner would have exposure, but the real question is whether the broker has the exposure.)

In an attempt to examine this area, the question arises with regard to special warranty programs. The most well-known warranty program is the Home Owner Warranty Program (HOW) which attempts to eliminate part of the controversy mentioned by simply allowing a warranty position for purchasers of new homes. (This type of concept is spreading, even with the used home area.)

One question which might eventually plague Realtors in this particular area, where a home ownership warranty program or similar program is sold, is whether that warranty program constitutes the sale of insurance. If it is the sale of insurance, that is, if a purchaser acquires this program and the program or warranty under HOW is insurance, then all the controls with regard to the sale of insurance would apply, such as a requirement to have the real estate broker–insurance salesperson licensed in the insurance field. There would be other requirements that would also come into play. In an attempt to examine this area and determine whether a real estate broker would be required to be licensed for insurance purposes, this author conducted a study at the University of Denver on this particular issue. A summary of this issue and some of the findings from that study follow.

The following article illustrates the basic concept of warranty programs relative to used homes. With this in mind, this material attempts to examine the problems in this area in general, and the specific issue as to whether a warranty program constitutes insurance. If it does constitute insurance, obviously the real estate broker must take those steps necessary to comply with the law.

On the other hand, if the program does not constitute insurance, there are nevertheless areas of liability and concern for the licensee. The following material helps to develop some of these considerations.

HOME OWNER WARRANTY PROGRAMS: DO SUCH PROGRAMS CONSTITUTE INSURANCE?

As the caption of the article indicates, the genesis of this review is to examine the question as to whether a home owner warranty program on *used* homes constitutes insurance for state law purposes.

Many independent companies are currently selling programs wherein, for a given charge or premium, they agree to provide coverage of one sort or another relative to certain items on used residential property. For example, the Equitable Home Warranty Maintenance Program provides that for a given premium, such as $250.00, a one-time fee, they will provide a one-year warranty relative to repair requirements that occur within that one year. Such coverage would include garage door openers, garbage compactors, central air conditioning, electrical work, exhaust fans, certain heating work, plumbing work, structural work, and a number of other items.

The Equitable program is not unlike many other programs which offer similar types of coverage. The attraction for a seller is, obviously, to enable him to "insure" (no pun intended) the condition of the home. The seller knows that a purchaser would be less reluctant to buy if he knew the heating, electrical, plumbing, and other systems relative to the house were in proper working condition or were insured or covered in some fashion to assure the purchaser that he would not be subject to additional expenses, at least within the first year, relative to these items.

The purchaser obviously has the comfortable feeling of knowing these items are covered and is less concerned with this issue when purchasing a house. The obvious attraction for a real estate brokerage firm is to avoid the headache which might be concomitant with the sale of property. Real estate salespeople have been learning that they are prime targets for lawsuits when defects are discovered subsequent to a closing. In a typical situation a Realtor lists a house, finds a purchaser, closes the transaction, and then finds that the furnace does not work when it is first tested in the fall, after a purchase in July! Subsequently the purchaser argues that the broker knew or should have known that the furnace was not operative. The broker in turn finds himself in many instances involved in a lawsuit or in a position where he is required, for his own protection, to expend monies to repair the furnace. The broker may avoid this potential liability problem by the use of a warranty program, such as those mentioned herein.

Thus it is apparent that the purchaser, seller, and broker have great concern and potential benefits from this type of program. It is true that there is a premium involved, but the amount seems to be clearly acceptable, based on the number of programs that are springing up around the country. In any event, the issue does not seem to be the desire or need for the program, but rather whether these programs will be permitted to exist without the auspices of the Insurance Commissioner's Office or similar types of offices in the given state. This, of course, is the heart of the matter and the issue being examined in the subsequent portions.

IS IT INSURANCE?

The Problem. The issue, as mentioned before, is whether the programs put forth by these various companies constitute insurance. An example of many of the companies offering these types of programs, and a summary of some of these options, are provided in Appendix A of this chapter. The practical problem is whether the activities of these various companies constitutes insurance. There is no definitive position as to whether this type of program will constitute insurance, at least on a uniform basis throughout the United States. Therefore, reference must be made to the law of each state.

Insurance Defined. The traditional definition of insurance, as provided in *Black's Law Dictionary, Third Edition,* page 989, states: "A contract whereby, for a stipulated consideration, one party undertakes to compensate the other for loss on a specified subject by specified perils." The discussion goes on to state: "Insurance is a contract whereby one undertakes to indemnify another against loss, damage, or liability arising from an unknown or contingent event."

With this basic definition in mind, the issue is whether a company can distinguish its type of operation in these warranty programs as opposed to straight insurance, in the traditional form that the lay person might think of insurance. As such, some jurisdictions have created a distinction of insurance-type programs versus a warranty (see Appendixes A and B of this chapter).

Some states consider that insurance, of a general-risk capacity, should be distinguished from a warranty program in which certain repair work is undertaken. For example, if one purchases a television set and the picture tube does not function properly after six months, there may be a warranty, guaranty, or other agreement by the seller, manufacturer, or somone else to repair the unit. However, this type of program is generally distinguished from the warranty program in that the *same* party selling this set or someone related to that party, such as the wholesaler or the manufacturer, is making the warranty, as opposed to some third party who did not sell the unit.

It is clear that the warranty programs, or similar types of operations, partake of some of these characteristics as opposed to a straight "insurance" program. The latter may be a case with insurance for the possibility that fire damage may occur in the house. A program of compensation is purchased to protect the owner.

As indicated subsequently, some states have attempted to draw a distinction relative to the product or item being sold, as opposed to the general insurance concept. Some states, however, are not willing to accept this distinction. The table in Appendix B of this chapter illustrates the position of those states on the subject of whether these warranties constitute insurance.

EFFECT OF THE ISSUE

If Warranties Are Insurance. 1. Licensing of the Vendors: If it is determined that the warranty programs in question constitute insurance, obviously those parties who are selling the program must be licensed, assuming the state requires the licensing of parties selling insurance, which is traditionally the case. As such, real estate brokers must contemplate either dropping the program or requiring that a license be procured by all their salespeople who would be involved in the program. Since the program has become part of many sales in the normal course of business, this would generally require an additional expense, additional licensing procedures, study, examinations, and the normal items that are incident to a licensing program.

2. Insurance Company: If the warrantry program constitutes insurance, the parties who are marketing that program must be concerned with the

classification as an insurance company. That is, those companies, such as those described in the Appendix A, may all constitute insurance companies. Therefore, they must meet the statutory requirements of the given state relative to insurance companies, or otherwise be exempted. This classification may require bonding, net worth requirements, audited books, various controls, reporting rules, and much more. The costs for this type of activity, the amount of controls, and many other burdensome procedures may inhibit or eliminate the desire to work in this capacity.

If It Is Insurance, Who Will Control This Area? The additional practical point in this area is that if the sale of warranty programs constitutes insurance, who will oversee these types of programs? If it is insurance, most insurance commissioners or other officers handling the insurance aspect for the given state would oversee this type of program. However, since there is great overlap with the real estate area, there is often a question as to whether the real estate commission or other governing body over real estate activities should also oversee this issue. In those states where real estate and insurance are handled out of the same administrative office, this may not be a problem. However, more typically, real estate and insurance functions in the given state are in separate offices. As such, this creates a problem of jurisdiction and a question of overlapping activities. Coordination, of course, becomes a problem. This may indicate one reason why some jurisdictions, especially through some insurance commissioner's offices, have backed away from this problem. However, with the increased activity in this area, we may see greater activity in this area by those insurance commissioners who have thus far hesitated to respond to this question.

Consumer Effects. It seems as though this type of program can be an obvious advantage to a purchaser-consumer. If the program is prohibitive as a result of costs and other red tape, the argument is that the consumer will lose the benefit of this type of program, at least on some economical scale. The purpose of this chapter is not to examine this issue. However, this point has been raised by some of the companies that are attempting to develop a warranty-type program.

POSITIONS BY VARIOUS STATE COMMISSIONERS

Now that the essence of the problem has been set forth, it is worthwhile to review some of the comments and positions by various state commissioners. Keep in mind that the authority and general reference for these positions are indicated in Appendix B. Some of the more specific points are somewhat enlightening as to the views that are developing throughout the United States.

For example, one of the more straightforward positions by an insurance commissioner's office is that by Mr. Tharpe Forester, Deputy Commissioner for the State of Alabama, Department of Insurance. He states that their department has considered that a home owner warranty program does not constitute insurance, whether it is sold by an independent company or through a real estate firm. This very definitive position is the type of response that obviously makes the determination very simple. On the other hand, the response of the state of Colorado, J. Richard Barnes, Commissioner of Insurance, does not seem completely clear. Commissioner Barnes, in a letter of August 1, 1978 to this author, states:

> The expression "monetarily significant risk obligations for parts or materials needed for home repairs" means very simply that nothing is allowed beyond very minor items. These could be described as such things as window cleaning materials, floor scrubbing soap, a nail here and there, etc. as distinguished from new windows, new furnace boiler or blower, hot water tank, wood or roofing materials, etc.
>
> If someone were to ask us to set a dollar figure, that may be difficult, but certainly one would say that not more than $20 per house contract could be spent as incidentals.
>
> Let us make it clear that no independent contractor labor deal would be allowed under the warranty. Otherwise, it becomes insurance. All work must be done by and be capable of being done by the full time employees of the warranty maintenance company. By full time, we're referring to employees on whom FICA is paid and income taxes withheld, etc. The test is operational as well as organizational.

Commissioner Barnes states that they have taken what he calls a rather "firm position" with regard to this area. This is illustrated by a number of court cases that are pending on this issue. It is true that the state of Colorado, through Commissioner Barnes' office, has undertaken a number of lawsuits to challenge the operation of many real estate companies and warranty companies relative to their programs. The position by Barnes is clear in those cases: The item constitutes insurance. However, the standards to distinguish an operation as being insurance or not being insurance are not as clear as the Alabama position. This is evidenced by the following comment by Deputy Commissioner Brown, in a letter of July 21, 1978:

> Your client can contract for future personal labor services to be performed by it provided such are within the realistic personal physical capability of

your client to perform. No third-party labor indemnification organizational structure would be allowed on Insurance Code Exemption. A personal services contract exemption to Insurance Code application must follow much the·same format as a retainer agreement commonly utilized by law firms.

The statement seems to be distinguishing between a position in which personal labor services are to be performed and contracts with third parties. This seems to prohibit contracts with independent contractors. However, it does not seem that clear relative to employee contracts. That is, could a warranty company avoid the insurance classification by coming in and having its own employees undertake the repair work called for under their contract with the seller of the home? Commissioner Brown goes on to state in his letter of July 21, 1978:

> Your client cannot contractually undertake monetarily significant risk obligations for parts or materials needed for home repairs. To do so is to promise an indemnity upon the occurrence of a determinable risk contingency which puts it squarely within the definition of insurance. . . .

A number of other states, as indicated in Appendix B, have stated that they have not made a judicial determination. For example, Mr. James Montgomery, in a letter of August 22, 1978, states that the District of Columbia has not taken a position on this.

Other states have passed statutes to resolve the matter of whether it is insurance within the general insurance law. This point is illustrated by the Florida position. It passed a home warranty law which requires companies to become licensed. The insurance commissioner's office for the state of Florida regulates those companies. Their position and that law are in Chapter 634, parts 2 and 3 of the Florida statutes.

The Florida approach may be the answer to this enigma. That is, rather than playing with mental gymnastics as to whether a program can be "distinguished" out of the definition of insurance, assuming the statute in the given state defines insurance, it may be more worthwhile, and of more help to practitioners, simply to undertake the regulation of this area if such regulation is desired by the legislators of the given state.

Many states, as indicated in Appendix B, have taken the position that whether the activities of the given warranty program constitutes insurance will be considered on a facts-and-circumstance test in each instance. This type of position has been stated in a letter from Mr. Steve Adams, Assistant Deputy Insurance Commissioner for the state of Georgia.

The opposite position has been taken by Mr. Robert A. Fraundorf, supervisor of the state of Idaho department of insurance. In his letter of August 11, 1978, Mr. Fraundorf states: "The State of Idaho considers *all*

Home Owner Warranty Programs to be insurance under the provisions of the Idaho Code" (emphasis supplied). This position makes it clear for practitioners that they will face a fight on this issue should they attempt a warranty program without meeting the insurance requirements of the state of Idaho.

Other state commissioners' offices or commissioners handling the area of insurance responded along the lines of those mentioned earlier. That is, they may have taken a very positive position that the program is insurance, is not insurance, or they may have vacillated somewhat on a facts-and-circumstances test.

Even within some states, the positions are inconsistent. For example, in the state of New York there have been various positions. In the initial study of this issue in 1976, the position by New York was that the warranty programs did constitute insurance. In fact, in a letter written by Mr. Bernard Goldstein, Office of General Counsel for the State of New York, it was stated that: "A number of third-party firms have attempted to issue warranty programs in New York to Purchasers of homes. All have been advised that such programs violate the insurance law and have been requested to cease and desist."

However, a recent letter of August 22, 1978 from Mr. Goldstein indicates that some things may be changing. Mr. Goldstein mentions that the earlier position still reflects the status of the insurance department. However, as Mr. Goldstein states, a recent decision, *Electronic Realty Associates, Inc. and Matt Jordan Realty, Inc.* v. *Lennon* (1978), holds that home owner warranty programs do not constitute insurance. That decision has been appealed by the Attorney General. A decision will be forthcoming in the near future.

A letter dated August 17, 1978, from Mr. Pasquantonio, staff attorney for the state of North Carolina, remarks that their basis for classifying home warranty programs as insurance is the fact that they are being offered by a third party, that is, someone other than the owner, manufacturer, or seller. Again this distinction seems to be an important point in a number of states.

CONCLUSION

It is clear at this point that most states are being asked to examine the issue of whether a warranty program constitutes insurance. In 1976 many states indicated that they had not faced this issue. With more and more jurisdictions being faced with warranty programs, it is clear that states can no longer duck the problem. Most jurisdictions that have expressed an opinion on this

issue, aside from a facts-and-circumstances test on each case, seem to indi-
rate that the item does constitute insurance. (This can be examined in more
detail through Appendix B, which illustrates each state.)

Because there is no uniform state law on this subject, an unlikely occurrence at this point, every warranty program that operates in various
states must meet this issue through *each* given state. However, this author is
informed that the National Association of Insurance Commissioners is reviewing this question and that some determination may be made in the
near future to support uniformity.

SECURITIES

A real estate broker can learn quickly that there are various other areas in
which he must be licensed, if, in fact, he wishes to participate in those areas.
For example, there may be a requirement to be licensed as an auto dealer
if mobile homes are sold. This depends on the given jurisdiction in question.
There may also be a requirement to be licensed in the insurance field if insurance is being sold, as discussed earlier with regard to home owner warranty programs or for that matter straight or normal types of insurance. In
this section we are concerned with the requirement for being licensed in the
real estate securities area when the real estate salesperson is selling what
constitutes a security.

The following discussion touches on this area of real estate securities
and the licensing requirements. Reference is once again made to the text of
this author entitled *Real Estate Securities, An Introduction,* published by
the Colorado Society of CPA's in 1976 updated 1977 and 1978, and now
conducted as a one-day seminar throughout the United States.

REALTORS: COMMISSION:
SECURITIES ISSUE

If real estate people have not had enough trouble attempting to collect a
commission in many cases in the past, they can now add to their dilemma
the potential of a defense by a seller, when attempting not to pay a commission, by hearing the argument that the real estate broker, although
licensed in real estate, is not licensed in securities, and therefore cannot collect a commission!

This position was asserted in *Lyons* v. *Stevenson,* 65 CA 3d 595, 135
Cal. Rptr. 457 (1977).

In this case, the court held that the broker was entitled to his commission for a given transaction, notwithstanding that he was not licensed as a securities broker. The issue in question was whether the sale involved a security, and therefore whether a securities license was necessary to collect a real estate commission.

Although the Realtor was successful in this particular case, since it was held that he was not dealing with a security, a Realtor can expect to face this issue in the future with regard to a transaction that may constitute a security. (For more details on when real estate can constitute a security, see *Real Estate Securities, An Introduction,* Levine, Mark Lee, *Colorado Society of CPAs,* 1976, updated 1977 and 1978.)

IN GENERAL—REAL ESTATE AS A SECURITY

Can real estate constitute a security?

The 1933 Securities Act (1933 Act) provides that security is "any note, stock, Treasury Stock, bond, debenture, evidence of indebtedness, Certificate of Interest, or participation of profit-sharing agreement, Collateral Trust Certificate, pre-organization certificate or subscription, transferable share, *investment contract,* voting-trust certificate, certificate of deposit for security, fractional undivided interest in oil, gas, or other mineral rights; or in general, any interest or instrument commonly known as a 'security,' or any certificate of interest or participation in, temporary or interim certificate for, receipt for, guarantee of, or warranty or right to subscribe to or purchase, any of the foregoing." (Emphasis supplied.)

The definition is so broad that it is clear, by many Court decisions, that real estate can be a security.

The major emphasis or force for interpreting that real estate would be a security has been on the label "investment contract." Generally speaking, an investment contract requires three elements:

1. There is an investment of money or other property.
2. The investment is made with the intent to use someone else's expertise, other than the investor.
3. The intent is to make a profit from such activity.

In *SEC* v. *W. J. Howey, Co.,* 238 U.S. 293 (1946), the United States Supreme Court emphasized the investment contract definition. Further, in Securities Act Release No. 33-4877, August 8, 1967, the SEC emphasized the same point by stating that under the Federal Securities Law an offering of a limited partnership interest or an interest in a joint profit-sharing real estate venture generally constitutes an offering of a profit-sharing arrangement or an investment contract which is a "security" within the meaning of Section 2(1) of the Securities Act of 1933.

The Release further reviews the Howey Case and states: "In other words, the investor provides the capital and shares in the risk and profit; the promoter or third party manages, operates and controls the enterprise, usually without active participation on the part of the investor."

It is clear that this broad language can easily result in real estate being classified as a security. For example, a condominium development formed by a partnership where the intent is to run the condominium for profit, can result in an interpretation that an investment contract exists and therefore the application of the securities rules under the 1933 Act and the 1934 Securities Exchange Act will apply.

Any transaction where the broad interpretive definition of an investment contract is met can result in a security.

If the transaction is classified as a security, as mentioned, the '33 and '34 Acts will be applicable unless an exemption otherwise applies.

There is often confusion when a party states that an exemption exists, such as a transaction which is exempt because of the "private offering rule." (The private offering exemption, under Rule 146 promulgated by the SEC, allows for the avoidance of registration requirements with regard to the security.) However, it does not eliminate the anti-fraud provisions nor does it eliminate the requirement under the 1934 Act of the broker/dealer being properly licensed.

Obviously, an explanation and examination of the details of this area is beyond the scope of this overview. However, the real estate investor and the promoter must be aware of the implications of selling an investment which fits the definition of a security via the investment contract or any of the other broad interpretive provisions, as noted.

It is an interpretive problem to determine whether an "investment contract" exists. It has been argued that it is a question of law and also a question of fact. Because there is no absolute standard for whether a security exists, and therefore the transaction cannot be quantified, the potential investor-developer should exercise great caution.

The report of the Real Estate Advisory Committee to the Securities and Exchange Commission (Chairman Dickey), Washington, D.C., states "The security is deemed to exist where there is a contract, transaction, or scheme whereby a person invests his money in a common enterprise and is led to expect profits from the efforts of a third party."

Thus, real estate could easily fit the above definition. If it does, the earlier laws mentioned under the Securities Act of 1933 and related acts may be applicable. The days of thinking that real estate is real estate and a security is a security, referring in the latter case to a stock or bond, is coming to an abrupt end. It is apparent that a security could easily exist in the form of real estate if it meets the above definitional elements.

This problem of applying securities law to what *had been* considered the independent field of real estate has been a perplexing problem. On October 12, 1972, the earlier mentioned report of the Real Estate Advisory Committee was submitted to the Securities and Exchange Commission's by then Chairman, Mr. William J. Casey. It was designed around the problems of whether real estate is a security, and in fact, if it is a security, how the field should be regulated. Should there be a separate real estate advisory board or some other group similar to the SEC to regulate securities as they apply to real estate, or should such activities be directly under the SEC without a separate board?

The Dickey Report made various recommendations:

1. Enhance investor protection;
2. Clarify and simplify rules and regulations to govern the distribution of real estate securities;
3. Develop a framework to achieve uniform regulation of real estate securities among the Commission and the various state and other regulatory agencies and authorities, to achieve the goals set forth in the report;
4. Create a broader understanding and acceptance by real estate people of the concepts including understanding their obligations and responsibilities when they are seeking equity financing from the general public.

The Dickey Committee also recommended establishing a permanent advisory committee to the SEC to coordinate real estate activity in the securities field.

Another question in the real estate and securities field is whether the securities concepts apply to rental pools (common group to handle rentals of condominiums). Specifically, one of the suggestions under the Real Estate Advisory Committee Report was:

"If a rental pool (that is, some agreement whereby the rental and management condominiums are handled for the owners) is offered with the purchase of the condominium or cooperative unit, registration should be required. The committee recognized that many knowledgeable persons engaged in condominium development feel such a rigid rule should not be adopted, but on balance, the Committee feels it is desirable."

There are many other recommendations in the Report with regard to the real estate securities field. For example, there are limitations with regard to sales literature and what should be disclosed therein. There is also a requirement to disclose conflicts of interest between the developer and *the subject* project *vis-a-vis* other projects the developer has that might conflict with or prohibit the development of the subject project, which the developer is trying to sell to one group as opposed to another.

There are also recommendations as to the amount of commissions and other fees that should be allowed a developer, limitations on when and how he receives the fee, and other controlling limitations with regard to commissions and benefits paid to the promoters of the projects.

[The above excerpt is reprinted with permission from *Real Estate Securities, An Introduction,* by Mark Lee Levine (Colorado Society of CPAs, 1977 and 1978).]

APPENDIXES

Appendix A illustrates a number of programs which currently exist relative to warranty programs. Keep in mind that references to warranty programs relate to used homes as opposed to new homes. For a discussion of the new home programs, see the article, "Does a Warranty Program for Homes Constitute the Sale of Insurance?" by Mark L. Levine in *Real Estate Fundamentals,* published by West Publishing Co., 1976. The tables here are certainly not an exhaustive study of all of the programs that exist. This appendix was prepared by one of the companies involved, Equitable Home Warranty Maintenance, Inc.

Appendix B states the responses made by various state insurance commissioners and other parties involved as to whether their state has taken a position on warranty programs and whether they constitute insurance. For further details or an examination of the actual correspondence, readers are requested to contact the author, Mark Lee Levine, 1150 Delaware Street, Denver, Colorado 80204, (303) 892-5891.

APPENDIX A

Program	Inspection Type	Repair Type	Insurance or Warranty	Princ. Purchasers	Approximate Number of Contracts in Effect 1-77
American Home Guard	O-R	OW	Warranty	Sellers	3,120
American Home Shield	O-R	SC	Warranty	Sellers	52,000
AMC Home Protection	D-INS	OW	Warranty	Buyers	538
Certified Home Inspection (CHIP)	D-INS	OW	Warranty	Buyers	1,248
ERA (Buyers Protection Program)	O-R	SC	Warranty	Sellers	17,466
Equitable Home Warranty Maintenance	WO-INS	SC	Warranty	Sellers	N/A
First Amer. Home Protection Service	S-INS	SC	Insurance	Sellers	N/A
Homestead Inspection Warranty	D-INS	OW	Warranty	Buyers	N/A
Pacific Cal-West	O-R	SC	Warranty	Sellers	10,400
Rollins Home Care	O-R	SC	Warranty	Sellers	1,840
St. Paul Home Protection	S-INS	SC	Insurance	Buyers	1,240

BA: Basic appliance—built-in garbage disposal, dishwasher, range and oven.
BMS: Basic mechanical system—central heating, interior plumbing, interior electrical.
BST: Basic structural—roof, wall, ceiling and floor structure, foundation, basements.
CA: Central air conditioning
R: Renewable.
NR: Nonrenewable.
O-R: inspected by owner or Realtor.
S-INS: short inspection by independent contractor.
WO-INS: inspected by warranty company employed inspectors.
D-INS: detail inspection by independent contractor.
SC: subcontractor.
WOMC: warranty company owned maintenance company.
OW: owner arranges repair and is reimbursed.

APPENDIX A—Continued

Program	Premium Cost for			Deduct or Service Charge	Coverage	Period Renewable
	$30K House	$70K House	$150K House			
American Home Guard	195	245	285	65–135	BA; BMS + CA; plumbing fixtures; BST and roof water penetration	1 yr; NR
American Home Shield	220	220	220	20–50	BA; BMS + CA and/or plumbing fixtures in some locations	1 yr; R
AMC Home Protection	180	210	275	250	BMS + CA; BST & roof water penetration	1 yr; R
Certified Home Inspection (CHIP)	110	215	285	100	BMS + CA; Bathroom fixtures; kitchen sinks; BST & roof water penetration; attached garages	1 yr; R
ERA (Buyers Protection Program)	110 260	180 260	270 390	25–100	BA + countertop blenders, central vacuum; BMS + plumbing fixtures; doorbells, CA; built-in wall units, water softeners	1 yr; NR
Equitable Home Warranty Maintenance	250	250	250	15	BA + intercom; garage door openers; compactors; BMS + CA; all electrical fixtures; exhaust fans	1 yr; R
First American Home Protection Service	217	293	527	100	BA; BMS + CA; plumbing fixtures; BST	1 yr; NR
Homestead Inspection Warranty Company	200	275	425	100	BMS + bathroom fixtures; laundry tubs; BST + roof water penetration; attached garages + breezeways	2 yr; R

Pacific Cal-West	210	210	210	15–20	BA + bathroom & kitchen fans; BMS	1 yr; R
Rollins Home Care	230	230	230	100	BA; BMS + CA; plumbing fixtures; sump pump	1 yr; NR
St. Paul Home Protection	100	140 210	300 450	25–50	Optional: BA; water softeners; BMS + CA; BST	1 yr; R

BA: Basic appliance—built-in garbage disposal, dishwasher, range and oven.
BMS: Basic mechanical system—central heating, interior plumbing, interior electrical.
BST: Basic structural—roof, wall, ceiling and floor structure, foundation, basements.
CA: Central air conditioning.
R: Renewable
NR: Nonrenewable

APPENDIX B—DO WARRANTIES CONSTITUTE INSURANCE?

State	Statutory Authority	Opinion by AG, etc.	Comm. Position	Footnotes
Alabama—Warranty, not ins.			Warranty	
Alaska				NR
Arizona—F&C	Senate 1196	F&C		Circular letter
Arkansas—F&C		F&C		
California				NR
Colorado—F&C but generally ins.	Yes	DDC	F&C	C-79609, Div. 8 C-70995, Div. 7
Connecticut				NR
Delaware				NR
D.C.—No determination			Letter	
Florida—Warranties *not* included in ins. code	Chapt 634	Leg.	*ibid.*	(1) But does have home warranty law.
Georgia—Warranties—Generally not ins.—F&C			Yes	Individual basis
Hawaii—Warranty, same as Ga.	Yes, AG	AG	*ibid.*	Exception
Idaho—All insurance	Yes	State	*ibid.*	All
Illinois—On individual basis, Either/Or—F&C			*ibid.*	

Indiana				NR
Iowa—Ins.	Yes	DC		C-84294
Kansas				NR
Kentucky—Ins.	Yes	Leg.		
Louisiana—Warranty, but on individual basis.			Ins.	Generally not ins.
Maine—On indiv. basis, F&C	AG		Comm.	
Maryland				NR
Massachusetts				NR
Michigan—Warranties and not ins. w/exceptions F&C			Mixed	Generally not ins.
Minnesota—Indiv. basis, F&C		Comm.	Indiv. basis	
Mississippi				NR
Missouri				NR
Montana—F&C		Comm.		
Nebraska—Ins.	Yes	AG	Ins.	
Nevada—Indiv. basis, F&C				Generally looks to risk outside of product
New Hampshire—Ins.	Yes	Leg.	Ins.	Regulations on homeowner warranties forthcoming
New Jersey				NR
New Mexico—Usually ins.	Yes	AG	Usually ins.	AG 73-70

APPENDIX B—Continued

State	Statutory Authority	Opinion by AG, etc.	Comm. Position	Footnotes
New York—Ins. w/exceptions		1977/3827 Supreme Ct.	Ins.	Exception—case law on appeal. Holds not ins.
North Carolina—Ins.	Judiciary	Judiciary	Ins.	
North Dakota—Probably ins.	Yes	Leg.		Century code Sec. 26-02-01
Ohio—No ruling—F&C				Under study.
Oklahoma				NR
Oregon—Ins.	Commerce Dept.		Ins.	Cease & desist order, proposed legislation.
Pennsylvania—Ins./F&C			Ins.	F&C
Puerto Rico				NR
Rhode Island—Ins. w/exception		Comm.	Ins. w/except.	If builder provides it, then not insurance
South Carolina—Warranty—normally not ins.		Comm.		Qualified definition
South Dakota				NR
Tennessee—Indiv. basis/F&C			Indiv. basis	
Texas—Indiv. basis			*ibid.*	
Utah—Not ins. generally				Exceptions

Vermont			NR
Virgin Islands			NR
Virginia			NR
Washington—Usually ins.	Yes	AG	Usually ins.	48.01.040
West Virginia			NR
Wisconsin—Placing controls on warranties	Legis.	Legislature		Limited certificate of authority to cover these items.
Wyoming—Appears as ins.	Yes		Pending	Various opinions, exceptions, 26-1-102

AG: attorney general.
Comm.: commission.
DDC: Denver district court.
DC: district court.
F&C: facts and circumstances.
ibid.: same as above.
ins.: insurance.
Leg.: legislature.
NR: no response.

CHAPTER 6

Governmental Controls
Discrimination
Interstate Land Sales
FHA

DISCRIMINATION

A Realtor's Liability—Antiblockbusting—Fair Housing Act of 1968. Another area of exposure to Realtors deals with the potential of violating the Federal Housing Act of 1968, Sec. 801 *et seq,* 42 USC Sec. 3601 *et seq* (1970).

The importance of this area is stressed in the case of *U.S.* v. *Bob Lawrence Realty, Inc.,* 474 F.2d 115 (5th Cir. 1973) Cert. Denied, 414 U.S. 826 (1973). This case, as indicated in the following pages, reviewed a fact situation wherein it was alleged by the Attorney General, bringing suit for injunctive relief against certain real estate firms as a result of antiblockbusting, that there was an issue of racial discrimination. The argument was that the Realtors who had been in the neighborhood in question arguably were involved in attempting to obtain listings while making representations to a predominantly white neighborhood that the neighborhood was changing and would be substantially black in population. As a result of these alleged tactics, the neighborhood in question became populated, in the majority, by blacks. The action in question was whether the real estate firm actually violated the antiblockbusting section of the Fair Housing Act of 1968, as mentioned earlier.

The trial court issued an injunction against the firm to prevent them from further acting. (The action was somewhat moot as to the given area, since the black population had risen. However, it was an attempt to affect further activities of a similar nature.)

On appeal, at least with the Bob Lawrence Realty case, the Fifth Circuit Court of Appeals sustained the position of the trial court on the injunction. There were various procedural questions raised in this particular case, although the important point for real estate professionals is to recognize a potential exposure when an action is undertaken in a given neighborhood that may be thought to be blockbusting in derogation of the federal laws.

One interesting question raised when discussing this case in a note in a Case Comment, Florida State University Law Review, 382 (1974), was how to determine whether blockbusting existed by the Realtor. The comment in the review indicates the requirement of scienter (intent) for blockbusting. This is contrasted with a spontaneous activity by the Realtors in an area in which they recognize that heavy sales may occur as a result of activity that has already taken place or apparently has started to take place. Thus, when is a Realtor to know when he is participating in blockbusting in contravention of federal law, or when in fact he is simply seeking listings in an area where selling seems to be heavy, possibly as a result of previous sales that may give an indication of panic selling?

UNITED STATES of America v. BOB LAWRENCE REALTY, INC., et al.,
United States Court of Appeals, 1973.
474 F.2d 115

* * *

GOLDBERG, Circuit Judge:

This case presents the first appellate challenge to the constitutionality of 42 U.S.C. § 3604(e), the "anti-blockbusting" provision of the Fair Housing Act of 1968, Title VIII of the Civil Rights Act of 1968, 42 U.S.C. § 3601 et seq. We find that § 3604(e) falls within the constitutional authority of Congress to enact legislation to enforce the Thirteenth Amendment and that § 3604(e) does not violate the First Amendment. The District Court enjoined appellant from violating § 3604(e). We affirm.

This action was brought by the Department of Justice pursuant to Title VIII of the Civil Rights Act of 1968, 42 U.S.C. § 3601 et seq., alleging that appellant, Bobby L. Lawrence, President of Bob Lawrence Realty, Inc., and four other Atlanta, Georgia real estate brokers had undertaken "block-busting" activities prohibited by 42 U.S.C. § 3604(e).

The government's complaint seeking injunctive relief arose out of all the defendants' solicitation activities in racially transitional areas in southeast Atlanta. It alleged (1) that the defendants participated, individually and collectively, in a pattern or practice of resistance to the enjoyment of rights granted by the Act, and (2) that a group of persons had been denied rights secured by the Act, raising an issue of general public importance. See, 42 U.S.C. § 3613. * * * The District Court held, * * * that the government's affidavits and documentary evidence were insufficient to make out an "individual pattern or practice" of violations by appellant, and granted summary judgment as to that issue. The District Court also held that triable issues of fact existed as to whether appellant had participated in a "group pattern or practice" of unlawful conduct and as to whether there had been a denial of rights secured by the Act to a group of persons raising an issue of general public importance. * * *

Shortly before the trial, consent decrees were entered against two of the five original defendants, and the action against a third was dismissed. The case as it pertained to appellant and the other remaining defendant then proceeded to trial. The District Court made the following findings of fact, which are more fully set out in its opinion. * * *

> Appellant is a real estate broker licensed by the State of Georgia to engage in the listing and selling real estate, * * * and employes twenty seven sales personnel who act as his agents. * * * During the period with which this action is concerned, appellant did business in the Candler Road—McAfee area in southeast Atlanta. Appellant was aware that this area has been a racially transitional area since 1968, approximately two years before the action was filed. Prior to 1968 the racial composition of the area was all white, but as blacks began moving into the area in 1968, whites began moving out. Two of appellant's sales personnel made representations prohibited by 42 U.S.C. § 3604(e) to four different individuals. Although these representations did not constitute an "individual pattern or practice" of violating the Act, they were made as part of a "group pattern or practice" of violating the Act by all agents in the area.

On December 27, 1971, the District Court issued its opinion and order enjoining appellant from further unlawful conduct, from which ruling only appellant appeals. * * *

On appeal to this Court, appellant launches a scatter gun attack on the District Court's order. * * *

I. CONSTITUTIONALITY OF SECTION 3604(e)

* * * This Court will give great deference, as indeed it must, to the congressional determination that § 3604(e) will effectuate the purpose of the Thirteenth Amendment by aiding in the elimination of the "badges and incidents of slavery in the United States." * * * Appellants have failed to present any argument that impugns the reasonableness of the

congressional determination. Indeed no such argument can be made in light of the role that blockbusting plays in creating and in perpetuating segregated housing patterns and thus in preventing ". . . a dollar in the hands of a Negro . . . (from purchasing) the same thing as a dollar in the hands of a white man." * * *

Blockbusting and the First Amendment

Appellant contends that § 3604(e) constitutes an unconstitutional prior restraint by Congress on the right to free speech. In rejecting this contention, the court below stated:

> "It is evident that the statute did not make mere speech unlawful. What it does make unlawful is economic exploitation of racial bias and panic selling. We conclude that the statute is one regulating conduct, and that any inhibiting effect it may have upon speech is justified by the Government's interest in protecting its citizens from discriminatory housing practices and is not violative of the First Amendment."

* * * Appellant argues that an individual cannot properly be enjoined from making racial representations to obtain the business of a potential seller when the racial statement presents the truth. But it is clear that just as "(t)he state can prohibit the use of the street for the distribution of purely commercial leaflets, even though such leaflets may have 'a civic appeal, or a moral platitude' appended." * * * The federal government may in some circumstances prohibit purely commercial speech made in connection with conduct which Congress can permissibly regulate or prohibit. Any informational value in a statement violative of § 3604(e) is clearly outweighed by the government's overriding interest in preventing blockbusting. * * * Appellant's second contention that the "group of persons . . . engaged in a pattern or practice of resistance to the full enjoyment of § 3604(e) . . . "must have engaged in a conspiracy or concerted action before the Attorney General has standing to sue is also erroneous. * * *

Blockbusting by its very nature does not require concerted action or a conspiracy to wreak its pernicious damage. There is, for example, no need for XYZ Realty to conspire with ABC Homes to set off a pattern or practice of activities violating the act. The sociological phenomenon of a transitional area * * * is enough to attract blockbusters intent upon culling all the profits that can be derived from the area. The very essence of the phenomenon is that a large number of competitors individually besiege an area seeking to gain a share of the market.

* * * The District Court finding that a group of persons was engaged in a pattern or practice of violating § 3604(e) demonstrates the efficacy of the Attorney General's decision that he had "reasonable cause to believe that any person or group of persons (was) . . . engaged in a pattern or practice of resistance to § 3604(e) * * *

III. PROPRIETY OF INJUNCTIVE RELIEF

* * * Appellant's argument that injunctive relief is improper in this action is apparently based on his belief that since he is totally innocent of any violation of the Act, he is being enjoined solely on the basis of activities of other real estate agents in the area, and furthermore, that equity should not intervene because there is no danger that he will violate the Act in the future. The District Court, however, explicitly found: (1) that appellant had violated § 3604(e); (2) that there was a group pattern of violating the Act by all the agents in the area; and (3) that appellant participated in that pattern or practiced. * * *

Along with its power to hear the case, the court's power to grant injunctive relief survives discontinuance of the illegal conduct. * * * It can be utilized even without a showing of past wrongs. But the moving party must satisfy the court that relief is needed. The necessary determination is that there exists some cognizable danger of recurrent violation, something more than the mere possibility which serves to keep the case alive.

* * * The District Court found that injunctive relief was appropriate. Appellant has not shown that the District Court abused its discretion. It does not appear that there was no danger of recurrent violation. * * *

IV. ATTORNEY'S FEES

* * * Appellant's contention that equitable principles require that the government pay its attorney's fees is utterly frivolous. The government's suit was neither harassing nor unmeritous. Equity does not require that the District Court grant attorney's fees to a party found to have violated a federal statute by blockbusting in a racially transitional area. * * *

V. CONCLUSION

The anti-blockbusting statute, § 3604(e), is an attempt by Congress to disprove the belief, held by many, that the Thirteenth Amendment made a promise the Nation cannot keep. Integrated housing is deemed by many to be an a priori requirement before our schools can be realistically integrated. * * * Brushing these polemics aside, it is indisputable that white flight is a blight upon the democratized society we envision and this Congressional Act is in the mainstream of that vision. We hold that § 3604(e) is a constitutional exercise of congressional authority to enact legislation to effectuate the Thirteenth Amendment. Any informational value that may be found in speech uttered in furtherance of blockbusting is clearly outweighed by the power of Congress to regulate the purely commercial activity of blockbusting. * * *

Affirmed.

ZUCH v. HUSSEY
United States District Court
E. D. Michigan, S. D., 1975
394 F.Supp. 1028

* * *

MEMORANDUM OPINION AND ORDER

KEITH, District Judge.

This is an action brought by residents of several communities in Northwest Detroit to seek a remedy for certain alleged violations of the Fair Housing Act of 1968, 42 U.S.C. § 3601 et seq. The matter is presently before the Court on the plaintiffs' Motion for a Preliminary Injunction.

The hearing on this motion lasted approximately ten (10) weeks, during which time the Court heard testimony from over fifty (50) witnesses. More than ninety (90) exhibits were admitted into evidence. After careful consideration of the matter and pursuant to the findings of facts and conclusion of law, the Court grants the plaintiffs' Motion for a Preliminary Injunction.

INTRODUCTION

Perhaps the single most significant factor operating in this case is the racial fear of the white residents of the areas involved. At times, this fear has become so irrational and pervasive that it reflects a hysterical community psyche. Fears which reach this proportion perhaps reflect accurately on racial relations in our city, but such fears alone cannot be the basis for finding a violation of the Fair Housing Act.

Throughout the ten (10) weeks of testimony, the defendants made several allegations about the plaintiffs' motives in bringing this action. One charge was that the plaintiffs were seeking to prevent further entry of blacks into their neighborhood. Another was that they were seeking to put certain real estate agencies out of business because they were dealing with blacks. The defendants sought earnestly to elicit testimony from the plaintiffs' witnesses and from their own witnesses to support these allegations. While the Court is of the opinion that violations of the Fair Housing Act were shown by the plaintiffs, it also believes that there was some evidence which supported the allegations of the defendants.

Witnesses testified that if their communities became significantly black, they would move. There was testimony about the initial reaction of the residents to the entry of the first black family into the Emerson Community. Frantic meetings were described in which racial hatred was vented and schemes were suggested to physically remove the black family from the community. There was also evidence that the officers of the

Emerson Community Homeowners Association (ECHO) * * * used their organization's newspaper to recommend certain favorite real estate agencies to their readers. There was also an admission by Vincent Zuch, one of the most active plaintiffs, that he was "at war with the real estate industry." This Court does not condone any of this. It is mentioned only to show the complexity of the issues involved.

The Court also observed that many of the witnesses had had little or no day to day interpersonal contact with their black neighbors. As a result, some of them exaggerated the significance of certain activities which they observed. * * * In part, these witnesses are victims of their own isolation, prejudice and ignorance. Their fears are products of the kind of racial isolation the Fair Housing Act was designed to end. The Court has taken all of this into consideration in reaching its decision.

I. FINDINGS OF FACTS

After considering the evidence offered by both sides at the hearing on the plaintiffs Motion for a Preliminary Injunction, the Court makes the following findings of fact and conclusions of law. * * *

A. THE AREA

This action involves an area of Northwest Detroit which lies west of predominantly black neighborhoods and east and south of predominantly white neighborhoods. It is bounded on the east by Southfield, on the north by Seven Mile Road, and on the west by Heyden Street between Seven Mile Road and Six Mile Road and thereafter by Evergreen Road. The southern boundary, generally, is a line running through Acacia Street. Approximately six thousand five hundred (6,500) families live in the area.

Within this area, there are several sub-communities. Perhaps the most important, to this action, is the Emerson Community whose residents are principally responsible for this law suit. Also included in this area are North Rosedale Park and Rosedale Park (also called South Rosedale Park and South Rosedale).

The plaintiffs produced ample evidence at the hearing to support their contention that the area in question was a racially transitional neighborhood, commonly referred to as a "changing neighborhood." To the layman, either expression is used and understood to mean that blacks are moving into an area.* * *

Prior to 1971, there were no minority families living in the Emerson Community and no more than three lived in the Rosedale Communities. The first black family moved into Emerson in 1971, purchasing a house on Edinborough Road. The present racial composition of the area is estimated to be between ten (10) and twenty (20) per cent black. The other two (2) communities have also experienced an influx of blacks, although somewhat less dramatically than what has occurred in the Emerson Community. While the total number has decreased, there has continued to be some movement of white families into the neighborhoods. There is no questioning, however, the contention that Northwest Detroit has undergone a striking shift in its racial composition in the last four (4) years.

In this context, the continued pace of such racial change in this area is critical. Areas in transition seem to experience rapid population turnover which in large part results from "panic selling," * * * The problem of panic selling arises where white residents succumb to perceived pressures to move out because blacks are beginning to enter the neighborhood. * * *

The testimony taken at the hearing indicates that there are white residents of Northwest Detroit who do in fact correlate the entry of black families with the incidence of lower class social pathology. From their testimony, there emerges the following psychological equation: The quantity of life in a community diminishes with the entry of minority families, particularly black families. It is these fears, and this psychology, that the defendants in this action are alleged to have exploited or attempted to exploit. * * *

The issue which arises at this point, therefore, is not whether the process by which white families are replaced by black families is either irrational or inevitable, as well it might be. The real issue in this litigation is whether the real estate industry should be allowed to enter into the process and, for commercial advantage, artificially hasten or at least accelerat the rate of population turnover and the pace of racial change. As the Fifth Circuit so accurately noted in United States v. Bob Lawrence Realty, Inc., * * *

> "The sociological phenomenon of a transitional area is enough to attract blockbusters * * * intent upon culling all the profits that can be derived from the area. The very essence of the phenomenon is that a large number of competitors individually besiege an area seeking to gain a share of the market." * * *

The concept of a racially transitional neighborhood is critically important to this litigation, because it is within this context that the activities of the real estate industry, in general, and the defendants, in particular, must be scrutinized. From the evidence before the Court, it appears that if the real estate industry is allowed to operate unchecked, the pace of racial transition will be manipulated in a way that will irreparably distort any chance for normal and stable racial change.

B. THE PLAINTIFFS

The plaintiffs are a multi-racial group of homeowners, overwhelmingly white, who live in one (1) of the three (3) subcommunities which constitute the area in question. The white plaintiffs have lived in their respective communities for varying lengths of time; the black moved into the area.

C. THE DEFENDANTS

The defendants are a group of incorporated and unincorporated real estate agencies and a number of individual real estate salespersons. All of the defendants operate in the Detroit Metropolitan area, and all operate or have operated in the area in question. * * *

STEERING AND BLOCK-BUSTING

1. EARL KEIM REALTY COMPANY

The defendant Earl Keim Realty (Keim) is a sole proprietorship owned by Brian P. Hussey. Its principal office is at 22727 Michigan Avenue in Detroit, with branch offices at various locations in Detroit, Redford and Southfield, Michigan. The defendants Virginia Greenwood, Helen LePage, Ethel Wallace and Roy M. Wilson, III are or were at one (1) time employed by Keim Realty as salespersons.

Mrs. Marilyn A. Waddell, a resident of the Emerson Community for over five (5) years, testified that she was approached by a woman in May of 1972 while she was working in her yard. The woman, who was not identified by Mrs. Waddell, but whom the attorneys for the plaintiffs identified in their proposed Findings of Fact as Helen LaPage, introduced herself to Mrs. Waddell as a salesperson working for the defendant Keim. The witness testified that the woman asked her if she knew "what" was moving in next door to her; Mrs. Waddell replied that she knew "who" was moving in and that she had met her next door neighbors and felt that she was going to like them. The family next door was black. The woman indicated that Keim had sold a house recently on her block and directed Mrs. Waddell's attention to a Keim sign in a yard about three (3) houses from her own. She told Mrs. Waddell that she could not live with "them" and left. Mrs. Waddell was subpoenaed by the plaintiffs to testify. * * *

The second witness to testify against the Keim Realty Company was Earnest Bago, also a resident of the Emerson Community. Mr. Bago visited the Keim office on Seven Mile Road and Inkster Road in June, 1972, and again on July 3, 1972. He testified that he went to the realty office because he had heard rumors of objectionable activities by real estate salespersons in his community. Among these rumors was one that salespersons were showing houses to black customers at night with lights on and the windows unobstructed.

June, 1972, visit.

Mr. Bago, posing as an out-of-towner, spoke initially to defendant Ethel Wallace. He indicated that he was interested in buying a house in the Emerson area. The defendant said she would be happy to show him such a house, indicating, however, that Emerson was not in her office's area.

Mr. Bago asked Ms. Wallace if the Echo area was integrated and was told that this could be answered better by the Keim office on Grand River and Outer Drive. "They know where the concentrations of blacks are," she was reported to have said.

Nothing further was discussed at this meeting.

July 3, 1972, visit.

Mr. Bago telephoned the Keim office before his second visit and talked to a person whom he identified as the defendant Virginia Greenwood. Before the witness arrived at the office, Ms. Greenwood had called Ms. Wallace, who was not present, to identify the witness as the person with whom she had talked earlier. Ms. Greenwood told the witness that she had checked with Ms. Wallace and that she would assist him.

On the desk in the office was an open map. Mr. Bago went to this map and pointed out the area in which he was interested. The defendant asked if Mr. Bago had lived in Detroit before; he replied that he had not.

The defendant then told him that they had some nice areas in which he may be interested outside of Detroit. "The school system is poor in Detroit," she was supposed to have said. She continued, "Do you read the newspapers? Even the police are afraid to live in the area, and they are supposed to protect the rest of us."

On the map, Ms. Greenwood drew a line with a marker along Warren Avenue. In the towns of Inkster, Westland and one (1) other area (Wayne), she drew "X's" and also in an area of Livonia where there was a nearby race track. These were areas which the witness was told to avoid as well as the area south of Warren Avenue (see P. Ex. 19).

The witness asked why these areas should be avoided and was told that blacks live in Inkster and were moving into Garden City, Westland and Wayne. She suggested Livonia and Farmington as areas where there was a low crime rate and desirable conditions under which to raise a family.

The defendant gave the witness two (2) listings books, one (1) for Detroit and one (1) for Farmington (P. Exs. 20, 21), and he was told to take them home to compare the prices of homes in the suburbs with those in Detroit. Ms. Greenwood indicated that prices were lower in Detroit because blacks lived there. She said that the Rosedale Park area was kept white by not putting up "For Sale" signs.

The defendant related to the witness that her agency was a member of the United Northwestern Realty Association (UNRA), and they had to show homes in all white areas to blacks. Nevertheless, they were able to avoid having to sell to blacks by asking the owners to take the houses off the market temporarily.

Mr. Bago, after leaving the Keim office, immediately took the multi-list books to the plaintiffs' attorney to be used as evidence in this action. Theoretically, with access to these books, the witness had all houses listed therein available to him for purchase. Also, unknown to the witness at the time, the multi-listing services were apparently available to black brokers and salespersons who were members of UNRA. * * *

2. C. SCHUETT REALTY, INC.

Defendant C. Schuett Realty, Inc., (Schuett) is a Michigan corporation engaged, inter alia, in the listing and sale of real estate. Its office is located at 19228 West McNichols in Detroit. Defendants Ben B. Miller and Jerry O'Rourke are employed as salespersons by Schuett Realty.

Mrs. Dorothy Taylor, a plaintiff in this action and a resident of Northwest Detroit for over tweleve (12) years, testified that she visited the office of the defendant Schuett on June 24, 1972, to inquire about a four (4) or five (5) bedroom house for relatives who were planning to move to Detroit from Illinois. She spoke to the defendant Jerry O'Rourke.

Mr. O'Rourke told the witness that a home similar to the one in which her relatives were interested had just been sold to a nice "white family." He indicated that he did not have any others in the Northwest Detroit area. He then asked the witness if she was interested in selling her home; the witness said that she was not. Mr. O'Rourke handed her his card and told her that maybe she would change her mind.

Mr. O'Rourke talked with Mrs. Taylor mainly about the Brighton and Redford areas. He told her that the schools in Brighton were so much better and that Brighton had so much more to offer than Detroit. The entire visit lasted about thirty (30) minutes. * * * Mrs. Taylor was asked by Mr. Harper, an attorney for several of the defendants, whether Mr. O'Rourke made any representation to her regarding the entry or prospective entry of black families into her neighborhood. She replied that he had not, but that was probably what he wanted to say.

On re-direct, Mrs. Taylor was asked what she understood the defendant to mean when he handed her his card and told her that she may change her mind about selling her house in a year or so. She responded that she understood this to mean that the area was going to change her mind about moving. * * *

The plaintiff Frank O'Keefe, a resident of the Northwest Detroit area for several years, testified about a visit he made to the Schuett office on the corner of West Outer Drive and Six Mile Road in Detroit in the early summer of 1972. Mr. O'Keefe testified that at the office of the defendant he spoke to a salesperson identified as Mr. Ben Miller. Mr. O'Keefe testified that his purpose in making the visit was to determine how his community was "being handled" by the real estate industry. He had witnessed a very noticeable increase in real estate solicitation after a black family had moved into his neighborhood in the summer of 1971. He is a member of the Emerson Community Homeowners Association. After the black family moved in, Mr. O'Keefe testified, ten (10) to twelve (12) homes were sold on his block alone. "Many people abandoned the neighborhood," he added. Mr. O'Keefe is a member of the Emerson Community Homeowners Association (ECHO).

At the Schuett office, the witness approached the first salesperson he encountered and indicated that he was interested in a home in the ECHO area in the Twenty-Five Thousand Dollar ($25,000.00) range. The plaintiffs introduced into evidence the business card of Ben Miller, a salesperson for Schuett (p. Ex. 14). The witness pretended to be interested in a three (3) bedroom colonial type house.

The witness testified that Mr. Miller took out a book of listings for the Farmington and Livonia area. Mr. O'Keefe, however, directed the defendant's attention to a listing in a Detroit area book on Mansfield Street. The defendant's reaction, according to O'Keefe was, "You wouldn't want that home, the coloreds have moved in pretty good there."

The witness replied, "That doesn't bother me."

Mr. Miller then replied, concerning the area where the Schuett office was located, "This neighborhood is pretty good, the coloreds have moved in, but there are still some pretty good buys."

The entire visit lasted no more than five (5) minutes. Mr. Miller testified that he offered to drive the plaintiff around and show him houses in the Detroit area; the plaintiff admitted this. Mr. Miller also testified that almost all of his real estate sales were in the Detroit area and that he himself lived in an integrated area within the City of Detroit.

3. JOHN H. HUSSEY COMPANY

The defendant John H. Hussey Company (Hussey) was a Michigan corporation engaged in the business of listing and selling real estate. Defendants Jim Brady and Jim McNish were employed as salespersons by Hussey.

Michael R. Secord, a plaintiff in this action, moved into Northwest Detroit in June, 1972. At this time, he was working for Mr. Ernest Bago, another plaintiff. When he indicated that he was interested in moving from Clinton Township, Mr. Bago suggested to him that he inquire about buying a home in Northwest Detroit. In February, 1972, he visited the Hussey office on Six Mile Road and spoke initially to James Brady.

The witness testified that Mr. Brady told him not to look at houses east of Southfield because that was a changing area. Mr. Secord ultimately purchased a house in Northwest Detroit from Mr. James Delany of the Hussey Company.

Mr. Secord admitted that he was satisfied with the service rendered to him by Hussey's salesperson and agreed that neither salesperson refused to show him any house which he wanted to see. Mr. Secord also testified that he would not want to live in an area that was more than fifty (50) percent black, because as he put it, he did not "want to be in a neighborhood where he was excluded." * * *

Vincent Zuch, perhaps the most active plaintiff in this action and a resident of Northwest Detroit, made visits to four (4) real estate offices on June 23, 1972, among them the Hussey office on West McNichols and Evergreen. At the office of the defendant, he spoke to James McNish.

Mr. Zuch indicated to Mr. McNish that he was from Wisconsin where he had worked with a man who had lived in Detroit eleven (11) years ago. He said that he was now relocating to Detroit and that he was interested in purchasing a house. He had with him a hand drawn map, which he stated was prepared by a friend in Wisconsin. The map was supposed to indicate an area of Northwest Detroit near Six Mile Road and Huntington Road in which his friend suggested he might be interested.

Mr. Zuch testified that Mr. McNish told him that Detroit was "Zilch, it's out." He suggested that if the witness wanted a good place to live, he should go to Redford where he lived. The defendant added that Detroit was having problems, that property values were down and that blacks lived there. Mr. Zuch then ended the conversation by telling Mr. McNish that he had to leave and that he would return later that weekend with his wife. * * *

4. JOE E. NORWOOD NO. 1 INC.

Joe E. Norwood No. 1 Inc. (Norwood) is a Michigan corporation engaged in the business of listing and selling real estate. Its office is located at 17421 Telegraph, Detroit, Michigan. Defendant Mark Zehnder is employed as a salesperson by Norwood.

MRS. Susan Williamson, subpoenaed by the plaintiffs to testify, was visited by a man at her former home on Edinborough Road prior to February, 1972. She identified this man as being employed by "Norwood Realty." She said that the man was the same man who had sold the house next door to a black family in early 1972. She testified that the man came into her home and told her that he had just sold the house next door a black family. He told her that she could get a good price for her home if she sold now. Mrs. Williamson eventually sold her house and moved to Brighton, Michigan. * * *

On June 23, 1972, Mr. Vincent Zuch visited the office of Norwood on Telegraph and Grand River and posed as a businessman from Wisconsin in the same manner that was described during his visit to the defendant Hussey's office, supra. He discussed the purchase of a house in the Twenty-Five Thousand Dollar ($25,000.00) range with Mr. Mark Zehnder, a saleperson for Norwood.

Mr. Zuch testified that Mr. Zehnder told him that he had come to the right man. The defendant allegedly told Mr. Zuch that the exodus was on, that whites were moving out of Northwest Detroit, blacks were moving in, and, as a result, property values were going down. Mr. Zehnder told the witness that he should consider Farmington where the schools were better and the shopping just as good.

Mr. Zehnder testified that he suggested Mr. Zuch purchase a home in Farmington because that was where he lived. In his opinion, it was a nice place to live. He also testified that he thought the schools in Farmington were better than those in Detroit but that the shopping in Detroit was better than that in Farmington. He denied making any statement about the racial composition of either Detroit or the suburbs. Mr. Zehnder said that he recommended Farmington in the first place, because Mr. Zuch had requested that he suggest a nice place to purchase a home.

5. MAYFAIR REALTY COMPANY

The defendant Mayfair Realty Company is a Michigan corporation engaged in the business of listing and selling real estate. * * *

Mr. Daniel Maxwell, a resident of Northwest Detroit and a plaintiff in this action, testified that he made several visits to the office of Mayfair Realty located on Schoolcraft Road in Detroit. He testified that the first such visit occurred on July 2, 1972, at approximately 4:00 P.M. His interest in visiting the defendant's office was to find out about the "steering of people" by the defendant.

Mr. Maxwell recalled that he left his name and telephone number with a receptionist on the first visit after being told that no salesperson was available to assist him. He called the defendant's office a week later receiving no response to his visit. He was again told that no salesperson was available and that someone would call him later. He was never called. * * *

7. JOY REAL ESTATE COMPANY

The defendant Joy Real Estate Company is a Michigan corporation engaged in the business of listing and selling real estate. * * *

Mr. Vincent Zuch visited the office of the defendant Joy Real Estate Company and spoke to the defendant Windmueller on June 23, 1972. During this same period, he had visited three (3) other real estate offices in the Detroit area. Mr. Zuch testified that he posed as a businessperson from Wisconsin and that he related the same story to Mr. Windmueller that the Court has noted. * * *

According to Mr. Zuch, Mr. Windmueller recommended purchasing a house in the suburbs of Farmington where, in the defendant's opinion, property values were better than those in Detroit and where transportation was about the same. The defendant made this recommendation in spite of his belief that the plaintiff could get twice the house for his money in Detroit. Mr. Windmueller then went to a wall map to further demonstrate the difference in property value, pointing out, according to Mr. Zuch's testimony, that in the vicinity of Six Mile Road and the Southfield Expressway, blacks had moved in and property values were lower. * * *

8. MILLER BROS. REAL ESTATE

Miller Bros. Realty Company (Miller Bros.) is a Michigan corporation engaged in the business of listing and selling real estate. Its office is located at 2590 Puritan, Detroit, Michigan. The defendant Werner V. Cohen is a salesperson for Miller Bros.

Leo J. Elliott, a plaintiff in this action and a resident of Northwest Detroit, testified that he visited the office of Miller Bros. on Eight Mile Road in Detroit on June 28, 1972. He was accompanied by George Badeen, a sixteen (16) year old resident of Northwest Detroit. They were assisted at the Miller Bros. office by the defendant Werner Cohen.

Mr. Elliott, dressed in casual clothes and carrying a motorcycle helmet, was posing as a businessperson from Texas. He told Mr. Cohen that he was interested in a large house and indicated that he had seen several houses in the area near the defendant's office which he liked. Mr. Cohen, the manager of the office, took the witnesses into his office near the entrance of the building. There, the defendant is supposed to have mentioned the Detroit housing ordinance and to have told the witnesses that anywhere they might live in Detroit they would probably have black neighbors. * * *

9. BOWERS REALTY AND INVESTMENT COMPANY

The defendant Bowers Realty and Investment Company (Bowers) is a Michigan corporation engaged, inter alia, in the business of listing and selling real estate. The defendant Art Watkins was employed as a salesperson by the defendant Bowers at all times relevant to this action.

Ms. Marie Olson, a resident of Detroit and a witness for the plaintiffs, testified that in February, 1973, she was approached at her home by a man who identified himself as a Mr. Gill, a salesperson for the defendant Bowers. Mr. Gill, contrary to fact, is alleged to have told the witness that he had a buyer for her house. Ms. Olson told him that he must have made a mistake since her house was not for sale. The man persisted and finally told the witness that he could get her the money for the house by that night. Ms. Olson protested that her house was not for sale, despite the man's insistence that now was the time to sell while she could still get a good price. There was no further identification of the man other than his having told the witness that he was a Mr. Gill working for the defendant Bowers. * * * The defendant Bowers is also alleged to have conducted a solicitation campaign in Northwest Detroit involving flyers, telephone calls and door-to-door canvassing. * * * The plaintiffs alleged that they made requests to the defendant that these solicitations cease. The defendant denied the allegations but admitted that its agents solicit extensively. Ms. Daralyn Bowers, the manager of Bowers Realty, testified that her agents are trained to solicit listings but that they operate under tight control exerted by the defendant.

10. LAWRENCE C. HUMPHREY, d/b/a
FOUR STAR REALTY

Lawrence C. Humphrey, d/b/a Four Star Realty is a Michigan real estate brokerage firm engaged in the business of listing and selling real estate. Irvin Corley, Muriel Skinner and Mr. B. Clark are, or were, salespeople employed by Four Star.

Ms. Helen Stockton, a resident of Northwest Detroit, was called by the plaintiffs to testify about a visit to her home on November 7, 1973, by a man identified as Mr. B. Clark, a salesperson for Four Star Realty. Ms. Stockton testified that at approximately 10:45 A.M. her doorbell rang several times. When she answered it, Mr. Clark and an unidentified couple stood at her door. Mr. Clark told Ms. Stockton that he was there for an 11:00 A.M. appointment which she had made with him over the telephone. The witness testified that she had not made such an appointment and that she so informed the defendant. Mr. Clark then checked in his pocket and showed her that he had her address written down. Ms. Stockton asked him if he had her name; he said that he did not. He eventually conceded that a mistake had been made and he told Ms. Stockton that he would return to his office to check the source of the mistake. When Ms. Stockton moved into Northwest Detroit in 1969, one (1) black family lived on her block. At the time of her testimony, four (4) black families lived there. Many of her immediate neighbors, three (3) or four (4) families are retired persons. The testimony of Ms. Stockton was uncontradicted.

Mrs. Mildred Martin, a resident of Northwest Detroit for twenty-five (25) years, testified about a conversation between herself and Muriel Skinner, a salesperson for Four Star. The conversation occurred on July 29, 1972. Ms. Skinner approached the witness while she was working in her yard on the day in question, greeted her and asked if she was interested in selling her house. Mrs. Martin said that she was not. Ms. Skinner then commented on the neighborhood being nice. The witness responded that that was one of the reasons she was not interested in selling her home. Ms. Skinner gave the witness her business card and asked the witness to mention her to anyone she knew who might want to sell his house. Mrs. Martin thought that Ms. Skinner was black. * * *

UNREQUESTED SOLICITATION

The plaintiffs have also complained about unrequested mail solicitations from various defendants. These solicitations do not refer to race, but the plaintiffs argue that under the circumstances of the communities' transition from all white to racially integrated, such solicitations convey to the recipients the idea that their communities are becoming unstable. As a result of their tendency to exploit racial fear, solicitations have the effect of speeding up the exodus of white residents from the area. The purpose of the defendants in sending these solicitations is to influence the recipients to sell their homes so that the defendants may thereby profit from such sales.

The kinds of solicitations involved in this action vary. Some contain pictures of the salespeople, some contain phrases designed to appeal to the fear that the residents may have for their personal safety, and others and thinly veiled attempts to appeal to racial prejudice. These solicitations are in the form of letters and cards and are addressed either to specific people or to "occupant." Some are general in their references to the area in which the recipient lives and others are specific to the point of indicating that the sender has sold a house on the recipient's block.

Many examples of these solicitations were introduced into evidence. One addressed to "resident" carried the legend, "WE THINK YOU MAY WANT A FRIEND FOR A NEIGHBOR . . . KNOW YOUR NEIGHBORS" * * *

The plaintiffs also allege that various of the defendants have engaged in telephone solicitations in Northwest Detroit. They tried to introduce testimony regarding several of these telephone conversations in which direct references were made to race. * * *

II. CONCLUSIONS OF LAWS

* * * 3. The Fair Housing Act of 1968, 42 U.S.C. § 3601 et seq. was designed to provide, within constitutional limit, for fair housing throughout the United States. * * * Congress' intention in passing the Act was to end the unfairness of racial discrimination forever; it should, therefore, be liberally construed.

Since its passage, the Act has been interpreted to ban all racially discriminatory conduct by real estate agents in the sale and rental of housing. * * *

Steering on a racial basis ("steering") is prohibited by that portion of Section 3604(a) of the Fair Housing Act which makes it unlawful to "otherwise make unavailable or deny, a dwelling to any person because of race." This section makes it unlawful to steer or channel a prospective buyer into or away from an area because of race. Unlawful steering or channeling of a prospective buyer is the use of a word or phrase or action by a real estate broker or salesperson which is intended to influence the choice of a prospective property buyer on a racial basis. * * * Where choice influencing factors such as race are not eliminated, freedom of choice in the purchase of real estate becomes a fantasy. * * * It is the freedom of choice for the purchaser which the Fair Housing Act protects. Hence, race need not be the sole reason for the defendant's conduct if it is an element of that conduct. * * *

Accordingly, any action by a real estate agent which in any way impedes, delays, or discourages on a racial basis a prospective home buyer from purchasing housing is unlawful. * * *

It is the opinion of this Court that when a real estate agent actively undertakes an effort to influence the choice of a prospective home buyer on a racial basis, whether on his own initiative or in response to the buyer's initiative, the agent either directly or indirectly discourages the prospective home buyer from purchasing a home in a particular area. Where available housing has been traditionally denied to blacks because of their race. This conduct tends to perpetuate racially segregated communities. The Court, therefore, concludes as a matter of law that steering is a violation of Section 3604(a) of the Law. * * *

The purpose of this section is to prevent individuals from preying upon the fears of property owners in racially transitional areas and thereby inducing the kind of panic selling which results in community instability. * * *

Section 3604(e), therefore, is aimed at both overt "blockbusting" and other uninvited solicitations in racially transitional neighborhoods where it can be established (1) that the solicitations are made for profit, (2) that the solicitations are intended to induce the sale of a dwelling, and (3) that the solicitations would convey to a reasonable man, under the circumstances, the idea that members of a particular race are, or may be, entering the neighborhood.

It is a well known fact that racial tensions and anxieties are generated when blacks move into previously all-white neighborhoods. It is also well known that many real estate agencies attempt to exploit such a situation by making repeated, uninvited solicitations for the sale of homes. In most instances, this activity (commonly referred to "blockbusting") has proven to be an effective means of stimulating the sale of homes in racially transitional neighborhoods. It does so by capitalizing upon the racial fears of whites, reminding them that blacks are moving into the area. * * *

This Court is well aware of the racial fears which exist in a community into which black families are entering for the first time. The testimony in this action has underscored the instability which results from these fears, and it is this instability upon which the real estate industry preys. * * *

The plaintiffs have alleged that in several instances the defendants refused to deal with prospective "buyers" because they were black. In each of the instances complained of, however, the "buyer" was in fact a tester. In order for a "refusal to deal" to occur, the plaintiff must be a bona fide purchaser; this is clear from the language of the statute. * * *

The defendants, throughout the ten (10) weeks of hearings and in their post-hearing briefs, emphasized that all of the witnesses, with the exception of Mr. Michael Secord, were testers. This is irrelevant. There is no requirement in the Fair Housing Act that the prospective buyer, except in the case of a refusal to deal, be a bona fide purchaser. * * *

The evidence resulting from the experience of testers is admissible to show discriminatory conduct on the part of the defendants. The Fair

Housing Act of 1968 was intended to make unlawful simpleminded as well as sophisticated and subtle modes of discrimination. It is the rare case today where the defendant either admits his illegal conduct or where he sufficiently publicizes it so as to make testers unnecessary. For this reason, evidence gathered by a tester may, in many cases, be the only competent evidence available to prove that the defendant has engaged in unlawful conduct. * * *

The defendants have also raised objections to the testimony of several witnesses because the witnesses initiated either the contact with the realtor or the discussion of race. This is irrelevant. * * * The discriminatory conduct of the real estate salespersons is attributable to the real estate agency under the doctrine of respondeat superior and because the duty to obey the law is nondelegable. * * * Injunctive relief is appropriate in this case in order to insulate the community from any further exploitation by these defendants during the pendency of this action. Injunctive relief is a severe remedy and should be granted in only the most extreme situations. The Court is convinced that this is such an extreme situation. The Court must necessarily balance the harm to the defendants against the harm to the public if the injunction is not granted. By this decision, therefore, the Court has concluded that the public interest is paramount. * * *

III. SPECIFIC CONCLUSIONS OF LAW
(The Court addressed the actions of each defendant)

A. Violations of 42 U.S.C. § 3604(a).

* * * The following conduct constituted violations of 42 U.S.C. § 3604(a):

1. The Conduct of Bernard O'Laughlin as agent of Lexington House Realty testified to by James Irvin.
2. The conduct of Roy M. Wilson, III, agent of Brian Hussey, d/b/a Earl Keim Realty of Detroit, testified to by Richard Cartwright.
3. The conduct of Ben B. Miller, agent of C. Schuett Realty, Inc., testified to by Frank X. O'Keefe.
4. The conduct of James Brady, agent of John H. Hussey Co., testified to by Mike Secord.
5. The conduct of Virginia Greenwood, agent of Brian Hussey, d/b/a Earl Keim Realty of Detroit, testified to by Ernest Bago.
6. The conduct of Mark Zehnder, agent of Joe E. Norwood Company No. 1, testified to by Vincent Zuch.
7. The conduct of Arnold Windmueller, agent of Joy Real Estate Company, testified to by Vincent Zuch, subject to the limitation noted by the Court, supra, at page 1042.
8. The conduct of Bill Willis, an agent of Mayfair Realty, testified to by Vincent Zuch.

9. The conduct of Jim McNish, an agent of John H. Hussey Company, testified to by Vincent Zuch.

B. Violations of 42 U.S.C. § 3604(e).
   The following conduct constituted violations of 42 U.S.C. § 3604(e):

1. The conduct of Irwin Corley as agent of Lawrence Humphrey, d/b/a Four Star Realty, testified to by Barbara and Thomas Herrod.
2. The conduct of Mr. Clark, agent of Lawrence Humphrey, d/b/a Four Star Realty, testified to by Helen Stockton.
3. The conduct of Artincus Watkins, agent of Bowers Realty & Investment Company, testified to by Mary Finneren.
4. In view of the foregoing conclusions of law and findings of facts, the Court concludes as matter of law that the racial atmosphere in the area in question is such that a solicitation for a listing, made for profit and with the intention of inducing the sale of a dwelling, would convey to a reasonable man the idea that members of a particular race are or may be entering the area in question, and thus violate 42 U.S.C. § 3604(e). * * *

REALTORS' EXPOSURE UNDER TITLE VIII OF THE CIVIL RIGHTS ACT OF 1968

The Realtor will see additional exposure arising as a result of the broker directing or guiding potential purchasers in violation of Title VIII of the Civil Rights Act of 1968, 42 USC Sec. 3601 *et seq.* Such direction of purchasers may include a bias as a result of religion, sex, ethnic background, racial trends, or various other standards that are prohibited under the act.

The important point for a Realtor to note, as illustrated in the previous case, is that a violation of this act subjects the Realtor to exposure in the form of civil and criminal sanctions.

In the particular area of racial steering, one article that analyzes this issue is Note, 85 *Yale Law Journal* 808 (1976). This note emphasizes the violation under the federal law where brokers direct purchasers as the result of racial considerations. The act requires a "color blind" standard, as indicated in the note (that is, color is not to be a factor).

In another article by R. Helper, entitled "Racial Policies and Practices of Real Estate Brokers," Mr. Helper emphasizes the general areas where Realtors seem to develop "an exclusion ideology." These may include:

1. Most whites do not want black neighbors.
2. Property values decline as black residents enter white neighborhoods.
3. Integrated neighborhoods eventually become resegregated.

4. Whites are hurt financially and socially by sales to blacks in white area.

5. Selling to blacks in white areas is an unethical business practice.

The broker who engages in such ideology will not only face the potential wrath of the courts as a result of the act mentioned but will also be in violation of ethical standards promulgated by the National Association of Realtors. [See National Association of Realtors, *Realtors' Guide to Practice Equal Opportunity In Housing* 23 (1973).]

Consider what patterns may develop for direction of purchasers as a result of sex, marital status, race and so forth.

For additional sources with regard to a violation of the Title VIII of the Civil Rights Act of 1968, and related issues, see National Association of Realtors, *Realtors Guide To Practice Equal Opportunity In Housing* 23 (1973); National Advisory Commission on Civil Disorders, Report 225 (1968); National Neighbors, *Racial Steering: The Dual Housing Market and Multiracial Neighborhoods* 3 (1973); the various hearings regarding the National Association of Realtors, and related issues before the Subcommittee on Housing and Urban Affairs of the Senate Committee on Banking and Currency, 90th Congress First Session 337 (1967), and sequel hearings; and the earlier-referred to note in the *Yale Law Journal.*

REALTORS' EXPOSURE: "FOR SALE" SIGNS

Another area in which a Realtor may have exposure is if the Realtor potentially acts in violation of a local ordinance or statute that prohibits certain types of activities, such as a given form of advertising. This was the issue which was raised in the *Linmark Associates, Inc.* v. *Township Willingboro* case. This was decided in May of 1977 and addressed the issue as to whether the local ordinance could prohibit "for sale" and "sold" signs on certain residential property.

The purpose for this statute seems to have been to attempt to prevent the flight of white homeowners from a racially integrated area, which arguably would become less and less populated by whites should "for sale" signs be allowed, which would thereby support a flight appearance.

The Willingboro case illustrates the "for sale" issue. The case, however, should be addressed, implicitly, with the general concept of the development of law, and a Realtor should consider taking a stand on an issue, even though there may be exposure. In this particular case, the Realtor was successful.

LINMARK ASSOCIATES, INC.
and
William Mellman
v.
TOWNSHIP OF WILLINGBORO
and
Gerald Daly
97 S.Ct. 1614 (1977)

* * *

Syllabus

A township ordinance prohibiting the posting of real estate "For Sale" and "Sold" signs for the purpose of stemming what the township perceived as the flight of white homeowners from a racially integrated community held to violate the First Amendment. Virginia Pharmacy Bd. v. Virginia Citizens Consumer Council, 425 U.S. 748, 96 S.Ct. 1817, 48 L.Ed. 2d 346. Pp. 1617-1621.

(a) The ordinance cannot be sustained on the ground that it restricts only one method of communication while leaving ample alternative communication channels open. The alternatives (primarily newspaper advertising and listing with real estate agents, which involve more cost and less autonomy than signs, are less likely to reach persons not deliberately seeking sale information, and may be less effective) are far from satisfactory. And the ordinance is not genuinely concerned with the place (front lawns) or the manner (signs) of the speech, but rather proscribes particular types of signs based on their content because the township fears their "primary" effect—that they will cause those receiving the information to act upon it. Pp. 1618-1619.

(b) Moreover, despite the importance of achieving the asserted goal of promoting stable, integrated housing, the ordinance cannot be upheld on the ground that it promotes an important governmental objective, since it does not appear that the ordinance was needed to achieve that objective and, in any event, the First Amendment disables the township from achieving that objective by restricting the free flow of truthful commercial information. * * *

3 Cir., 535 F.2d 786, reversed.

* * *

Mr. Justice MARSHALL * * *

This case presents the question whether the First Amendment permits a municipality to prohibit the posting of "For Sale" or "Sold" signs when the municipality acts to stem what it perceives as the flight of white homeowners from a racially integrated community.

Petitioner Linmark Associates, a New Jersey corporation, owned a piece of realty in the Township of Willingboro, N.J. Petitioner decided to sell its property, and on March 26, 1974, listed it with petitioner Mellman, a real estate agent. To attract interest in the property, petitioners desired to place a "For Sale" sign on the lawn. Willingboro, however, narrowly limits the types of signs that can be erected on land in the township. Although prior to March of 1974 "For Sale" and "Sold" signs were permitted subject to certain restrictions not at issue here, on March 18, 1974, the Township Council enacted Ordinance 5–1974, repealing the statutory authorization for such signs on all but model homes. Petitioners brought this action against both the township and the building inspector charged with enforcing the ban on "For Sale" signs, seeking declaratory and injunctive relief. The District Court granted a declaration of unconstitutionality, but a divided court of appeals reversed. *Linmark Associates, Inc.* v. *Township of Willingboro,* 535 F.2d 786 (CA3 1976). We granted certiorari, _____ U.S. _____, 97 S.Ct. 351, 50 L.Ed.2d 307 (1976), and reverse the judgment of the Court of Appeals.

I

The township of Willingboro is a residential community located in southern New Jersey near Fort Dix, McGuire Air Force Base, and offices of several national corporations. The township was developed as a middle income community by Levitt and Sons, beginning in the late 1950's. It is served by over 80 real estate agents.

During the 1960's Willingboro underwent rapid growth. The white population increased by almost 350%, and the nonwhite population rose from 60 to over 5,000, or from .005% of the population to 11.7%. * * *

At the trial in this case respondent presented testimony from two real estate agents, two members of the Township Council, and three members of the Human Relations Commission, all of whom agreed that a major cause in the decline in the white population was "panic selling"—that is, selling by whites who feared that the Township was becoming all black, and that property values would decline. One real estate agent estimated that the reason 80% of the sellers gave for their decision to sell was that "the whole town was for sale, and they didn't want to be caught in any bind." J.A. 219a-220a. Respondents' witnesses also testified that in their view "For Sale" and "Sold" signs were a major catalyst of these fears.

William Kearns, the Mayor of Willingboro during the year preceding enactment of the ordinance and a member of the Council when the ordinance was enacted, testified concerning the events leading up to its passage. * * * According to Kearns, beginning at least in 1973 the community became concerned about the changing population. At a town meeting in February 1973, called to discuss "Willingboro, to sell or not to sell," a member of the community suggested that real estate signs be banned. The suggestion received the overwhelming support of those attending the meeting. Kearns brought the proposal to the Township Council, which requested the Township Solicitor to study it. The Council also contacted National Neighbors, a nationwide organization promoting integrated housing, and obtained the names of other communities that had prohibited "For Sale" signs. * * *

Rather than following its usual procedure of conducting a public hearing only after the proposed law had received preliminary Council approval, the Council scheduled two public meetings on Ordinance 5-1974. The first took place in February 1974, before the initial Council vote, and the second in March 1974, after the vote. At the conclusion of the second hearing, the Ordinance was approved unanimously. * * *

Although the ordinance had been in effect for nine months prior to trial, no statistical data was presented concerning its impact. Respondents' witnesses all agreed, however, that the number of persons selling or considering selling their houses because of racial fears had declined sharply. But several of these witnesses also testified that the number of sales in Willingboro had not declined since the ordinance was enacted. Moreover, respondents' real-estate-agent witnesses both stated that their business had increased by 25% since the ordinance was enacted. * * *

II
A

The starting point for analysis of petitioners' First Amendment claim must be the two recent decisions in which this Court has eroded the "commercial speech" exception to the First Amendment. In *Bigelow* v. *Virginia,* 421 U.S. 809, 95 Ct. 2222, 44 L.Ed.2d 600 (1975), decided just two years ago, this Court for the first time expressed its dissatisfaction with the then-prevalent approach of resolving a class of First Amendment claims simply by categorizing the speech as "commercial." * * * "Regardless of the particular label," we stated, "a court may not escape the task of assessing the First Amendment interest at stake and weighing it against the public interest allegedly served by the regulation." Ibid. After conducting such an analysis in Bigelow we concluded that Virginia could not constitutionally punish the publisher of a newspaper for printing an abortion referral agency's paid advertisement which not only promoted the agency's services but also contained information about the availability of abortions. * * * One year later, in *Virginia State Board of Pharmacy* v. *Virginia Citizens Consumer Council, Inc.,* 425 U.S. 748, 96 S.Ct. 1817, 48 L.Ed.2d 346 (1976), we went further. Conceding that "(s)ome fragment of hope for the continuing validity of a 'commercial speech' exception arguably might have persisted because of the subject matter in the advertisement in Bigelow," id., at 760, 96 S.Ct., at 1825, we held quite simply, that commercial speech is not "wholly outside the protection of the First Amendment." * * *

Respondents contend, as they must, that the "For Sale" signs banned in Willingboro are constitutionally distinguishable from the abortion and drug advertisements we have previously considered. It is to the distinctions respondents advance that we now turn.

B

* * * If the Willingboro law is to be treated differently from those invalidated in Bigelow and Virginia Pharmacy, it cannot be because the speakers—or listeners—have a lesser First Amendment interest in the subject matter of the speech that is regulated here. Persons desiring to sell their homes are just as interested in communicating that fact as are sellers of other goods and services. * * *

C

Respondents do seek to distinguish Bigelow and Virginia Pharmacy by relying on the vital goal this ordinance serves: namely, promoting stable, racially integrated housing. There can be no question about the importance of achieving this goal. This Court has expressly recognized that substantial benefits flow to both whites and blacks from interracial association and that Congress has made a strong national commitment to promoting integrated housing. * * *

. The record here demonstrates that respondents failed to establish that this ordinance is needed to assure that Willingboro remains an integrated community. * * *

The constitutional defect in this ordinance, however, is far more basic. The Township Council here, like the Virginia Assembly in Virginia Pharmacy, acted to prevent its residents from obtaining certain information. That information, which pertains to sale activity in Willingboro, is of vital interest to Willingboro residents, since it may bear on one of the most important decisions they have a right to make: where to live and raise their families. The Council has sought to restrict the free flow of this data because it fears that otherwise, homeowners will make decisions inimical to what the Council views as the homeowners' self-interest and the corporate interest of the township: they will choose to leave town. The Council's concern, then, was not with any commercial aspect of "For Sale" signs—with offerors communicating offers to offerees—but with the substance of the information communicated to Willingboro citizens. If dissemination of this information can be restricted, then every locality in the country can suppress any facts that reflect poorly on the locality, so long as a plausible claim can be made that disclosure would cause the recipients of the information to act "irrationally." * * *

Since we can find no meaningful distinction between Ordinance 5-1974 and the statute overturned in Virginia Pharmacy, we must conclude this ordinance violates the First Amendment.

III

In invalidating this law, we by no means leave Willingboro defenseless in its effort to promote integrated housing. The township obviously remains free to continue "the process of education" it has already begun. It can give widespread publicity—through "Not for Sale" signs or other methods—to the number of whites remaining in Willingboro. And it surely can endeavor to create inducements to retain individuals who are considering selling their homes. * * *

Reversed.

REALTORS' LIABILITY: HOUSING

Under the National Association of Realtors Code of Ethics, the Realtor cannot deny equal professional service to any person as a result of race, creed, sex, or country of national origin. This would be in violation of Article 10, and therefore subject the Realtors to sanctions under that provision.

This issue is extremely important with regard to the basic principle of discrimination in housing, as announced in the *Jones* v. *Mayer* case decided in 1968 by the United States Supreme Court.

The *Civil Rights and the Real Estate Salesman* pamphlet published by the National Association of Realtors in January, 1968, Form 111-829, emphasizes that the complaints against Realtors in this particular area often arise when the salesperson has used a basic fact that minority groups are moving into the neighborhood as a reason for the homeowner to list his property for sale so that he can get out while the price is still high.

Another argument that results in blockbusting and therefore is in violation of the federal act is when a salesman has engaged in an intensive telephone or mailorder campaign for listings in a changing neighborhood in which he implies the minority issue as a reason for buying or selling, depending on the given facts. Keep in mind that merely giving the *impression* that panic selling exists or will exist can be sufficient for a violation.

GOVERNMENT—FEDERAL ACTS— INTERSTATE LAND SALES

Interstate Sales and the Realtors' Exposure. As is true with any profession, the Realtor must be aware of many laws that affect the business. If the Realtor is involved in a sale of unimproved ground, not otherwise exempt, the Interstate Land Sales Full Disclosure Act of 1968 can apply. This act promulgates regulations and controls out of the Office of Interstate Land Sales central office in Washington, which controls this particular body of law administered under HUD as the primary controlling body.

The important point in this particular area, without attempting to go into the complete act, is to emphasize that where unimproved ground is sold and registration is required under the act mentioned, the Realtor must be aware of the requirement to give a copy of the property report to the purchaser. The property report must give important details as to the unimproved ground being purchased. That detail would include such factors as the amount of paved roads, water conditions, sewer, general weather conditions in the area, and much more. Should the report not be given and should the Realtor participate in this activity, there are penalties, both civil and criminal, that can be levied against the Realtor. For more details on this particular act, see *Real Estate Fundamentals,* by Levine, Mark Lee (West, 1976).

Federal Housing Administration. It is possible for a real estate broker to not only feel the sanctions imposed by a civil suit, but to also find that there may be federal and state criminal actions for violations of his duties. In addition, a real estate broker may also lose his license as a result of improprieties. This point was illustrated in the Valencia case, Supreme Court decision out of New York in 1977. In the Valencia case, the question is raised as to what sanctions may be imposed on a real estate broker, Burke, when that broker prepared FHA mortgage application forms with false information. This case follows.

VALENCIA v. CUOMO
Supreme Court, Appellate Division, 1977.
394 N.Y.S.2d 284

* * *

MEMORANDUM BY THE COURT.
Proceeding pursuant to CPLR article 78 to review so much of respondent's determination, dated October 3, 1975 and made after a hearing, as (1) revoked petitioner William Burke's real estate broker's license on the ground of demonstrated untrustworthiness and (2) directed petitioners Jerome Stern and Madison Valencia Group, Inc. (Madison) to comply with a certain condition within 30 days and provided that their licenses would be revoked on the ground of demonstrated untrustworthiness in the event of such failure.

Determination confirmed insofar as reviewed and proceeding dismissed on the merits, with costs. The time within which petitioners Madison and Stern are to comply with the condition contained in the determination under review is extended until 30 days after entry of the order to be made hereon.

Jerome Stern is president and representative broker of Madison. William Burke is secretary of that corporation. In response to an advertisement, Mrs. Thelma Swingearn contacted Burke about securing a second mortgage for her home. As a result of his dealings with Mrs. Swingearn, Burke prepared three FHA mortgage applications, all containing false information. The second and third applications were prepared after the previous ones had been denied. During the time that Burke was filing the FHA applications with little success, Mrs. Swingearn was attempting to raise cash from other sources since Burke would not help her obtain a personal loan. Burke referred Mrs. Swingearn to a lender, from whom she received a loan at a usurious rate.

Eventually the first mortgagor (sic., mortgagee) foreclosed on Mrs. Swingearn's home and the home was purchased at the foreclosure sale by George Rosen, who had participated in the usurious loan to Mrs. Swingearn. At her request, Rosen sold the home to Mrs. Swingearn's daughter and son-in-law, who had obtained the money to purchase the home from the FHA pursuant to the third loan application filed by Burke at Mrs. Swingearn's direction. Burke was asked by Rosen, through Rosen's attorney, to close the sale since it was Burke who had prepared the loan application. Madison received a $1,620 commission.

* * * The determination that Burke was involved in the usurious loan to Mrs. Swingearn was supported by substantial evidence * * * The determination of "untrustworthiness" or "incompetency" * * * is also substantiated by Burke's failure to independently verify the information that he allegedly received from Mrs. Swingearn. Although we have held that a broker is not responsible for preparing a false application where the misstatements are contrived by the applicant * * * in the instant case Burke had reason to believe, at least as to the second and third FHA mortgage applications, that the information was false. It was not improper for the Secretary of State to conclude, under the circumstances, that Burke had an obligation to seek independent verification of the misinformation.

* * * Under the circumstances of this case, the penalty imposed was not so disproportionate to the offense as to be shocking to one's sense of fairness * * *

MAGNUSON-MOSS WARRANTY ACT

As is true with the general consumer movement, we have seen additional activity in the consumerism area with regard to additional federal laws. Because personality can be important with the purchase of realty, such as a home built with all of the kitchen appliances included, this area is important for the real estate licensee, builder, leader, and others who deal in this field. One of the more important new federal laws that protects the consumer with regard to consumption of consumer products and warranties on those products is the Magnuson-Moss Warranty Act. This act, sometimes referred to as the Lemon Law, applies to retailers and the warranties they might make to consumers. This act, published under 15 United States Code, Section 2301, *et seq.,* provides for a federal law to protect consumers if they buy a "lemon."

Enacted in January of 1975, the rules apply to products manufactured on or after July 4, 1975. There are a few other special dates, but this is the general effective date for the act.

However, even though this date is the general application date, there are provisions in the act providing that rules are to be issued by the Federal Trade Commission. These rules have various effective dates with regard to disclosure of warranties and other matters connected with the protection of the consumer on warranties. As mentioned, the function of the act is to protect the consumer with regard to products being purchased for consumer use. This would include the warranty information the consumer receives, the competition in warranties in general, the prevention of deceptive actions by retailers with respect to warranties, an attempt to induce or increase the incentives being provided for by manufacturers as to reliability of products themselves, and a means of developing within the retailers and other parties making warranties a method of settling disputes on warranted goods. In connection with this position, the act provides for rules and regulations on warranties.

Under Section 101(6), a written warranty is covered under consumer products. A written warranty is: "any written affirmation of fact or written promise made in connection with the sale of the consumer product by a supplier to a buyer which relates to the nature of the material or workmanship and affirms or promises that such material or workmanship is defect-free or will meet a specified level of performance over a specified period of time," or

"Any undertaking in writing in connection with the sale by a supplier of a consumer product to refund, repair, replace, or take other remedial action with respect to such product in the event that such product fails to meet the specifications set forth in the undertaking which written affirmation, promise, or undertaking becomes part of the basis of the bargain between a supplier and a buyer for purposes other than resale of such product."

Generally speaking, the duties under the Magnuson-Moss Act provide that those warrantors who desire to issue a warranty on consumer products through a written warranty have certain duties. The warrantor is generally the producer of the goods, although it can also include retailers. Once again, the act covers certain rules with regard to a warrantor giving a written warranty as to consumer goods.

Therefore, the question arises as to what is a *consumer good* or *consumer product*. The act provides a consumer product, under Section 101(1) includes "any tangible personal property which is distributed in commerce and which is normally used for personal, family, or household purposes (including any such property intended to be attached to or installed in any real property without regard to whether it is so attached or installed)."

Thus the meaning of consumer goods is very broad and is very similar to much of the language used in the Uniform Consumer Credit Code.

Example —————————————————————————————————

Mrs. Housewife purchases a TV set. A written warranty is given to her with regard to the life of the picture tube and certain labor that will be given in conjunction with the replacement of the picture tube.

This particular sale of a TV set is a consumer good or product as indicated above. It is also within the Magnuson-Moss Act, since there is a written warranty.

Sometimes it is difficult for the consumer to know whether the item he purchased is a consumer product and covered under the act or might be real estate and not covered. As a result of this problem, the Federal Trade Commission has issued general rules or guidelines to attempt to resolve some of these ambiguities. As such, an ambiguity in this type of area, such as whether something constitutes real estate or personal property to fall within a consumer, that is, within the act and giving the consumer protection of Magnuson-Moss.

Example —————————————————————————————————

Mr. Purchaser acquires an automobile to use it in business and for pleasure. The automobile has a defect in the engine. The question is whether the defect is covered under Magnuson-Moss. This raises the more general question as to whether the product falls within a consumer product, for personal use. In this case the product is being used for personal and for business use. The position as interpreted under the guidelines would probably be in favor of coverage, since the guidelines seem to stress the normal use of the product to be controlling to determine whether it is covered under the act.

Remember that the act covers written warranties and not a general statement of policy about the customer's needs and general acceptance of the consumer product. Consumer satisfaction in general would not be covered.

Example ───────────────────────────────────

Mr. Purchaser acquired a TV set. On the back of his receipt there was a statement "satisfaction guaranteed or you will receive a refund of all of your money." Mr. Purchaser used the TV for one month, but he was not satisfied with the nature of the color on the set. He did not think the picture was as crisp and clear as it should be.

Mr. Purchaser brought the set back to the seller and requested his money back in accord with the statement made on the receipt. Could he receive his money back?

He might be able to receive his money back under the theory of general contract law. However, the Magnuson-Moss Act would not protect the consumer in this case, because the act does not apply as to the short written statement that was given. The statement is not specific enough as to the product and it does not relate to a specific period of time or remedies that are permitted. This does not mean that there might not be other actions by the warrantor that might bring the TV set within the Magnuson-Moss Act. For example, a separate written warranty might bring the TV set within the act.

The statement in the example was too general. If the statement had been more specific as to the time for refund, such as allowing a refund if the claim was made within thirty (30) days, it might have been sufficient to bring it within the act.

What is the designation of the types of warranties? Under the act, if a product cost the consumer more than $10.00, excluding tax, there must be a designation of the warranty. That is, when a written warranty is given and is within the act, the warranty must be clearly and conspicuously designated to be either a *full* warranty, which deals with the duration or time of the warranty or a *limited* warranty. This is under Section 103 of the act.

When the warranty is deemed to be a full warranty, there are certain minimum standards that are included. The warrantor must agree to correct any defect without charge if there is a default, malfunction, or failure to conform with a written warranty. See Section 104. Further, 104(a) (2) provides there cannot be a limitation on the length of the implied warranties.

An additional requirement is that there cannot be any exclusion or limitation of consequential damages unless those limitations are printed in a very conspicuous manner on the face of the warranty. This is provided by Section 104(a) (3).

If the product cannot be repaired within a reasonable period of time, the warrantor must allow the consumer to choose between a refund or replacement of the product. One question is, what amount of reasonable effort can first be made by the warrantor to repair the item before the warrantor must give a selection of refund or replacement of the product itself?

There are other limitations under the full warranty. For example, the warrantor will owe the duties indicated to the original purchaser and to anyone who comes into the product and is a consumer of the product within the warranty period. That is, the warranty cannot be limited to the original purchaser, but must be transferable to other transferees during the warranty period.

Under Section 104(b) (1), the warrantor cannot impose a duty on the consumer with regard to the goods, unless the duty is reasonable. Obviously, the warrantor would not be responsible under the warranty if the damage was improperly caused by the unreasonable actions of the consumer.

Example

Mr. Purchaser, consumer, acquires an automobile for personal use. He fails to heed the warranty requirements under the written full warranty. This includes the requirement to change oil, regulate the oil pressure, and similar items. Eventually, there is engine damage. The consumer seeks a replacement automobile or repair to the engine as a result of the damage.

Obviously, this would not be covered by the warrantor, since the warrantor might make a full warranty as to engine damage within the given period of time. If the damage can be traced to the unreasonable use and actions of the consumer failing to maintain the property in accord with the instructions of the warrantor, there is no liability [Section 104(c)].

Simply because Magnuson-Moss covers the written warranty does not mean that it abrogates state laws as to other warranties. The act continues all state rights and remedies allowed to consumers. There are some exceptions, such as allowing the Magnuson-Moss Act to control with regard to disclaiming implied warranties and the duration of those warranties. These will control as opposed to state law.

Under Section 108, there are limitations on disclaiming implied warranties. For example, the supplier cannot disclaim or modify, except as provided within the act, any implied warranty to a consumer with respect to the consumer product if the supplier makes a written warranty to the consumer with respect to such consumer product or at the time of the sale, or within ninety (90) days thereafter the supplier enters a service contract with the consumer which applies to the consumer product.

One exception under the act under Section 108 (b) provides that implied warranties may be limited as to time, by limiting them to the duration of the written warranty if that limitation is deemed to be conscionable (fair) and is set forth in clear and unmistakable language. It must be prominently displayed on the face of the warranty itself. If a warranty disclaimer is attempted in derogation of the rule mentioned, it is ineffective for purposes of the Magnuson-Moss rule and for state law.

Because of this rule, it changes the Uniform Commercial Code Rule under Section 2-316, which had previously allowed the supplier to disclaim implied warranties by using specific writings or expressions, by the buyer's examination of the goods, or by course of dealing. The Magnuson-Moss Act now specifically changes this rule.

Who is affected by the Magnuson-Moss Act? As indicated, those who are making warranties are generally affected by the act. However, the Magnuson-Moss Act covers retailers because they can be "suppliers" within the meaning of the Magnuson-Moss Act. Further, if the retailer gives service contracts or gives written warranties on consumer products, they are also covered under the act.

Special disclosure rules. As has been true with many federal and state acts passed in recent years, the public must be informed of their rights. In the past, we generally assumed that one who was concerned with the law would investigate the rights and remedies the law might give him. However, that position seemed to have been unreasonable. Many individuals—consumers and others—might not have been aware of the rights and remedies provided to them by law. As such, the Federal Consumer Credit Protection Act, the Uniform Consumer Credit Code, and many other laws, such as the Real Estate Settlement Procedures Act, require that many disclosures be given to the general public. This same trend of thought has been continued in the Magnuson-Moss Act, under which disclosures must be given to consumers as to the rights that they have under the warranties.

In general, the warrantor, such as the manufacturer, must give certain warranties and must provide retailers with certain information and materials they can use to comply with the disclosure rules under the act. The warrantor can provide a copy of the written warranties with every consumer product, by providing some sort of attachment to the product which contains the full text of the warranty. They might also print the warranty on the product itself. They could also provide a notice, sign, or some other poster that discloses the consumer product warranty and offers a copy of the written warranty with the product.

When products are sold through the mail, there are different options for complying with the disclosure requirements to let the consumer be aware of the warranties. Generally speaking, the warranty must be disclosed in the catalog with close proximity to the description of the product itself or in some information section of the catalog that is clearly referenced by each product to let the consumer be aware of the disclosure of the warranty information within the catalog.

The obvious information that must be included would be such things as identification of the names and addresses of the warrantors, the identity of the parties to whom the warranty is extended, what the warrantor will do in case the product is defective, the items covered by the warranty, the exclusions or exceptions with regard to the warranty, the steps that the consumer must take to obtain performance of the warranty, a description of the remedies available to the consumer if performance is not undertaken by the warrantor in accord with his warranty; the time period covered by the warranty; what the consumer must do and the expenses he must bear with regard to the warranty; what is clearly covered and not covered under the warranty; a clear statement of the elements of the warranty, which would not mislead a reasonable, average consumer as to the scope of the warranty; the time period in which the warrantor will undertake his actions to perform; informal dispute or settlement procedures which are offered by the warrantor, if any; and certain other items.

How can the consumer be sure that he will receive the benefits under the act? The enforcement provisions under the Magnuson-Moss Act provide for an action by the Federal Trade Commission, the Attorney General, and by consumer actions. In other words, the FTC and the United States Attorney General can bring actions to enforce the rules of this act, or the individual consumer can bring his own action.

In addition, when the consumer brings an action, he can seek, as part of his damages or judgment, the costs and expenses he incurs, including attorney fees. There are special procedural limitations with regard to bringing actions, such as bringing an action in a federal court. In this case, the amount in controversy must be at least $50,000.00. However, there are other sources or actions by the consumer. Once again, the FTC could bring an action or the consumer could seek a remedy under informal procedures set by the warrantor. The consumer could also seek an action in a state court.

Other Limitations and Rules. The act also prevents the warrantor from making a warranty conditional upon the consumer using an article or service which is identified by brand, trade name, or corporate name, unless those items are provided without charge under the warranty.

Example ————————————————————————————————

Mr. Purchaser acquires a new automobile. Under the provisions of his full written warranty, there is a statement that all mechanical, maintenance, lubrication, and so forth must be undertaken by an authorized dealer of the warrantor. Thus if Mr. Purchaser requires certain repairs on his warranted item, they must be undertaken by the warrantor's representatives, only.

Is this a proper act by the warrantor? On the assumption that the cost for this type of service is not provided by the warrantor, and there will be a charge to the consumer, this action is improper.

———————————————————————————————————————

This "tie-in" prohibition is improper under the act, unles the FTC waives that requirement and allows the warrantor to provide for a tie-in because of the nature of the goods themselves. It is unlikely that the FTC will provide for very many waivers of this type.

CHAPTER 7

Unauthorized Practice of Law

How far can a real estate practitioner proceed without violating the state laws for unauthorized practice of law? What can the broker do in the way of preparing contracts, closing papers, deeds of trust, mortgages, and other legal documents? How much tax advice can a Realtor give, if any, before he is in the unauthorized practice of law area?

These and related issues face the real estate professional on a day-to-day basis. Many firms have hurdled this problem by having legal counsel on retainer or by otherwise having matters reviewed by counsel. This may be a possible solution in many instances, but for the smaller firm, the sudden needs required in a situation in which counsel cannot be obtained on a timely basis, and in many other circumstances, necessitate some basic guidelines as to how far a Realtor can go without being in the area of unauthorized practice of law.

This topic is a never-ending issue which has been examined by all states in some fashion or other. The question is, of course, not restricted to real estate licensees, but arises in many fields, such as mortgage banking, building business, tax fields by accountants acting, and much more.

The following material illustrates some of the cases in this particular area and also examines the practical implications of unauthorized practice of law in addition to ethical and state restrictions on the same.

Some of the following material has been reproduced from *Handbook on Real Estate Law* by Mark Lee Levine and Kenty Jay Levine, published by Professional Publications and Education, Inc. (1978).

129

UNAUTHORIZED PRACTICE OF LAW— REALTORS' EXPOSURE

This particular area examines the very basic question of when a Realtor is in violation of the law because he has been practicing law. In other words, when he has gone beyond the scope of acting as·a Realtor and is now acting as an attorney, unlicensed to do the same.

The cases which follow illustrate the concerns of both the Bar Association and Realtors with regard to unauthorized practice of law. One of the pragmatic problems is to determine at what point a Realtor is in fact entering the area of practice of law.

Many standards have been developed in the various states with regard to this issue of practice of law by a Realtor. Some states take a very restrictive view and prohibit the Realtor from being involved in almost any document preparation, whether it be the contract for the sale, the deed, deeds of trust or mortgages, notes, or other documents. On the other hand, the other extreme of the continuum is to allow the Realtor to prepare the documents just mentioned, so long as they are in standard approved form, generally approved by the Real Estate Commission of the given state. The latter state could be illustrated by the Colorado position; the prior might be illustrated more so by the Ohio position. In any event, there is a substantial difference between states, and although this is true with any case which might be read, it is particularly true with regard to the area of unauthorized practice of law. The reader must be very cognizant of the differences that exist from state to state and be aware that the cases illustrate a general principle which must be refined to the given state in question.

The issue of unauthorized practice of law generally arises in real estate transactions in which documents are prepared by the Realtor, and it is argued that this is beyond the scope of the Realtor and is the practice of law.

Keep in mind that this issue of violating the practice of law standards is not restricted to the real estate field. Bar associations have challenged title companies, insurance companies, CPAs, and many other groups with regard to this issue. As for the Realtor, there are a great number of articles and support items discussing this issue as to unauthorized practice. Having the general question stated, we can proceed to a few cases which illustrate the point. For further reference, it is suggested that the reader consult the sources in the footnote noted herein.*

* For additional sources with regard to unauthorized practice of law, see a collection of sources in the American Law Reports: 53 A.L.R. 2d 788 (1957). See also 13 A.L.R. 3d 1137 (1967); 13 A.L.R. 3d 812 (1967); and 34 A.L.R. 3d 1305 (1970),

MORLEY v. J. PAGEL REALTY & INSURANCE
Court of Appeals of Arizona
rehearing Denied July 16, 1976
550 P.2d 1104

* * *

OPINION

KRUCKER, Judge.

This was an action by appellants, Clifton and Mary Morley, against appellees, J. Pagel Realty & Insurance (Pagel Realty), Shirley Tripett, a real estate salesperson employed by Pagel Realty, and Western Surety Co., the surety on Pagel Realty's bond. Also named as defendants were Lawrence P. Hayden, dba Old West Realty and Lawrence P. Hayden and JoAnne Hayden, husband and wife. * * * From an adverse judgment rendered by the trial court on stipulated facts, appellants have perfected this appeal. We reverse.

Appellants owned a three-bedroom home in the Warren area of Bisbee, Arizona. On March, 1973, they listed their property for sale with Pagel Realty through appellee Shirley Tripett. The asking price was $15,000, payable as follows: "DOWNTERMS $3,000 will carry at 8% interest with 15 yr Stop." Pagel Realty's commission was to be six percent.

In April of 1973, Tripett obtained a written offer from Lawrence and JoAnne Hayden. It provided for a purchase price of $15,000, with a $2,500 down payment and the balance payable as follows:

"$12,500.00 by buyers executing in favor of sellers a demand note payable at not less than $100.00 per month. Buyers reserve the right to pay more than $100 per month on said note without penalty. Interest rate on the note will be 8%. The note will be all due and payable 10 years from date of closing.

Tripett showed the written offer to appellants without giving them any advice concerning its contents. On April 20, 1973, appellants signed the written offer.

---

and earlier cites under those A.L.R. reports which give a very good collection of the history of this area. There are also other numerous articles in this area, such as Comment, California Real Estate Brokers: Conveyancing Forms: The Unauthorized Practice of Law, 35 S. Cal. Rev. 336 (1962); see also a collection of these articles in Note, 40 Cincinnati Law Rev. (1961). For a discussion of the Colorado position which is a more lenient position for Realtors, see *Conway-Bogue Realty Investment Co.* v. *Denver Bar Association,* 135 Colo. 398, 312 P.2d 998 (1957). The Realtors' position against unauthorized practice of law is mentioned in the Code of Ethics promulgated by the National Association of Realtors.

The closing took place on May 14, 1973. On that date Lawrence and JoAnne Hayden executed a promissory note for $12,500, naming appellants as payees. The form used for the note included the words "This note is secured by a mortgage on real property," but these words were crossed out.

Sometime during the next six months the Haydens deeded the property to a third party for cash, defaulted on the note, and went bankrupt. Appellants thereafter brought this action against Pagel Realty and Tripett, alleging that they had breached their fiduciary duty to appellants, had negligently represented appellants in the sale of their land, and were grossly negligent in failing to protect appellants' interests.

On January 15, 1975, counsel for the parties submitted the case to the trial court on the following stipulation:

"That the defendant Triplett (sic), a licensed real estate salesman, acting as agent for the defendant, Pagel, carried a Deposit Receipt and Agreement, which is in evidence, to the plaintiffs, Worley (sic) and delivered it to them without giving any advice concerning the contents of the agreement." Counsel also stipulated that the only legal issue was: ". . . does the issue of giving advice by the defendant, or any of them, to the plaintiffs, to the effect that the promissory note should be secured by a realty mortgage constitute the illegal practice of law; and, if so, is that a complete defense to the plaintiff's claim?"

Counsel also stipulated that if appellees were held liable, the amount of damages would be $11,900.00.

On June 3, 1975, the trial court ruled in favor of appellees by minute entry. On September 17, 1975, formal judgment was entered which stated:

". . . the court concludes and finds that the giving of advice by the defendants, or any of them, to the plaintiffs, to the effect that the promissory note should be secured by a Realty Mortgage, would constitute the illegal practice of law."

This appeal presents two distinct questions for our consideration: (1) independent of any question of unauthorized practice of law, whether a real estate agent who shows his clients a written realty purchase offer that contemplates satisfaction of a substantial portion of the purchase price with an unsecured promissory note has a duty to tell his clients that the purchase price should be secured by a mortgage; and (2) whether a real estate agent who tells his clients that the purchase price of their property should be secured by a mortgage thereby engages in the unauthorized practice of law.

We recently discussed the duties of a seller's real estate broker in *Vivian Arnold Realty Co.* v. *McCormick*, 19 Ariz. App. 289, 506 P.2d 1074 (1973):

"A real estate agent owes a duty of utmost good faith and loyalty to the principal, and one employed to sell property has the specific duty of exercising reasonable due care and diligence to effect a sale to the best advantage of the principal—that is, on the best terms and at the best price possible. * * * He is also under a duty to disclose to his client information he possesses pertaining to the transaction in question. * * *

No Arizona decisions have delineated the exact extent of a real estate broker's duty to his client in a situation like the one that occurred here. * * * However, several analogous decisions from other jurisdictions suggest what that duty should be. The Oregon courts have said that a real estate broker must make a full and understandable explanation to his client before having him sign any contract. * * *

In *Duncan* v. *Barbour*, 188 Va. 53, 49 S.E.2d 260 (1948), a real estate broker submitted an amended purchase offer to his client without disclosing that it failed to accord with the client's wishes in three crucial respects. The court upheld denial of the broker's commission. It stated:

". . . it was the duty of the agent to disclose to his principal the vital differences in the terms and conditions of sale contemplated by the parties. This duty was not discharged by simply handing to the owner an unsigned contract and directing his attention to one specific change. It was his duty to inform his principal of all facts which might influence his principal in accepting or rejecting the offer." 49 S.E.2d at 265.

In *Reese* v. *Harper*, 8 Utah 2d 119, 329 P.2d 410 (1958), defendant was a farmer with little business acumen. He owned a farm that was subject to $15,000 in liens. He listed the farm for sale with plaintiff, a real estate broker, and asked $45,000 for it. Plaintiff showed defendant a third party's written offer of $30,000, which states on a separate line that there were to be no encumbrances. Defendant understood that the purchaser would pay him $30,000 and also pay off the liens; in fact, the offer required defendant to discharge the liens out of the $30,000 purchase price. Plaintiff did not explain the terms of the offer, and defendant signed it after cursorily examining it. Defendant later refused to go through with the deal, and plaintiff sued for his commission. The court affirmed judgment for defendant. It rejected plaintiff's argument that he had no duty to "coddle and spoonfeed" defendant, holding that plaintiff violated his duty to:

". . . apply his abilities and knowledge to the advantage of the man he serves; and to make full disclosure of all facts which his principal should know in transacting the business." * * *

From Prall and Starkweather we learn that a real estate broker must make some kind of explanation of the offer he procures for his client. Duncan tells us that if the offer varies from the terms of the listing the broker must so inform his client. And from Reese we discover that a person acting as broker for an inexperienced client must employ all his professional ability and knowledge to make sure the client understands the "facts" that will materially affect his desire to sell in accordance with the terms of a purchase offer. * * * In the case at bench, appellants seek to hold appellees liable for failing to inform them that the Haydens' offer contemplated no security and that a mortgage should be required. Although this information might be beyond the average person, it is common knowledge in the real estate business. We think that as part of appellees' duty to effect a sale for appellants on the best terms possible and to disclose to them all the information they possessed that pertained to the prospective transaction, appellees were bound to inform appellants that they should require security for the Haydens' performance.

The second question we are faced with is whether a real estate broker who tells his client he should require a mortgage thereby engages in the unauthorized practice of law. In *State Bar of Arizona* v. *Arizona Land Title & Trust Co.,* 90 Ariz. 76, 366 P.2d 1 (1961), supplemented, 91 Ariz. 293, 371 P.2d 1020 (1962), our Supreme Court gave the following general definition:

> ". . . those acts, whether performed in court or in the law office, which lawyers customarily have carried on from day to day through the centuries must constitute 'the practice of law.' " 90 Ariz. at 87, 366 P.2d at 9.

In the State Bar case the court said such acts include the direct or indirect giving of advice relative to legal rights and liabilities. * * *

In determining what constitutes "legal advice" or "acts . . . which lawyers customarily have carried on from day to day throughout the centuries," the following language from *Gardner* v. *Conway,* 234 Minn. 468, 48 N.W.2d 788 (1951) is helpful:

> "The line between what is and what is not the practice of law cannot be drawn with precision. Lawyers should be the first to recognize that between the two there is a region wherein much of what lawyers do every day in their practice may also be done by others without wrongful invasion of the lawyers' field.
>
> * * *
>
> The development of any practical criterion, as well as its subsequent application, must be closely related to the purpose for which lawyers are licensed as the exclusive occupants of their field. That purpose is to protect the public from the intolerable evils which are brought

upon people by those who assume to practice law without having the proper qualifications." * * *

Appellees intimate that appellants would require real estate brokers to discuss with their clients the merits of all the various available security devices. We do not read appellants' argument so broadly. The only duty appellants contend for is a duty to warn the untutored vendor that he should require some form of security in the contract of sale. The giving of such banal advice by real estate brokers creates no danger to the public. We hold that under the circumstances that arose in this case, a real estate broker would not engage in the unauthorized practice of law by telling his clients that the purchase price of their property should be secured by a mortgage. * * * Our holding today is a narrow one and should not be read to extend beyond the situation presented by the facts of this case. It is reinforced by Art. 26, § 1 of the Arizona Constitution. Having achieved, by virtue of this provision, the right to prepare any and all instruments incident to the sale of real property, including promissory notes, real estate brokers and salesmen also bear the responsibility and duty of explaining to the persons involved the implications of these documents. Failure to do so may constitute real estate malpractice.

Reversed and remanded with directions to enter a judgment in favor of appellants in the amount of $11,900, plus costs.

LEGAL AND OTHER COUNSEL

The importance for the real estate agent to ensure that the client, or any other parties involved in a real estate purchase and sale, is represented by legal, tax, and other counsel cannot be overly stressed.

First, there are state laws, which might insist on the broker's suggesting and recommending legal and other counsel. That is, a number of states require the agent to recommend that the parties obtain legal and other counsel. However, even if the state law does not insist on this recommendation, it is a consideration that should apply in almost all instances. In addition, the Realtor code of ethics suggests that the Realtor consider recommending legal counsel. Therefore, there may also be an ethical requirement, if the agent is a member of the National Association of Realtors and is following their code of ethics. Once again, however, it is in the best interest of the real estate professional and the parties involved to recommend counsel, whether it is required by state law or the ethical requirements.

Inasmuch as the real estate agent is normally not an attorney (and even if the licensee is an attorney he can generally not represent the parties in the transaction as both an attorney and as a Realtor) the licensee should be cognizant of the needs of the parties and recommend counsel. In addition, recommending counsel can be rewarding as an insulator to the licensee. Thus, if the Realtor has recommended legal counsel, tax counsel, and other representatives and they have not been brought in at the election of the party or parties involved, the Realtor can show that he did recommend such counsel and that the same was not elected or chosen by the parties involved. Incidentally, it is important that the recommendation to obtain counsel be in writing, preferably in the contract. For example, the language might read: "All parties are advised to seek legal, tax, and other counsel to consider the implications of this agreement. Said advisors should be sought and consulted with prior to the execution of this agreement."

Real estate agents must become more aware of the exposure they face as a result of adverse implications that may arise subsequent to the execution of this contract. For example, if the treatment of the given transaction by a seller results in adverse tax implications to that seller, the seller may turn his vengeance on the agent, arguing that the agent should have informed the seller of adverse tax implications or at least suggested competent advisors to aid the seller.

It is interesting to note that most sellers will consider themselves to have a degree of sophistication, except when it is to their advantage not to assert that sophistication. This, of course, is true with purchasers and is also true with agents who find themselves in a position of trying to defend by lack of expertise. That is, we all are inclined to assert a degree of expertise in given areas or at least to hide our lack of knowledge. However, when it becomes legally advantageous to show a lack of knowledge in a given area, this certainly is brought to the forefront. An example might be a seller who did not realize that by taking a given amount of cash in a transaction, he would not qualify for an installment sale under Code Section 453 of the Internal Revenue Code of 1954, as amended. The seller might or might not have been aware of installment sale implications in the past, but certainly if he wishes to take a position that he has been damaged as a result of his lack of being able to use the installment sale technique, he may plead his lay position and argue that the agent, the "expert" in real estate, should have informed him of this particular point or at least have suggested legal and other counsel.

These points typify the concern that should be felt by real estate agents in recommending legal, tax, and other counsel, whether or not the same is required by state laws or ethical consideration. This makes the case all the stronger for agents to recommend counsel. However, the protection for the licensee in insulating his position by indicating that if there was an error, someone else with greater expertise, namely the tax attorney, the CPA, or someone else, should have noted the given consideration, may act as a backstop and protector for the agent. One might simply say that what we are trying to do is shift the buck to someone else. This is a valid point; the agent may in fact be trying to escape. I suppose the considerations are: (1) It may not be bad for the agent to attempt to shift the buck. (2) The agent is somewhat insulated. (3) The agent also would generally not have the expertise of the attorney or CPA, assuming qualified attorneys and CPAs, and therefore it is a justifiable ground to in fact shift the burden or buck in the given transaction.

The practical issue in this area, once again assuming that state and ethical requirement do not require the recommendation of counsel, is that the agent might be hesitant to recommend legal, tax, or other counsel simply because such recommendation may deter, or in fact destroy the potential sale and/or purchase. In representing a seller, it may come down to a given tax point that cannot be hurdled, and therefore the counsel advises the seller not to complete the transaction. As such, this obviously may cost the real estate agent a commission.

On the other hand, there are valid concerns by the agent that the given tax or other advisor might not be realistically informed under the circumstances and may blow the deal when in fact it should not have been blown. The advice given may be defective, it may be that the problem could have been hurdled, it may be that the attorney or other parties are unrealistic in the demands, such as insisting on a higher interest rate than that that can reasonably be obtained or other difficult and unreasonable positions might be asserted by counsel.

Many Realtors have read such publications as Robert Ringer's text on *Winning Through Intimidation* or a sequel to it. Mr. Ringer emphasizes the concern just mentioned: the possibility that the attorney or other party may destroy the transaction unreasonably. That is, many times transactions in fact should not be completed because there is a defect under the circumstances. However, just as often, if not more so, many attorneys or other counsel are not realistic in attempting to solve the problem. In addition, some counsel go beyond the scope of their position, such as an attorney advising on legal issues who also attempts to weigh certain economic considerations such as the value of the property in its highest and best use and other marketing concepts that are generally outside the scope of the attorney's review.

Many Realtors have heard the statement made by an attorney to his client that: "You are selling this property for too low a price. It is worth substantially more." This type of statement indicates that the attorney, in most circumstances, is exceeding his boundaries and is in the marketing area as opposed to the legal implications that he should be reviewing, along with other tax and related issues.

In any event, a Realtor would be well advised to recommend counsel who can support the needs of his client. It is helpful for the Realtor to suggest to his client or parties involved that when obtaining legal, tax, and other counsel, the selection should be made with parties who are reasonably familiar with real estate transactions as opposed to a general practitioner who might not have the expertise in this particular field.

If a conflict does result and the Realtor feels the counsel is being unreasonable, it may be worthwhile to suggest that the client select an additional opinion by other counsel of the client's choice. This action is no different than selecting an additional opinion when obtaining medical or other types of advice.

How should counsel be obtained? What if your client agrees that he should select some advisors to oversee the legal, tax, and other ramifications in the transaction, but does not know any such individual? It is possible that the Realtor may know someone to recommend given names. There is some danger to this, in that the seller or purchaser may look to the Realtor as somewhat of a guarantor of the actions by the counsel. That is, since the Realtor recommended the party, the client may look to the Realtor as warranting the actions and knowledge of the given counsel.

There are other sources for selecting counsel. Most jurisdictions have bar associations, accounting groups, and other professional organizations that list members in their group. There can also be a selection of parties through word of mouth, general reference with the banker or other advisor, and other parties who might deal with this type of need on a day-to-day basis. Obviously, confirming the background and the expertise of the given counsel is an important point. Confirmation might be through other parties who have used this particular counsel, interviewing with the counsel in question, looking to the background, certifications, formal educational training, and other items which bear on the reputation and expertise of the given counsel.

When all is said and done, there is no absolute guarantee that the counsel selected will in fact be able to do the job in a manner acceptable to the client. Nevertheless, these are some means of selecting advisors.

As mentioned, there are a number of lawyer referral services and other referral services for counsel. A quick check in the telephone book under attorneys or legal counsel may produce a reference number, such as a metropolitan lawyer referral service, which can forward brochures and other information on the topic of selecting counsel.

To reiterate, it is very important that the Realtor recognize the insulation and protection obtained when the client has adequate counsel. This may prevent a later suit against the Realtor because of some adverse question that was not seen by the Realtor, such as an easement issue, questions as to surveys, adverse ownership questions, title issues in general, tax questions, security as to mortgages, deeds of trust, security agreements, financing statements, questions on default, defects in the closing papers, questions as to covenant not to compete, federal and state laws of disclosure, and much more. The Realtor can shift much of this responsibility to a party trained in this area, and the Realtor can feel more comfortable in learning and producing in his area of expertise, namely that of marketing. This is not to say the Realtor should not be cognizant of and informed on legal, tax, and related issues. However, the Realtor may find the learning process much more tempered by having experts guide the parties through this transaction, rather than learning on a case-by-case method as a result of suits or other controversies.

CHAPTER 8

Liability and Effect on Commissions & Licensing

COMMISSIONS AND RELATED LIABILITY ISSUES

Commissions and Title Issues. An additional concern is the liability, or one might say the necessity, of a real estate broker to determine the status of title by a seller. Consider, for example, the situation in which a real estate broker lists a property from the party who was alleged to be the owner. The representation by the owner is that in fact he does own the property. The broker procures a ready, willing, able purchaser, who is willing to purchase according to the terms of the seller. It is later discovered, near closing, that the owner of the property in fact does not have a good title. The question is whether the real estate broker is entitled to a commission and whether the real estate broker has any responsibility to the third-party purchaser, if in fact the owner does not have good title to the property. Although only the question of the commission is discussed in the following case of *Mayberry* v. *Davis,* the point made by the Minnesota court seems to solve the issue.

MAYBERRY v. DAVIS
178 N.W.2d 911
Tom MAYBERRY and Ed. G. MUTSCH, d.b.a. Ed. G. Mutsch Realty,
Appellant,
v.
Donald E. DAVIS, Respondent.
* * *
Supreme Court of Minnesota
* * * 1970.
* * *

OPINION

OTIS, Justice.

Plaintiffs have been awarded a verdict of $2,400 in an action to recover a real estate commission. The Court granted a new trial and thereafter ordered judgment notwithstanding the verdict. Plaintiffs appeal from the judgment.

The subject of this litigation is a farm consisting of some 158 acres in Rosendale Township, Watonwan County. Title was in Waldron C. Davis, when he died December 21, 1965. His heirs and their undivided interests were as follows: His widow, Grace Corliss Davis, one-third; his son, Donald E. Davis, defendant herein, two-ninths; his daughter, Corliss Davis Wilfley, two-ninths; and a daughter, Winifred Davis Hover, two-ninths.

In August 1966, plaintiff Tom Mayberry approached defendant and his mother with a view to securing a listing for the sale of the farm. A nonexclusive oral agreement was reached by the parties by which defendant undertook to pay plaintiffs 5 percent of $2,400 if plaintiffs effected a sale which would net the estate $48,000.

In May, 1967, plaintiffs produced two buyers, Melvin Hobbs and Howard Quick, who were ready, willing, and able to divide and purchase the farm in two tracts on the terms to which plaintiffs and defendant had agreed. By that time, the final probate decree had been entered and title had vested in defendant, his mother, and two sisters. For reasons which are not clear, defendant's sisters did not sign the purchase agreements. In August 1967 defendant advised plaintiffs that the property was no longer for sale and in March 1968, the farm was conveyed to defendant and to one Lowell J. Hurley.

The only issue for determination is whether or not the fact that plaintiffs entered a listing agreement with defendant, knowing he was not vested with complete title, relieved defendant of his obligation to pay a commission if those having the remaining interests declined to join. We hold the defendant's inability to perform was not a defense. Accordingly we reverse.

In granting a new trial, the Court relied on language in *Fosbroke* v. *National Exch. Bank,* * * * and *Rees-Thomson-Scroggins, Inc.* v. *Nelson,* * * * However, in the Fosbroke Case, the Court merely held that preliminary negotiations between the parties did not give rise to a commission where substantial conditions had not been agreed on when the property was sold through other channels. There, we said, among other things, that the broker "must bring the minds of the buyer and seller to an agreement for a sale and the price and terms upon which it is to be made." * * * The Trial Court concluded that plaintiffs did not bring the minds of the sellers and the buyer to an agreement. However, as we view the law, it was not necessary to bring all of the owners and the buyers together as long as the broker produced purchasers who were willing and able to perform on the conditions prescribed by the particular owner who contract with the broker. This principle was suggested in *Sherwood* v. *Rosenstein,* * * * where we held that a wife's refusal to join in a conveyance did not deprive a broker of his commission to which the husband had agreed. * * *

It is fundamental that a broker may not be denied his commission merely because the transaction he has negotiated is not consummated for reasons beyond his control. * * *

While there is a split of authority, we are of the opinion that the better-reasoned cases permit recovery. * * *

Finally, a case similar to the matter before us is *Cincinnati M & M Realty, Inc.* v. *Uckotter.* There, as here, the defendant and his sister each had an undivided interest in real estate when defendant entered a listing agreement. The defendant sought to defeat the broker's recovery by claiming the broker knew the state of the title before securing a purchaser. The Ohio Court held that the broker, having done what he was employed to do, had earned his commission and was under no obligation to contact the defendant's sister to induce her to complete the transaction.

We concur in the view that one who contracts with a broker to secure the sale of property which the principal does not own takes the risk of incurring an obligation to pay a commission if title cannot be perfected. It is not the duty of the broker to determine ownership unless he expressly agrees to do so. If the principal has reason to doubt his capacity to produce good title, he may not induce the broker to perform services which prove to be futile. The principal is in a better position than the broker to determine what imperfections there are and what signatures must be obtained to bring about a valid conveyance. Consequently, we hold that plaintiffs' knowledge of outstanding interests in other heirs was not a bar to recovering their commission. Accordingly the verdict is reinstated.

Reversed.

* * *

Commissions and Conditions. One additional area of exposure that is common to real estate brokers is the potential of losing a commission because of the wording of contracts. Importance of a condition precedent is illustrated in the following *Barrett* v. *Duzan,* a decision out of Arizona in 1976. Conditions, therefore, are important to any real estate broker who is preparing contracts or aiding in the preparation of contracts. Sometimes conditions cannot be avoided, but at least the broker should be aware of the affect of a failure of a condition, such as illustrated in the Barrett case.

BARRETT v. DUZAN
Court of Appeals of Arizona, 1976.
559 P.2d 693

* * *

OPINION

DONOFRIO, Presiding Judge.

This is an appeal by Don J. Barrett dba Don Barrett Agency from a judgment of the Superior Court denying him recovery of his action against the Appellees/Duzans for a real estate commission on an exclusive listing agreement.

On May 9, 1972, Appellees were the owners of a certain restaurant and lounge located in Prescott Valley, Arizona, known as the Coachlight Inn. On that date, they entered into an exclusive listing agreement for the sale of this property with the Appellant, who was a duly licensed broker under the laws of Arizona. This listing contained an asking price for the Inn of $195,000.00, and gave to Appellant the "sole and exclusive rights to sell, present any offer he may receive, or to exchange, or to rent or lease" the property.

It also provided that in the event the realtor produced a purchaser in accordance with the terms of the listing, or "in the event a sale is made by owner," during the term of the listing agreement then for services rendered the Appellees agreed to pay the Appellant ten percent (10%) of the list price, or of any lesser price which the Appellees accepted. The term of the listing agreement was for a period of 180 days. The agreement was irrevocable.

Following the execution of the listing agreement, Appellant commenced the performance of his obligations thereunder and referred the listing to the Multiple Listing Service of Prescott, and during the month following the signing of the listing agreement of the Coachlight Inn was advertised by Appellant in the Los Angeles Times, the Chicago Tribune and the Arizona Republic.

On May 27, 1972, Gordon Suggs became the manager of the Coach-light Inn, and shortly thereafter became aware that the Weedons and Herrells, (with whom the appellees were dealing) were prospective pur-chasers of the Inn. Suggs formed an interest in obtaining the Inn himself, and, being aware that the Appellant had an exclusive listing on the Inn, worked with and through the Appellant in negotiations between himself and the Appellees. Appellant obtained appraisals on both the Inn and on Mr. Suggs' property. It is to be noted that the Appellees gave this ap-praisal to the Weedons and the Herrells who later based their offer upon it.

After these appraisals of the Inn and of Suggs' property were ob-tained, Appellant took Appellee Mrs. Duzan to inspect the Suggs prop-erty. Thereafter Appellant participated in several discussions with Mr. Suggs and Mrs. Duzan in attempting to work out an exchange agreement. No written agreement was ever reached between the Appellees and Mr. Suggs. Mr. Suggs never became a ready, willing and able buyer of the Coachlight Inn.

Sometime in June, 1972, the Weedons and Herrells entered into nego-tiations with the Appellees for the purchase of the Inn. The Weedons and Herrells were aware of Appellant's exclusive listing agreement, but, from the very beginning of their negotiations with Appellees, they made it clear that they would not deal with a realtor. Mrs. Duzan, thereafter, actively participated in negotiations with the Weedons and Herrells. Mrs. Duzan told the Appellant that the Herrells and Weedons did not want Appellant at the negotiations.

The Appellees, the Herrells and the Weedons ultimately reached an agreement on the purchase and sale of the Inn. The agreed purchase price was $160,000.00.

After an oral agreement had been reached between the Appellees, the Herrells and the Weedons, but prior to September 1, and with Appellees' prior knowledge and consent, attorney John Burke called Appellant. Mr. Burke informed him that the amount of the commission involved was proving a difficult point for the Appellees, and that if Appellant would accept $7,500.00 the sale could be closed. That conversation was followed on August 29, 1972, by a letter from attorney Burke to Appellant. The letter requested that Appellant execute an agreement to accept $7,500.00 as commission for the sale of the Weedons. Appellant immediately ex-ecuted the requested agreement.

On September 1, 1972, Appellees, the Weedons and the Herrells ex-ecuted an agreement for the sale and purchase of the Coachlight Inn. An escrow for the transaction was also opened on September 1, 1972. The contract of sale was subject to the Weedons and Herrells applying and obtaining a conventional mortgage refinancing loan from Great Western Bank in the amount stated in the escrow instructions.

Pursuant to the sales agreement, the Appellees bound themselves to deliver title to the Inn at the close of escrow. The Weedons and Herrells took possession of the Inn and operated it until November 7, 1972 when the Weedons and Herrells were informed that they had been unsuccessful in obtaining financing with Great Western Bank. The property was returned to Appellants who in turn deeded in lieu of foreclosure to the guarantor on the mortgages existing against the property.

* * * We first deal with the issue wherein Appellant/Broker urges that when the owners of the Coachlight Inn entered into the exclusive listing contract, the owners severed their right to independently produce a sale of the property. With this contention, we must disagree.

In the original listing agreement, the language of the contract specifically and clearly recognized the possibility that the Appellees might independently produce a sale of their own property. However, the contract provided that any sale by the owners would still generate a commission for the Broker/Appellant.

The pertinent provision of the listing contract reads:

"In the event the Realtor produces a purchaser in accordance with the above terms and conditions, or in the event a sale is made by Owner(s) or through any other agent during the terms of this exclusive listing, then for services rendered the Owner(s) agree to pay to the realtor ten percent (10%) of the above price or of any lesser price which Owner(s) accept." (Emphasis added)

Also the escrow instructions dated September 1, 1972, provide for the real estate broker's commission on the Appellees' independently derived sale.

Appellant is seeking recovery under two theories. One theory is for the contractual commission claimed due as the result of securing a ready, willing and able purchaser under the exclusive listing agreement. The second theory is in the alternative for $7,500.00 provided for in the modification of the terms of the listing agreement.

Inasmuch as the validity of the modification itself is questioned we will deal with this issue next. The escrow instructions refer the reader to a letter signed by Appellant on August 29, 1972, approximately three days before escrow was opened. This letter states that:

"The undersigned hereby agrees to accept Seven Thousand Five Hundred Dollars ($7,500.00) as and for total commission which shall be due the DON BARRETT AGENCY in connection with the sale of the premises known as Coachlight Inn, located at Prescott Valley, Arizona.

It is understood that the aforesaid sale of the Coachlight Inn will be handled through American Title Insurance Company under Escrow #121,875 and that the above referenced commission shall be remitted to said DON BARRETT AGENCY at the close of said escrow.

DATED at Prescott, Arizona this 29th day of August, 1972.
DON BARRETT AGENCY
By /s/ Don J. Barrett"

* * * There is no doubt that the parties to a contract may by their mutual agreement modify a contract between themselves. Our Supreme Court holds that, " * * * any detriment to promise, or benefit to promissor, constitutes a valid and sufficient consideration for a new promise which would in effect modify terms of the original agreement." * * *
* * * The modification between Appellant and Appellees only changed the amount of commission due on a binding sales agreement. Both parties had benefits and detriments arising from the modification agreement. Appellant would enjoy the success of a sale and have his burden of promoting the property lifted. On the other hand, he would suffer in the respect that he would be agreeing to accept less commission than expected. Appellees would benefit because of the proposed sale of their property. However, they would suffer in the respect that the sale would be substantially less than was contemplated at the time the listing was entered into. Everything in this case pointed to a valid mutual agreement between the parties. In addition, evidence shows that the Broker was not against the sale by the Owners even though it was of a lesser sum than the listing's asking price. In fact, he did everything to promote the sale, and executed the agreement to reduce his commission on the very same day that he was requested to do so. Never once did he voice a breach of contract on the part of the Appellees, but did everything in his power to promote the actions of the Appellees.

The one crucial remaining question is whether Appellant is entitled to a commission under any of these theories.

* * * In this connection his entitlement to a commission must be examined in light of the sales agreement. We would agree that, "it is the almost universally accepted rule of law that, in the absence of a specific contract to the contrary, when a real estate broker has brought together the parties to a sale or exchange of real estate, and they have agreed fully on the terms and entered into a binding contract for such sale or exchange, his duties are at an end and his commission is fully earned, and it is immaterial that the parties to the contract rescind mutually or that one of the other thereof defaults and the sale or exchange is not fully effected." (Emphasis added). *Lockett* v. *Drake,* 43 Ariz. 357, 360, 31 P.2d 499, 500 (1934). Cf. *Donaldson* v. *LeNore,* 112 Ariz. 199, 540 P.2d 671 (1975). However, this case is not the case at bar.

The facts in this case clearly show that the parties entered into a contract that was subject to the new buyers obtaining a refinancing loan from Great Western Bank. * * * Furthermore, the trial judge found that the sales agreement was a conditional contract in which the condition was never met. * * *

* * * From our review of the agreements, we agree with the lower court's finding that the sales agreement was a conditional rather than a binding sales contract. We are by no means holding that a binding contract is a prerequisite to the Broker earning his commission. It is elementary law that when a Broker presents a purchaser who is ready, willing and able to buy on the exact terms authorized by the seller, a Broker is entitled to his commission regardless of whether a contract is subsequently executed. * * * There are, however, numerous cases dealing with the issue of whether a real estate broker is entitled to a commission upon the entrance of the listed owner into a conditional sales contract for the listed property. * * * Our Supreme Court stated, " * * * where as here, a broker presents a buyer who executes a conditional contract and is willing to buy only if and when condition is fulfilled, a commission is not earned." * * *

* * * We see no difference whether the owner or the real estate agent procured the buyer. A conditional sales agreement does not vest the commission promised the agent until that condition is satisfied. The condition in this case was never satisfied, and the appellant's commission never vested.

For the hereinabove reasons we find that the Findings of Fact and the Judgment of the lower court are correct as a matter of law. Affirmed.

FREBERG, JR. v. CALDERWOOD
Supreme Court of Oregon, 1976
552 P.2d 545

* * *

PER CURIAM.

This is an action on a promissory note, with a counterclaim for a real estate broker's commission. The case was tried before the court, sitting without a jury. The trial court entered judgment in favor of plaintiff on the principal action and also on the counterclaim, based upon findings that defendant had breached his fiduciary duty as a real estate broker, thereby forfeiting his right to a commission. Defendant appeals. We affirm.

Defendant's sole contention on this appeal is that

" * * * (T)he trial court was in error in holding that defendant breached his fiduciary duty to plaintiff and therefore is not entitled to commission that would otherwise be due on the sale of plaintiff's property."

* * * Because of direct conflicts in the testimony we must bear in mind that in determining whether there was sufficient evidence to support the findings of the trial court in favor of the plaintiff all conflicts in the testimony must be resolved in his favor and he is also entitled to the benefit of all inferences which may be reasonably drawn from such evidence. * * * We have reviewed the testimony and hold that the findings and the decision by the trial court were supported by substantial evidence. Because the trial judge prepared a written opinion reviewing the evidence and stating the basis for his decision, with which we agree, it would serve no useful purpose to summarize the somewhat lengthy testimony in detail.

In essence, we find that there was evidence to support findings by the trial court as follows: Defendant, a real estate broker is Rosenburg, had a listing for the sale of real property belonging to plaintiff, a resident of Florida. Defendant received a written offer for the purchase of that property from his own partner and mailed that offer to plaintiff. Before that written offer was received by plaintiff defendant learned of another possible offer by a third party, a Mrs. Siegel, who was then told by defendant that it was too late to make an offer because the property had already been sold. A better written offer to purchase the property was then made by Mrs. Siegel also offered $5,000 to defendant's partner for his interest in his offer to purchase the property. That $5,000 offer was refused and she was told that defendant's partner had already bought the property. That $5,000 offer was "probably mentioned" to defendant by his partner. * * * Even if defendant did not know of that offer of $5,000 or that plaintiff could get more for his property by selling it to Mrs. Seigel than by accepting the offer of defendant's partner, the trial court could properly find that those facts must have been known by defendant's partner and were thus imputed to defendant. * * * Neither defendant nor his partner informed plaintiff of such facts. Plaintiff only learned of the offer by Mrs. Siegel as the result of a telephone call from her to his wife. On that occasion Mrs. Siegel told plaintiff's wife that a written offer was in the mail and asked that plaintiff wait until it was received before making a decision. At that time plaintiff had received the written offer from defendant's partner, but had not yet received the better written offer from Mrs. Siegel, which he later accepted.

Although much of the foregoing testimony was contrary to testimony by the defendant, who also testified that plaintiff had "verbally accepted" the offer by his partner, the trial court was not required to believe his testimony.

* * * On this state of the record we agree with the trial court in holding that defendant failed to satisfy the burden of proof imposed upon his as a real estate broker under the rule stated by this court, * * * to show that he had performed his fiduciary duty to plaintiff to make a full disclosure of all material information concerning the prospective sale of plaintiff's

property. It follows that defendant was not entitled to demand payment of a commission on that sale.

Affirmed.

LICENSING CONTROLS

FLUSHING KENT REALTY CORP. v. CUOMO
Supreme Court, 1976.
390 N.Y.S.2d 146

* * *

MEMORANDUM BY THE COURT.

* * * After a hearing, found that petitioners had demonstrated untrustworthiness and (1) suspended their licenses for a period of one month or, in lieu thereof, imposed fines in stated amounts and (2) directed the petitioners (except Pat Pescatore) to reimburse the complainant in the sum of $722.10, as a condition to the reinstatement of their licenses. * * *

The complainant was shown a residence by the petitioner Pescatore, who was employed by the petitioner Flushing Kent Realty Corp. The petitioners Marani and Ain where the principals of Flushing Kent. Thereafter, without the knowledge of the petitioners, the complainant negotiated for the purchase of the residence directly with the owner and finally purchased. The contract of sale made no provision for the payment of a broker's commission to the petitioners. After the closing, the complainant told the petitioners that the sale had been consummated.

An action was then commenced to recover the commission, naming the complainant and the former owner as defendants, on the theory that they had conspired to deprive the petitioners of the commission. That action was compromised, both defendants therein contributing to the amount of the settlement. The complainant then filed a grievance against the petitioners and the respondent determined that the petitioners had demonstrated untrustworthiness.

The determination rests upon the conclusion that the petitioners were guilty of harassment in bringing the action against the complainant. The fact is that the complainant negotiated with the owner in the absence of the petitioners, knowing that they would be entitled to compensation if the complainant purchased the property. Further, the complainant entered into the contract, making no provision for payment of a commission and not designating the petitioners as brokers.

The complainant did not inform the petitioners that the contract had been signed until after the closing of the sale. When the petitioners consulted their attorney, they were advised by him to sue the complainant as well as the owner. * * *

Under the circumstances, a finding that the petitioners exhibited untrustworthiness is not supported by substantial evidence. The petitioners were not guilty of harassment against the complainant by joining him as a defendant in the action to recover a commission. The bargaining by the complainant with the owner in the absence of the petitioners, the failure to provide for the petitioners in the contract of sale and the failure to communicate with the petitioners until after the closing, were grounds upon which the complainant might be considered by the petitioners' attorney to be liable to the petitioners. Otherwise the petitioners' right to compensation, and their remedies by action, might be seriously inhibited if their decision to bring suit could be followed by disciplinary proceedings. A genuine dispute negates the finding of harassment. * * * Hence, the determination must be annulled. * * *

REQUIREMENT FOR LICENSING

The failure to obtain a license in the real estate area, where a license is required, may not only defeat a commission, but may also defeat the enforceability of any contract arrangement affected by the licensing requirement. This issue is examined in the Reed case, which follows, and emphasizes the importance of the licensing requirement.

No. 73-101
Jacob W. Reed, a/k/a Bill Reed v. Kedric M. Bailey
COLORADO
(524 P.2d 80)

Decided April 30, 1974.   Rehearing denied May 21, 1974.
Certiorari denied July 22, 1974.

Opinion by JUDGE RULAND.

Defendant appeals from a judgment requiring him to account to plaintiff for certain funds obtained from the sale of patented mining claims. We reverse.

Insofar as material here, the record reflects that Frank Richardson owned three patented mining claims in Ouray County, Colorado. Richardson executed a written agreement with plaintiff and defendant in the nature of a net listing wherein he agreed to accept $30,000 for sale of the mining claims; the agreement further provided that plaintiff and defendant would divide equally any amount in excess of $30,000 which could be obtained for the claims. In conjunction with execution of this agreement, a second written agreement (captioned "Option to Purchase") was signed wherein Richardson agreed to sell the same claims to defendant and another for $60,000 on specified terms of payment. Apparently the second agreement was not intended as a sale but rather as a device to promote a sale to third parties.

Based on this transaction, plaintiff and defendant solicited purchasers for the claims, and defendant was ultimately successful in securing a sale of the property. Defendant subsequently refused to account to plaintiff for any of the proceeds. The present case was then filed for an accounting based upon the first written agreement.

Neither plaintiff nor defendant is licensed to sell real estate in Colorado, as required by 1969 Perm. Supp., C.R.S. 1963, 117-1-1. Although the Trial Court recognized that failure to obtain the required license precluded either party from prevailing in an action against Richardson for compensation, see *Benham* v. *Heyde,* 122 Colo. 233, 221 P.2d 1078, the Trial Court concluded that it should enforce a division of the proceeds received by defendant. We disagree.

Since plaintiff is not licensed as a broker or real estate salesman pursuant to Colorado statute, the original agreement between Richardson, plaintiff, and defendant constitutes an illegal contract. * * * Hence, plaintiff is precluded from seeking judicial assistance to enforce the contract. * * *

The judgment is therefore reversed and the cause remanded with directions to dismiss plaintiff's complaint.

Regulation of Licenses. The issue in the Kostika case, a New York decision, is whether the penalty imposed by the secretary of state on a real estate broker was improper under the circumstances.

Factually, the broker, Kostika, sold a three-family residence, which she owned, to Mrs. Hanel. Although Kostika was licensed, she did not inform the purchasers that she was licensed. Even the advertising for the sale of the property did not indicate that Mrs. Kostika was licensed. (Actually, the property in question was held by Rubegold Realty Co.) At the time Mrs. Kostika was to convey the property to Mrs. Hanel this fact of the license, held by Mrs. Kostika, was discovered by Mrs. Hanel, the purchaser.

As a result of this activity, the Hanels complained to the Regulator Board for Licensees. The question is the type of sanction, if any, that can be and should be imposed against Mrs. Kostika for her action.

Do you feel that Mrs. Kostika has any responsibility under the laws of your state with regard to her actions? Consider how she might have avoided this by giving a disclosure of her position. However, is there a duty to make this disclosure in your state?

KOSTIKA v. CUOMO
Court of Appeals of New York, 1977.
394 N.Y.S.2d 862

* * *

WACHTLER, Judge.

The sole issue presented in this case is whether the penalty imposed by the Secretary of State against the petitioner real estate broker was " 'so disproportionate to the offense, in light of all the circumstances, as to be shocking to one's sense of fairness' " * * * The Appellate Division found that the secretary's $200 fine was an adequate punishment but that his direction that, as a condition for the removal of the suspension of petitioner's real estate broker's license, the broker be compelled to repay the $15,050 profit she made on the resale of certain property was an excessive sanction and, therefore, should be set aside. We are of the opinion that the Appellate Division erred in setting aside the secretary's determination that the $15,050 profit be returned.

In April, 1974, the petitioner, Mrs. Miriam Kostika, sold a three-family residence which she owned in Forest Hills, New York, to Mr. and Mrs. Hanel. Mrs. Kostika was at that time a licensed real estate broker, although she never informed the purchasers of that fact and indeed used her maiden name, Miriam Schwecky, in all her dealings with the Hanels, despite the fact that Mrs. Hanel had on several occasions asked petitioner if she was a real estate broker. In addition, in connection with her attempts to sell the premises in question, during the winter of 1973-1974 Mrs. Kostika placed an advertisement in the New York Times. This advertisement did not indicate either Mrs. Kostika's name or the fact that she was a licensed real estate broker or dealer in real property.

On April 1, 1974, title passed to Mrs. Kostika from the Rubegold Realty Co. for the purchase price of $61,000. At a simultaneous closing, Mrs. Kostika transferred title to the same premises to the Hanels for a purchase price of $76,050. It was not until this point that the Hanels became aware that Mrs. Kostika was a real estate broker.

Subsequently, the Hanels complained about Mrs. Kostika's conduct to the Department of State and an investigation by the Division of Licensing Services ensued. A hearing was convened pursuant to section 441-e of the Real Property Law to determine the validity of the alleged violations raised in a formal complaint filed by the investigator. Mrs. Kostika was charged with having violated both section 175.6 of the Rules and Regulations of the Department of State promulgated pursuant to article 12-A of the Real Property Law (19 N.Y.C.R.R. 175.6) and with a violation of section 396-b of the General Business Law.

Section 175.6 of the Rules and Regulations of the Department of State clearly requires that "(b)efore a real estate broker sells property in which he owns an interest, he shall make such interest known to the purchaser." Section 396-b of the General Business Law requires: "Any person, firm, corporation or association, or agent or employee thereof, hereinafter called person, who, being engaged in the business of dealing in any property, makes, publishes, disseminates, circulates or places before the public or causes, directly or indirectly, to be made, published, disseminated, circulated or placed before the public, in this state, any advertisement respecting any such property, in any newspaper, magazine, or other publication, or over any radio station or television station, unless it is stated in any such advertisement that the advertiser is a dealer in such property or from the context of any such advertisement, it plainly appears that such person is a dealer in such property so offered for sale in any such advertisement * * * is guilty of a misdemeanor."

Mrs. Kostika appeared in person at the hearing and was represented by counsel. Both sides were given the opportunity to present witnesses and offer evidence, and at the conclusion of the hearing, the hearing officer found that Mrs. Kostika had demonstrated untrustworthiness. Pursuant to section 441-c of the Real Property Law the hearing officer declared that Mrs. Kostika's license be "suspended for a period of three months or in lieu thereof to pay a fine to the department (of State) in the sum of $200." The officer further determined that "(a)t the end of the period of suspension or upon payment of the fine the aforementioned license shall be further suspended until such time as the respondent (Mrs. Kostika) has presented proof satisfactorily to the Department that she has returned to Mr. and Mrs. Hanel the sum of $15,050."

The Secretary of State confirmed the determination of the hearing officer in all respects. In modifying the secretary's decision, the Appellate Division found that there was substantial evidence in the record to support the finding of untrustworthiness, correctly noting that it is not the province of the court to substitute its judgment for that of administrative agency. * * * Yet, that court struck down the secretary's ruling that the broker be compelled to disgorge the profit made on the transaction, requiring only that the $200 fine be paid and noting that in their opinion it did not appear that the purchasers had been overcharged for the property. * * * Where, as here, the administrative agency's determination is based upon substantial evidence, the penalty imposed is a matter of discretion to be exercised solely by the agency. Of course, this discretion is not to be completely unfettered. * * * It has long been settled in our State's jurisprudence that a fine or penalty imposed by the administrative agency is not to be disturbed unless it is clearly disproportionate to the offense and completely inequitable in light of the surrounding circumstances. Thus, the "shocking to one's sense of fairness" test was developed in the case law.

* * * Applying these guidelines to the case now before us, the conclusion is inescapable that the penalty imposed by the Secretary of State should have been allowed to stand. It cannot be gainsaid that the public at large has an interest in being protected from unreliable and untrustworthy real estate brokers engaging in somewhat less than arms-length and honorable sales practices. The responsibility for effectively providing that protection has been delegated to the Secretary of State * * * Accordingly, the secretary must be accorded broad discretion in imposing penalties designed to safeguard the public interest and discourage real estate brokers from engaging in shadowy practices * * *

In the instant case, the sanction imposed by the secretary is well-suited to these ends. One can hardly fathom a more effective means of removing the incentive for engaging in devious conduct, and thereby protecting the unwary purchaser from being over-reached or defrauded, than a penalty which insures that the malefactor is denied the fruits of his misdeed. Further, it cannot outrage one's sense of fairness that the impact on the broker here was disproportionate in that she was compelled to return her ill-gotten profit and pay a fine of $200—a net loss to her of $200. Hence, there was no basis for upsetting the determination of the Secretary of State.

Accordingly, the judgment of the Appellate Division should be reversed and the Secretary of State's direction that the petitioner be required to disgorge the profit made on the transaction should be reinstated.

CHAPTER 9

Agency Dual Capacity Duties

AGENCY

If a real estate agent acts in a dual capacity for both the seller and the purchaser, this may be proper in the given jurisdiction in question, but all jurisdictions require a disclosure of this fact to the parties in question, such as the seller and purchaser.

This point was evidenced in a recent decision of *Meerdink* v. *Krieger,* 550 P.2d 42 (1976). In this case the Washington court of appeals held that the real estate broker was responsible for damages for failing to disclose the relationship.

CONFLICT OF POSITION

Might a real estate broker find himself in conflict of position if he is recommending the purchase of property to a prospective purchaser, and the real estate broker has listed multiple pieces of property that may meet the needs of the purchaser? That is, if the broker has two or more pieces listed and two or more pieces meet the requirements of the prospective purchaser, is the real estate broker then in a conflict of position; and if so, what is the effect of this position? This issue is discussed in the Samuels case, in which a real estate broker is suing for his commission. The last sentence is the key to the court's position.

ROBERT N. SAMUELS, INC. v. ALPHONSO A. MICHAELS
Court of Appeals of Louisiana, 1975.
315 So.2d 63

* * *

REDMANN, Judge.

Plaintiff appeals from the dismissal on the merits of its claim for a real estate agent's commission. We affirm.

On the night of January 19, 1972, defendant landowner contacted plaintiff real estate agent's president and sole shareholder, and signed a "listing agreement" granting plaintiff the exclusive right to sell (sic) and promising a 10% commission on any sale or lease of defendant's property during the six-month time of the agreement.

Early January 20 plaintiff's president (hereafter referred to as plaintiff) went to Florida, returning January 30. Meanwhile (perhaps on January 28), defendant and his ultimate lessee, Argeros, met through an architect who had done work for both. Argeros informed defendant of his interest in leasing defendant's land, and defendant informed plaintiff thereof on his return that Argeros had already made an offer (on January 28) on other land a block away. Because plaintiff also had a listing from the owner of that land, plaintiff informed defendant that his sense of professional ethics prevented his pursuing negotiations with Argeros for defendant. Accordingly, with Argeros' offer on the other land was termed unacceptable by that landowner's counter proposal of February 3, defendant negotiated with Argeros with no assistance from plaintiff. Argeros testified that, even after he and defendant on February 6 reached a verbal understanding, of which plaintiff was informed by Argeros, plaintiff continued to urge Argeros to lease the other land rather than defendant's land.

* * * Assuming that plaintiff's "exclusive right to sell" might entitle him to a commission on a lease procured by the owner alone * * * we find our case substantially identical to Latter & Blum, Inc. v. Ocean Drilling & Expl. Co., La. App. 1973, 272 So.2d 53, writ refused 275 So.2d 784. Although our listing agreement did not expressly oblige the agent to make reasonable efforts to find a (buyer or) lessee, such an obligation must be implied if the agreement is to be enforceable. * * * If ethical obligations to another client prevented pursuit of the prospect defendant himself brought to plaintiff's attention, those ethical obligations might explain declining to perform for defendant, but they do not entitle plaintiff to a commission from defendant under a contract plaintiff not only declined to perform but actively breached.

Affirmed.

ON APPLICATION FOR REHEARING

PER CURIAM.

Refusing defendant's application for rehearing, we do amend our decree to specify that costs of appeal are to be borne by appellant.

The possibility of representing both sides and the duty to disclose the same is discussed in the Monty case. Consider the basic concept of a dual agency and see if this matches with the reasoning of the court.

MONTY v. PETERSON
Supreme Court of Washington, 1975.
540 P.2d 1377

* * *

UTTER, Associate Justice.

This is an appeal from a judgment entered in a nonjury trial in favor of the plaintiffs (respondents), Ralph and Karin Monty, in a suit for the amount of a real estate broker's commission paid by them to defendants (petitioners) Lewis W. Shurtleff and Shurtleff, Inc. The trial court found for the Montys, who claimed that the defendants had negligently failed to inform them of restrictive covenants materially affecting the value of a parcel of land they received in a real estate transaction in which they employed the defendants. It held that defendants' nondisclosure rendered them liable for the full amount of the commission they received, regardless of the actual damages respondents incurred.

The Court of Appeals did not reach the merits of petitioners' argument due to the improper form of their brief. Review was granted by this court, however, to reach the issue of the proper amount of damages for negligent nondisclosure by a real estate broker. We reverse the judgment of the trial court and hold that, where a broker acts in good faith but negligently fails to disclose to his client a fact material to the transaction and no question of divided loyalty is involved, the proper measure of damages is the actual harm caused to the client by the broker's negligent omission. * * *

The series of transactions that gave rise to this lawsuit began when respondents retained petitioners as their agent in listing an apartment house they owned for sale. Shortly after he had been retained by respondents, petitioner Shurtleff was retained by another couple, Ward and Viola Peterson, who wished to sell a small parcel of property (called the "Monson lot") and invest in some more extensive real estate. Mr. Shurtleff informed the Petersons of the availability of the respondents' property and obtained from them an earnest money offer to purchase it which he presented to respondents. After lengthy negotiations, they accepted it. The purchase price of the respondents' property was $55,000, $5,650 of which was paid by transferring the Monson lot to them. * * *

The Monson lot was zoned for duplex construction, and at all times all the parties were aware that this fact was material to respondents' valuation of it. It was also, however, subject to private covenants that restricted its use to single-family dwellings. Neither petitioners nor respondents were aware of these restrictions until they received the preliminary title report on the property. At that time petitioner Shurtleff mentioned the restrictions to respondents, but did so in a manner that (according to the findings of the trial court) did not adequately call to their attention the effect the covenants might have on their valuation of or plans for the property.

When, after the transactions were completed, the respondents became aware of the covenants and their import, they discussed the matter with petitioner and obtained a $680 rebate from the Petersons. They apparently were not satisfied with this partial settlement, and although the covenants diminished the value of the lot to them by only $850 and they had received $680, they filed this action against petitioners for the full amount of the broker's commission they had paid them, $3,300. The trial court awarded them this full amount. * * *

Petitioners' liability for failing to adequately advise their clients of the significance of the covenants on the land they purchased is not in issue here. Agents have a duty to exercise care in dealing with their principals and are liable for any damage caused by a breach of that duty. * * * The only question before us is what the measure of damages for breach of that duty should be in the circumstances of the instant case. * * * In most situations, an agent's negligence renders him or her liable only for the actual damages it causes the principal. * * * In *Mersky* v. *Multiple Listing Bureau,* * * * however, we recognize a limited exception to this rule in cases where agents negligently or intentionally fail to disclose to their principals facts bearing on their interests in the matters in which they are employed and their ability to maintain undivided loyalty to the principal. We held in Mersky, at page 233, 437 P.2d 897, that nondisclosure of a familial relationship between an agent and the person with whom he was dealing on the principal's behalf rendered him liable for the full amount of the commission he received "(h)owever inadvertently this failure (to disclose) occurred." * * *

Mersky was viewed as controlling by the trial court on the question of measure of damages in any case of nondisclosure by an agent, and its rule was applied to the facts here even though there was no potential conflict of interest by the agent involved. In so doing, the court misinterpreted Mersky's holding. There we heavily emphasized that what was involved was nondisclosure of a fact that impugned the agent's ability to exercise undivided loyalty in representing his principal's interests. * * *

We therefore hold that petitioners were liable only for the actual damages caused by their negligent failure to inform respondents of the covenant and their significance. It appears to be undisputed that, after they received the $680 settlement from the Petersons, respondents' net loss due to their ignorance of the covenants was $170. The award in their favor should have been limited to that amount, and the judgment in favor of respondents for the full amount of the brokers' commission paid petitioners was therefore excessive.

The decision of the trial court is reversed. * * *

AGENT IS AGENT FOR PURCHASER OR SELLER

In the case of Warren, the suit is brought by a purchaser who alleges breach of certain duties by "his" real estate agent. The real question in the case is whether the real estate agent is the agent for the purchaser or agent for the seller. It is clear that many purchasers are confused as to whom the real estate agent is representing. This is illustrated in the *Warren* v. *Mangels Realty* case, 23 Ariz. App. 318 (1975).

WARREN v. MANGELS REALTY
23 Ariz. App. 318
533 P.2d 78

* * *

OPINION

KRUCKER, Judge.

* * * The undisputed facts are as follows. On or about August 13, 1969, Bea Padilla (hereinafter referred to as Padilla), owner of the real property involved in this action, and Mangels Realty entered into an agreement which contained the following terms: (1) the broker was given the exclusive right to sell the property for a period of 24 months; (2) Padilla agreed to accept a minimum price of $107,000 for the property with a standard realty commission of six percent to be paid upon that amount and any amount in excess of the minimum sum would be

divided equally between her and the realtor; and (3) Padilla had the right to terminate on 90 days' written notice. The agreement was executed by Taraldson, a salesman for the broker, and also provided that the listing would be automatically terminated in the event that Taraldson not remain in Mangels' employ.

At the end of 1970 or the beginning of 1971, Taraldson showed the Padilla property to appellant, Frank Warren (hereinafter referred to as Warren). Taraldson had previously acted as salesman for Mangels in connection with the sale of two other parcels in Tucson to Warren and in each instance the seller had paid the commission.

After seeing and investigating the property, Warren submitted a written offer to Padilla, through Mangels, to purchase the property at a price of $240,000 on terms and subject to rezoning and the performance of certain drainage work. On March 9, 1971, a new offer was submitted by Warren to purchase the property for $232,000 on terms and subject to rezoning, but without requirement of any drainage work. The price reduction and the elimination of the drainage work requirement was the result of Warren's contacts and discussions with the owners of adjacent property, whom we shall refer to as the Johnston group, concerning their working together to solve a mutual drainage problem.

On March 24, 1971, Padilla, through her attorney, gave Mangels written notice of termination of the listing agreement effective 90 days from that date. Although Warren was aware that Mangels had an exclusive listing on the property, he was not aware of the terms of the listing agreement until April 5, 1971, when he was furnished a copy by Mangels.

Padilla refused to accept the Warren offers of February 4 and March 9 for several reasons: she did not like the rezoning contingency, was upset at the size of the broker's commission, and did not want to sell to someone from California. Warren and Mangels verbally agreed that Warren would pay Mangels a $25,000 commission so that Padilla could receive a sales price of $232,000 net, but this agreement was never reduced to writing nor submitted to Padilla. Warren never retracted the rezoning condition from his previous offers.

On or about April 10, 1971, Taraldson advised Warren that the Johnston group had been in contact with Padilla and that she was willing to sell to them provided she was released from any liability to Mangels for commission. On April 14, 1971, Warren and his employee, Colbourne, met with the Johnston group, Mangels and Taraldson in the office of Mangels' attorney in an effort to arrive at an agreement by which the Johnston group would purchase the property from Padilla and then share it with Warren. * * * The Johnston group was to purchase the property for $232,000 and a $35,000 commission was to be paid to Mangels by Warren and Johnston. Either later that day or the following day, Johnston and Padilla executed a sales agreement under the terms of which the

Johnston group purchased the property from Padilla subject to the obligation of the Johnston group to obtain a full release from Mangels. (Mangels did not participate in this transaction.) On April 15, again in the office of Mangels' attorney, Johnston advised Warren that he did not recognize any agreement with him and was buying the property independent of any claim of interest by Warren.

The Johnston group then proceeded to negotiate with Mangels, through Mangels' attorney, to obtain a release of Padilla with regard to the Padilla-Mangels commission agreement. Mangels made various attempts to protect Warren but Johnston refused to execute any agreement with Warren concerning the Padilla property. Ultimately, Mangels agreed to execute a release of Padilla in exchange for the obligation of the Johnston group to pay Mangels $64,250.00 (The total commission which Mangels would have been entitled to receive on the $232,000 sale under the terms of the listing agreement would have been $70,000.00.)

Warren's testimony on deposition was that the only basis for his complaint against Mangels was the failure to prevent the sale by Padilla to the Johnston group, i.e., Mangels should not have executed the release. * * * Appended to the motion for summary judgment were affidavits executed by Mangels and Taraldson. Each stated that during the life of the listing agreement between Mangels and Padilla, there had been no communication to Padilla that the affiant was acting as an agent for Warren. These affidavits are uncontroverted in the record. * * *

Whether or not an agency relation exists is a question of law for the court where the material facts from which it is to be inferred are not in dispute. * * * If, on motion for summary judgment the record before the court shows there is no genuine dispute as to any material fact and that only one inference can be drawn from those undisputed material facts, and based on the undisputed material facts, the movant is entitled to judgment as a matter of law, summary judgment is appropriate. * * *

The record clearly reflects that the relationship between Padilla and Mangels was that of principal-agent. Therefore, as to Padilla, a fiduciary relationship existed and Mangels owed to her a duty of utmost good faith and loyalty. * * * When Mangels undertook to represent Padilla in the sale of her property, Mangels was precluded from acting on behalf of Warren without Padilla's consent. * * * The uncontroverted affidavits reflect that Padilla had not consented to Mangels' representation of Warren in the Warren-Padilla negotiation concerning the subject property and Warren's mental characterization of Mangels as his "agent" could not by some magic process convert Mangels into one.

There is no question that Warren knew that Mangels had been engaged by Padilla as exclusive agent to effect the sale of her property. As stated in *Ledirk Amusement Co.* v. *Scheckner,* 133 N.J.Eq. 602, 33 A.2d 894 (1943):

" 'As a general rule, though subject to many exceptions, the same person may not represent opposite parties. An agent employed by one party is presumed, throughout the transaction, to be acting for that principal and not for the opposite party. * * * the fact that one party puts faith in the agent of another does not shift the agency.' " * * *

Under the circumstances of this case, Warren could not enforce any claim against Mangels for breach of duty as Warren's agent. * * *

Furthermore, if Warren's claim against Mangels was predicated upon the Warren-Johnston transaction, assuming such existed, there likewise is no claim for relief. Construing the evidence most favorable to Warren's point of view, the most that can be said is that Mangels was attempting to bring Warren and Johnston together. Therefore, Mangels was no more than a "middleman" and no fiduciary relation to Warren existed. * * *

We find no error in granting appellee's motion for summary judgment and therefore affirm. * * *

AGENCY—DUTIES

Realtors' Liability—Disclosure of Fiduciary Interests. Although there are numerous cases reflecting the Realtors' enigma regarding his inability to collect a commission, this issue arose in an indirect manner in the Aeschlimann case. In this case, the broker counterclaimed for his commission, and the argument by the seller, to attempt to avoid paying a commission, was that the broker-defendant failed to disclose his fiduciary duty to the plaintiff as to having an interest in and to a corporation that was allegedly related to the transaction. The court quickly disposed of this issue, as illustrated in the following case.

Warner J. AESCHLIMANN and Martha A. Aeschlimann,
husband and wife, Appellants,
v.
Bruce ROSBACH et al, Respondents.
Supreme Court of Oregon
* * *

* * *

BRYSON, Justice.

This is a suit for foreclosure in which defendant Bruce Rosbach counterclaimed for a real estate broker's commission. Defendant Bruce

Rosbach was plaintiff's real estate broker. Defendant Deborah Ann Rosbach, daughter of Bruce Rosbach, is the current title holder of property sold by plaintiffs through Bruce Rosbach to the J.L.F. Corporation. All the foreclosure issues have been resolved, and this appeal involves only defendant Bruce Rosbach's counterclaim for the broker's commission allegedly owed to him by plaintiffs for his participation in the sale to the J.L.F. Corporation.

In their answer to defendant's counterclaim, plaintiffs alleged, inter alia, that defendant violated his fiduciary duty to plaintiffs by failing to disclose to them that he had some "interest, ownership or control in J.L.F. Corporation" at the time of the sale. The Trial Court made findings of fact and conclusions of law as follows:

" * * *

"That at the time of the sale, out of which the said promissory note arose, the Defendant Bruce Rosbach had no interest in, ownership or control of the J.L.F. Corporation, as alleged in the Plaintiffs' first reply.

" * * * * "

Judgment was entered in favor of defendant Bruce Rosbach on his counterclaim.

Plaintiffs contend that the Trial Court erred in not requiring the defendant Bruce Rosbach to introduce written evidence of his disclosure to the plaintiffs of defendant's interest in the property and plaintiffs' informed consent to defendant's continuing to proceed as the broker. Inasmuch as the Trial Court found the defendant had no interest, plaintiff's contention is irrelevant.

Affirmed.

NEFF v. BUD LEWIS COMPANY
Court of Appeals of New Mexico, 1976.
548 P.2d 107

* * *

OPINION

SUTIN, Judge.

Plaintiff sued defendants, real estate broker and salesmen, claiming damages for misrepresentation of material facts, and for defendants' failure to disclose facts, regarding defects in the heating and cooling system of a building purchased by plaintiff. Defendant Bud Lewis Company counterclaimed against plaintiff for brokerage and lease commissions.
Defendants appeal from an adverse judgment in favor of plaintiff, and plaintiff appeals from an adverse judgment in favor of Bud Lewis Company.

A. Findings of Fact and Judgments

The trial court found:

On August 1, 1970, plaintiff purchased the Autrey Plaza Building from Cecil and Ellen Johnston. Defendants acted as agents for plaintiff in this transaction, and a fiduciary relationship existed between plaintiff and defendants. Latent defects existed in the heating and cooling system from the time of the construction of the building. Prior to plaintiff's purchase, defendants had managed the building for Johnston and had knowledge of continuing problems with the heating and air conditioning system of the building. They failed to communicate them to the plaintiff and concealed the facts when inquiry was made by plaintiff. Defendants represented to plaintiff that there was no problem or inadequacy in the heating and air conditioning system at the time of purchase and that all problems had been resolved. The lower court held that plaintiff relied on defendants' representations and was damaged.

Plaintiff was required to expend the sum of $37,249.80 to correct the deficiencies in the heating and cooling system of the building.

Plaintiff owed defendants $3,070.08, plus interest from August 1, 1972, at 6%, for a real estate commission. Plaintiff owed defendants $7,246.44 for a lease commission as of April 1, 1975, and further payments that come due and payable under the terms of a lease commission agreement. The trial court found that defendant Bud Lewis Company was entitled to an offset of the two commissions against plaintiff's judgment.

Judgment was entered for plaintiff in the sum of $25,732.89 plus costs and interest at 6% per annum from April 1, 1975, until paid.

B. Plaintiff's Case

1. Evidence in support of court's findings on plaintiff's case.

Prior to the purchase of the Autrey Plaza Building by plaintiff, Bud Lewis managed the building for Johnston. He had recommended to Johnston that about $10,000.00 be expended to repair the heating and cooling system and this was done. It was a revamp of the first and second floor system. This problem was inherent in the construction of the building. After this expenditure, Johnston continued to have problems with the heating and cooling system. Three other additional expenditures were incurred. Defendants were also acquainted with numerous complaints by tenants of the building. However, defendants assured plaintiff that the condition of the building was excellent, that it was well constructed and functioning well, and that the heating and cooling system had been checked; that there was no problem with the inadequacy of the system and that all problems had been resolved.

The building was purchased August 1, 1970. Thereafter, Bud Lewis Company managed the building for plaintiff. In December, 1971, the Bud Lewis Company told plaintiff of numerous complaints. At a conference plaintiff was told, for the first time, that the whole heating system was defective.

Plaintiff engaged Bridgers and Paxton Consulting Engineers to make a study of the problem and report. After the study and report were presented, the construction firm of Corzine and Rapp performed the work.

2. Defendants failed to disclose all material facts.

* * * First, defendants contend that they did not fail to disclose to plaintiff any material facts. We disagree. There was a conflict in the evidence.

Defendants rely primarily upon a letter dated June 10, 1970, from Johnson Service Company to defendant Gibson. This letter was attached to the exchange contract of the same date between plaintiff and Johnston under which contract plaintiff agreed to acquire the Autrey Plaza Building, and was reviewed by plaintiff and his attorney. It briefly explained some of the problems the Johnson Service Company had with the Aarkla-Servel heating and cooling units which served this building.

The trial court considered this evidence in arriving at its decision. The court also found that this letter did not disclose all material facts within the knowledge of defendants, facts upon which plaintiff relied. Despite the problems set out in the Johnson letter of June 10, 1970, defendants represented that, at the time plaintiff purchased the property, all of the problems had been resolved.

The trial court's belief, based on substantial evidence presented below, that defendants failed to disclose all the material facts within their knowledge, foreclosed defendants' position on appeal. "A broker is a fiduciary, holding a position of great trust and confidence, and is required to exercise the utmost good faith toward his principal throughout the entire transaction . . . (A) real estate broker is under a legal obligation to make a full, fair and prompt disclosure to his employer of all facts within his knowledge which are or may be material, or which affect his principal's rights and interest or influence his action relative to the disposition of the property." * * *

Defendants failed to comply with this rule. They failed to disclose all material facts.

3. Plaintiff relied on defendants' statements.

* * * Second, defendants contend that plaintiff did not rely on the statements of defendants, but made an independent investigation prior to the purchase. Defendants rely on the testimony of their own witnesses to establish this independent investigation. Our duty is to view the evidence most favorable to plaintiff. In doing so, we affirm the trial court on the point that plaintiff relied upon the statements of defendants.

4. Contributory negligence of plaintiff is not an issue.

* * * Third, in its conclusion of law No. 14, the court recited that its decision was based upon the "negligent omission and breach of duty on the part of defendants to make full disclosure to plaintiff of inadequacies

in the heating and cooling system of the Autrey Plaza Building." Defendants contend that if the appellants were guilty of negligence, plaintiff was guilty of contributory negligence which was a proximate cause of plaintiff's damage. We disagree. * * *

Justifiable reliance by plaintiff is the issue, and we must agree with the trial court that plaintiff had a right to rely on the defendants' representations that the Autrey Plaza Building was in excellent condition and that all problems with the heating and cooling system had been resolved.

We hold that contributory negligence is not a defense. The doctrine of negligent misrepresentation did not afford the defendants a defense of contributory negligence.

5. Damages were proven by the evidence.

Fourth, defendants contend that no damage has been proven by the evidence. This point is without merit.

Plaintiff's judgment is affirmed.

C. Defendant Bud Lewis Company's Counterclaim

1. Defendant Bud Lewis Company was not entitled to payment of commission on real estate transaction.

* * * On July 30, 1970, Bud Lewis Company and plaintiff entered into an agreement for the payment of a commission to this defendant for the consummation of the transaction between plaintiff and Johnston. The amount of the commission was $5,116.80, payable in semi-annual installments of $511.68 at 6% interest. Plaintiff paid four installments of principal and interest up to and including August 1, 1972.

Defendant Bud Lewis Company contends that the denial of this commission would constitute unjust enrichment, and that it would be inequitable and improper. * * *

Bud Lewis Company profited by plaintiff's prior payments on the commission, which plaintiff did not seek to recover. * * * It would be unjust enrichment for defendant to be allowed an additional profit of principal and interest in the sum of $3,545.93 awarded Bud Lewis Company by the trial court. This part of the judgment for defendant Bud Lewis Company is reversed.

2. Defendant Bud Lewis Company was entitled to commissions on lease agreements.

* * * Johnston and plaintiff entered into an agreement called "Assignment and Assumption." Johnston assigned leases to plaintiff subject to ten commission agreements in which Bud Lewis Company was broker. The commission agreements provided Bud Lewis Company with a real estate commission for the consummation of leases for tenants obtained in the Autrey Plaza Building, and an additional commission for any renewals or extensions of the leases. The terms of each lease varied.

Bud Lewis Company commissions, earned for leases obtained, did not fall within the constructive trust doctrine. Judgment is affirmed for Bud Lewis Company in the sum of $7,264.44 as of April 1, 1975, and for further payments that come due and payable under the terms of the lease agreements.

D. Conclusion

Judgment for plaintiff in the sum of $37,249.80 is affirmed. The off-set for Bud Lewis Company in the sum of $3,545.93 and interest is reversed. The offset for Bud Lewis in the sum of $7,264.44 and further payments due and payable is affirmed.

IT IS SO ORDERED. * * *

The Duty of a Broker for His Agents. In the Martin case, the factual situation involved the Martins, who owned a lot in Arizona City. Subsequent to their purchase of this lot they were contacted by John Foley, with a proposition to have a home constructed on a lot in question in Arizona City. The agreement was to have Foley build a home on a lot to be acquired by the Martins. Foley would in turn market the property and give a $4,500 profit to the Martins. It was also agreed that if Foley was not successful in this profit venture, he would at least pay a $3,000 profit to the Martins. Foley failed to abide by the agreement. The issue of agency arose because the Martins were looking to the broker-principal of Foley, that is, Althoff, the agency where Mr. Foley was licensed as a salesperson. The issue is whether the principal, the Althoff Agency, is responsible for the acts of Mr. Foley in failing to comply with his agreement. This raises the more basic question as to the liability of a principal for acts of its agent.

Under the facts given, would you consider that they would be responsible for the acts of Foley? What other answers would you need to make your decision? These issues are examined in the following Martin case. It also illustrates the potential exposure for a real estate broker when "hanging" licenses of inactive or only passively active salespeople.

MARTIN v. ALTHOFF
Court of Appeals of Arizona, 1976.
557 P.2d 187

* * *

OPINION

DONOFRIO, Presiding Judge.

This is an appeal from an order of dismissal with prejudice granted in favor of appellees R. H. Althoff Agency and General Insurance Company of America and against the Martins, appellants.

The facts necessary for a determination of this case are as follows: Appellants Martin are, and were at the time the actions took place, residents of Colorado. In July, 1966, they purchased a lot in Arizona City as an investment. In June, 1972, they were contacted by one John T. Foley with a proposition concerning the construction of a single family unit on their lot. The crux of the proposition was that (a) the appellants trade their present lot for another lot in Arizona City; (b) Foley would build a home on the newly acquired lot; and (c) Foley would then sell the home and lot. The agreement stipulated that if the sale did not produce $4,500 profit for the appellants, Foley would then purchase the property himself at a price which would give the appellants a $3,000 profit.

Foley failed to abide by the agreement and the appellants instituted litigation against him which resulted in a default judgment against Foley in the amount of $51,490.00.

* * *

From 1970 until late 1971 or early 1972, Foley was a real estate salesman for the Althoff agency (appellee). The affidavits in support of the motion to dismiss show that Foley terminated this relationship with Althoff at that time and left them. After leaving the Althoff agency Foley entered the construction business and had no further contact with the appellees. During his employment with appellees, Foley's license was held by appellees, pursuant to the statutory requirement.

After Foley left the Althoff agency, Althoff continued to hold Foley's license and did not return it to the real estate commissioner pursuant to A.R.S. 32–2128.

Appellants argue that appellees are liable for Foley's action based on the following: First, a significant part of the transaction between Foley and appellants was governed and controlled by various sections of the Arizona Real Estate Act; second, Foley was acting as a real estate salesman under the brokerage of Althoff and not in his individual capacity, and finally, Althoff was Foley's principal and liable for his actions against the appellants.

Appellee General Insurance Company's liability is based on its status as Althoff's surety.

* * * In order for the appellants to establish appellees' liability for Foley's actions they must first show that some portion of the transaction among themselves and Foley involved actions regulated by our statutes governing real estate transactions * * * and that Foley was acting as Althoff's agent. If they cannot do so, their basis for attaching liability to appellee fails.

* * * In this connection appellees argue that because of a prior case deciding this same issue the appellants are estopped to raise it in this proceeding by virtue of the doctrine of collateral estoppel. * * * We must * * * pass upon the issues of this appeal, particularly, the critical issue as to whether the failure by the broker Althoff to return salesman Foley's license to the commission within ten days after he left the employ of the broker, renders the broker strictly liable for the wrongful acts of Foley.

* * * In determining the issues herein we are governed by the well-settled law that before a broker can be held liable for the acts of the salesman, the salesman must have been acting within the scope of the broker's employment.

* * * Bearing this in mind, we first dispose of the issue as to whether there is any agency relationship between the Althoffs and Foley. We have read the entire record, including the affidavits of the parties concerned, and the undisputed facts show that Althoff had no connection with the involved transaction and that no agency relationship has been shown. Our reading of the record shows, * * * that all of Foley's acts were done as a contractor under his contractor's license.

* * * We next turn to the question as to whether the failure to return the license as provided in A.R.S. 32-2128 imposes absolute liability on the broker for the acts of its former salesman. In reading the provisions of the Real Estate Act, we are unable to find that the Legislature intended that the failure to return the license within ten days should result in absolute liability on the part of the broker.

The statute in effect at the time * * * provided:

> " * * * A salesman's license shall remain in the possession of the employer until cancelled or until the licensee leaves his employ, when it shall be returned to the commissioner by the broker for cancellation."

The statute quoted above, and its later amendment, is silent as to return the salesman's license when the employment relationship is terminated. In our research we have not been able to find any statute in any of the other provisions of the real estate code which would hold a broker liable for the acts of his former salesmen simply because of the failure of the broker to return the license to the commissioner. * * * It is the rule of statutory construction that courts will not read into a statute something which is not within the express manifest intention of the Legislature as gathered from the statute itself, and similarly the court will not inflate, expand, stretch or extend the statute to matters not falling within its expressed provisions. * * *

In view of the foregoing, we would answer the second issue in the negative and hold that the broker's failure to return the licensee salesman's license after the termination of his employment with the broker does not per se impose civil liability on the broker so as to give the appellant herein a cause of action or claim for relief against the broker, and that the trial court did not err in granting dismissal of the complaint with prejudice.

Affirmed.

CHAPTER 10

Brokers—Internal Relationships

INTERNAL RELATIONS WITH BROKERS

The Harestad case, out of Oregon, illustrates the interplay of a partnership agreement between two licensed parties. Although this issue deals with the partnership and is not directly related to a brokerage position, it does illustrate the importance of concrete, written agreements between the parties. Had the parties clearly stated in writing their agreement, many of the controversies mentioned in this case would have been avoided.

HARESTAD v. WEITZEL
Supreme Court of Oregon, 1975.
536 P.2d 522

* * *

TONGUE, Justice.

This is a suit for an accounting upon the dissolution of a partnership. The principal issue is whether plaintiff is entitled to share as a partner in profits from the sale of an apartment complex in Beaverton built on land purchased by defendant in his individual name and financed by his funds. Defendant appeals from an adverse decree. We affirm.

Defendant assigns as error the findings and conclusions of the trial court and "portions of its decree" to the effect that the parties had agreed that the apartments were partnership property and that plaintiff, therefore, was entitled to a one-half interest in the apartments and in the profits from that sale.

The facts.

Plaintiff was a licensed real estate broker. Defendant was a licensed real estate salesman. Defendant had some $200,000 in funds available for investment in real estate projects. The property and funds available to plaintiff totaled approximately $40,000.

In August or September 1970 plaintiff and defendant made an oral agreement to be partners in the real estate and building business and opened an office with a sign which read: "Harestad & Co.—Realty—Builders—Residential-Commercial-Acreage." Defendant testified, however, that he was interested only in building houses and that there was no discussion of apartment complexes at that time. They then opened a partnership checking account with checks printed "Harestad & Co. Realty" with space for signatures of both partners on all checks. Defendant provided $1,500 in funds, a portion of which was used to open that account, and plaintiff gave him her note for $750, which she later paid. Each later contributed an additional $500.

In October 1970 a five-acre tract of unimproved land, suitable for the construction of an apartment complex, was purchased in the name of defendant, with funds provided by him. Defendant then made arrangements for an architect, for contractors, and for financing for construction of the apartments, based upon his financial statement and upon a note and mortgage signed by him. Construction was started in March 1971.

In July 1971, prior to completion of the apartments, the property, to include the apartments, was sold under an earnest money agreement naming defendant as the seller. The down payment, however, was deposited in the partnership account, as were the monthly payments under the subsequent contract of sale, dated May 1, 1972. The monthly mortgage payments were also paid from that account and defendant was reimbursed from that account for payments totaling $79,965 previously made by him as an individual.

Defendant testified that upon completion of the sale of the apartments (for $629,332) he thought that $15,000 would be a "fair commission" to the partnership, with the result that each partner drew $7,500 at that time. Plaintiff, however, denied that there was any discussion of a "commission" at that time and in defendant's deposition he had testified that when each partner drew $7,500 "there was no discussion" about it "being a commission." Plaintiff offered testimony that the usual commission on a sale for that price would have been considerably larger. In any event, after that withdrawal of $15,000 some funds remained for payment of remaining bills arising from the construction of the apartment complex.

It also appears that previous payments for items such as a payment to the City of Beaverton for a "plan check fee" and numerous payments to subcontractors were made by check from the partnership account and that payments previously received, such as a payment from the city for an easement through the property, two payments from insurance companies for vandalism damage to the apartments, and the balance of funds remaining after payments to contractors from loan funds in escrow from the lending agency were deposited in the partnership account.

Meanwhile, in August 1971, plaintiff and defendant signed a form "Articles of Co-Partnership" dated (by error) as of September 1, 1969 (instead of 1970), for the purpose of carrying on the business of "Real Estate and building" under the name of "Harestad & Co. Realty" and stating that the capital of the partnership "shall be $1,250 each," representing the amounts previously paid by each partner. Again, defendant testified that his intent in the use of the words "and building" was the building of houses.

There was also testimony, much of which was denied by defendant, relating to time and effort devoted by plaintiff in connection with the apartment project, including meetings with city officials in connection with permits; consultations with architects; selection of carpeting, tile and appliances; daily visits to the construction site; the keeping of all books and records for the project; and arrangements for payments to contractors to be made by the lending agency.

The income tax returns for the partnership and for the two parties as individuals are not entirely clear with reference to the apartment project. The only reference to that project in the 1970 partnership return is a deduction for a "plan inspection fee." However, the property for that project was not purchased until October 22, 1970, and construction did not start until March 1971.

With reference to the tax returns for 1971, plaintiff testified that in February 1972 she and defendant talked with Mr. Kaster, the accountant who prepared the partnership returns (who was also her personal accountant) about the handling of deductions for expenses from the apartment project and that the defendant's accountant told her that "it was a partnership item" and that it was proper for her in her individual return to claim a deduction for one-half of such expenses, which was then done in her tax return for 1971.

Defendant's tax return for 1971 also showed deductions so as to indicate a 50 per cent interest in the apartments. Defendant would explain this on the basis that he had "sufficient other deductions for that year so that he would have a refund coming and could not take advantage of everything he could have deducted." Mr. Kaster testified that he talked with defendant's accountant before preparing plaintiff's return for 1971. Defendant's accountant was not called as a witness. The partnership return for 1971 makes no reference to the apartment project.

The partnership return for 1972 showed as an account receivable the balance due from sale of the apartments. That return was prepared by Mr. Kaster. Plaintiff testified that she and defendant went together to meet with Mr. Kaster and with an attorney prior to the preparation of that return and took with them the records relating to the apartment project. Mr. Kaster testified that "she brought the books in." Defendant denied talking to Kaster until later. That tax return was apparently signed only by plaintiff and was subsequently objected to by defendant's attorney.

In August 1972 defendant had a heart attack and was unable to work "full time" again until the spring of 1973. On November 6, 1972, the partnership was terminated. At that time both parties went to see defendant's lawyer, who drafted a proposed dissolution agreement, under which plaintiff's one-half interest in the apartment project would have been recognized. Plaintiff testified that defendant "dictated" the terms of that agreement and that her only objection to it was that the handling of incoming contract payments and the making of mortgage payments should be done in escrow, but that defendant objected to that proposal and that "that is where our problem began." Defendant denied "dictating" the terms of that proposed draft agreement (which was received in evidence "under the rule"), or agreeing to its proposed terms. He testified that this was "the first time" he "became aware that she claimed an interest" in the apartments.

The subsequent dissolution agreement, as well as escrow instructions, both of which also recognized that interest in plaintiff, were then prepared by plaintiff's lawyer and were signed by both plaintiff and defendant, who testified, however, that when he signed he did not intend that the agreement be delivered and that later on the same day he tore "in two" that dissolution agreement and saw another lawyer. Since November 1972 defendant has retained all of the monthly contract payments. Under the facts of this case plaintiff is entitled to share as a partner in the profits from the sale of the apartment complex.

* * * Under the facts of this case, we believe that the purchase, development and sale of this apartment project was within the scope of the business of this partnership as defined by the express terms of the written partnership agreement to the effect that the purpose of the partnership was for the business of "real estate and building." And even if such a result is not clear from those terms of that written agreement, we believe that the same result must follow from the conduct of the partners and their course of dealing, as evidenced both by the testimony of the partners and others and by the numerous documents, as previously described. * * *

Finally, defendant contends that a partnership agreement extending to the apartment project "is one squarely within the ambit of the statute of frauds," so that oral proof of such an agreement is prohibited by the terms of ORS 41.580(1), (5), and was therefore inadmissible. * * *

It follows, in our opinion, that the scope of the business subject to that agreement could properly be proved by parol evidence.

Affirmed.

BROKER'S RELATIONS WITH OTHER BROKERS

The intent of this material is not to examine in detail the broker's responsibility or liability relative to brokers vis-a-vis other brokers. However, the following case of Hapsas Realty, Inc., a New Mexico decision, indicates at least one problem area of broker relationships, that of oral agreements to divide real estate commissions.

For more information on this area of the real estate licensees' practice, see *Real Estate Law,* written by this author with Kent Jay Levine.

HAPSAS REALTY, INC.,
Plaintiff-Appellant,
v.
MICHAEL J. McCOUN,
Defendant-Appellee,
579 P.2d 785 (New Mexico, 1978)

Hapsas Realty, Inc., plaintiff-appellant, brought an action for declaratory judgment against Michael J. McCoun, defendant-appellee on an oral contract to divide a real estate commission earned by the leasing of certain premises. Appellee denied the contract and affirmatively alleged that the oral contract, if any, was unenforceable. The trial court, pursuant to N.M.R.Civ.P. 56 (§ 21-1-1(56), N.M.S.A. 1953 (Repl. 1970)), granted summary judgment in favor of appellee on the grounds that an agreement between brokers to share or divide a commission must be in writing pursuant to § 70-1-43, N.M.S.A. 1953 (Repl. 1961).

Section 70-1-43 provides:

Any agreement entered into subsequent to the first day of July, 1949, authorizing or employing an agent or broker to purchase or sell lands, tenements, or hereditaments or any interest in or concerning them, for a commission or other compensation, shall be void unless the agreement, or some memorandum or note thereof shall be in writing and signed by the person to be charged therewith, or some other person thereunto by him lawfully authorized. No such agreement or employment shall be considered exclusive unless specifically so stated therein.

Thus, Section 70-1-43 requires any agreement "authorizing or employing an agent or broker to purchase or sell lands . . . or any interest in or concerning them" to be in writing. Whether this statute is applicable to a contract to share a commission appears to be a case of first impression in New Mexico.

Appellant argues that an oral contract to share commissions does not fall within the statute since such an agreement is not an employment or agency agreement to purchase or sell an interest in land.

Appellee contends that § 70-1-43 is applicable to all situations involving real estate commissions and that the statute is designed not only to protect property owners but also all persons who come within its provisions.

In *Yrissarri* v. *Wallis,* 76 N.M. 776, 418 P.2d 852 (1966) this Court held that § 70-1-43 was applicable to all persons who came within the statutory provisions and rejected a property owner's contention that the statute was intended to benefit only a property owner. In Yrisarri the property owner claimed an oral modfiication of a written agreement for a commission. However, whether an agreement to share commissions comes within the provisions of § 70-1-43 is a question which was not addressed by this Court in Yrisarri.

Several courts in other jurisdictions have construed statutes similar to § 70-1-43 as they apply to agreements between brokers to share commissions. In the early case of *Gorham* v. *Heiman,* 90 Cal. 346, 27 P. 289 (1891), the Supreme Court of California determined that a statute requiring written agreements authorizing or employing brokers was designed only to protect owners of real estate against unfounded claims of brokers. The statute was determined not to extend to agreements between brokers to cooperate in making sales for a share of a commission.

The present California statute, Cal. Civ. Code § 1624(5) (West 1973) requires a writing with:

> An agreement authorising or employing an agent (or) broker . . . to purchase or sell real estate, or to lease real estate . . . or to procure . . . a purchaser or seller of real estate or a lessee or lessor . . . for compensation or a commission.

This provision has been held not to be applicable to agreements to share commissions between brokers.

Ariz. Rev. Stat. § 44-101(7) (1967) requires a writing:

> Upon an agreement authorizing or employing an agent or broker to purchase or sell real property, or mines, for compensation or a commission.

The Arizona Supreme Court in *Bush* v. *Mattingly,* 62 Ariz. 483, 158 P.2d 665 (1945) determined that the statute was not applicable to agreements between brokers.

The former Michigan statute, Mich. Comp. Laws Ann. (1967), § 566.132(5) was construed in *Beznos* v. *Borisoff,* 339 Mich. 12, 62 N.W.2d 461 (1954). In Beznos the Supreme Court of Michigan held that the statute was not applicable to agreements between brokers. The then applicable statute provided for a writing with:

Every agreement, promise, or contract to pay any commission for or upon the sale of any interest in real estate.

Other states which have had an opportunity to construe statutes similar to § 70-1-43 have held that their respective Statutes of Fraud requiring a written agreement were not applicable to agreements between brokers to share commission.

The rationale of these decisions is that the applicable statutes were designed to protect the property owner-broker relationship. To the extent these courts have stated that these statutes are designed to protect only property owners we disagree. *Yrisarri* v. *Wallis, supra.* However, we do find that we are in agreement that such statutes do not apply to agreements between brokers to share a commission. The clear purpose of § 70-1-43 is to protect the owner-broker agreement to pay commissions but not to protect the brokers from themselves.

We therefore hold that § 70-1-43 is not applicable to agreements between brokers to share a commission. The summary judgment of the trial court is reversed and this case is remanded for further proceedings.

IT IS SO ORDERED.

CHAPTER 11

Recovery Funds / Bonds

REAL ESTATE RECOVERY FUND

One source of problems is to collect a debt that is held to be owing to a third party as a result of a suit against a Realtor. That is, even though the court may find that a Realtor is liable under a given circumstance, there is no assurance that the obligation can be paid by the Realtor.

With this problem and the interest of parties who are concerned with not only a suit against a Realtor but also collection of those monies in mind, many states have provided for bonding arrangements or real estate recovery funds. An article covering this topic and the implications to the same is discussed in the following pages.

As mentioned in the prelude to this area, it is possible that an injured party may receive a judgment against a real estate agent, but the judgment may be unproductive in the sense that the real estate agent has no fund. To avoid this problem, a real estate recovery fund has been established in many states. This issue and the right to recover from the real estate recovery fund is illustrated in the following Lemler case, 558 P.2d 591 (1976). Remember that the right to recover from a recovery fund depends on the law for each state, assuming it has such a fund.

Gerald C. LEMLER and Elizabeth H. Lemler, Individuals,
Plaintiffs-Appellants
v.
REAL ESTATE COMMISSION of the State of Colorado,
Defendant-Appellee,
and
The Damar Company, Inc., a Colorado Corporation, et al., Defendants.
* * *
Colorado Court of Appeals,
* * *

* * *

RULAND, Judge.

The sole issue on this appeal is whether payment may be obtained from the Colorado Real Estate Recovery Fund to satisfy a judgment entered against a corporation and its president as the result of fraud committed in connection with a contract to erect a residence upon the property of the plaintiffs. The Trial Court ruled that recovery was not available from the Fund, and plaintiffs appeal. We affirm the Trial Court judgment.

* * * This document reflects that plaintiff Gerald C. Lemler contracted with defendant the Damar Company, Inc., for the design, construction, and sale of a residence to be constructed by Damar on land owned by plaintiffs. Damar, now defunct, was a Colorado corporation engaged in both the sale of existing homes and custom construction and sale of home. Damar held a corporate real estate brokers license pursuant to § 12-61-103(7), C.R.S. 1973, and defendant Daniel Indgjer, as president of Damar, was the officer authorized to act as a broker for the corporation.

Plaintiffs performed their obligations under the contract with Damar consisting of payment of an earnest money deposit, preparing a foundation for the residence, and installing tile and plumbing fixtures. However, Damar defaulted on its obligations to plaintiffs. Plaintiffs filed a complaint alleging fraud, and recovered judgment by default against Damar and Indgjer in the amount of $2,160. Being unsuccessful in their efforts to collect the judgment, plaintiffs joined the Colorado Real Estate Commission as a party defendant pursuant to § 12-61-303(2), C.R.S. 1973 (1975 Supp.), and applied to the Court for an order directing payment of the judgment from the Fund.

Insofar as pertinent her, § 12-61-302(1), C.R.S. 1973 (1975 Supp.), authorizes payment from the Fund for any final judgment of up to $50,000 entered against a licensed real estate broker for fraud in the performance of any act for which a license is required. Plaintiffs rely upon §§ 12-61-101(2) (a) and (b), C.R.S. 1973, which require a license for any corporation which is engaged in, or attempts to engage in, selling or offering to sell "real estate, or interest therein, or improvement affixed thereon."

While plaintiffs concede that the licensing statute is penal in nature because of the criminal penalties involved in violation of its terms, * * * they contend that the statute must be given a liberal construction under the circumstances of this case because the provisions governing the Fund are remedial in nature and are designed to protect persons defrauded by licensed brokers or salespersons. Based upon this premise, plaintiffs first argue that their contract with Damar constituted Damar's attempt to sell real estate improvements even though the improvements were to be affixed to the property in the future and that, therefore, a license was required. We find no merit in this contention.

Even if we were to disregard the penal nature of the licensing statute, * * * we may not ignore the intent of the General Assembly as evidenced by the obvious meaning of the words employed in mandating which transactions are covered by the statute. * * * The phrase "real estate . . . or improvements affixed thereon" refers to improvements situate on real estate at the time of the sale or attempted sale.

The construction of that phrase urged by plaintiffs would lead to absurd results. An appliance such as an electric range which both seller and buyer recognize will be built into the wall of a kitchen owned by buyer may constitute a fixture or improvement. * * * Under plaintiffs' construction of the licensing statute, any merchant who sells such appliances would have to obtain a real estate broker's license. Such was clearly not the intent of the General Assembly.

In the alternative, plaintiffs claim that the construction contract constituted a sale or attempt to sell "an interest" in real estate and thus a broker's license was required. In support of this argument, plaintiffs assert that a builder holds "title" to a structure he is building until the structure is completed and transferred to the landowner. We reject this contention also.

Under the circumstances of this case, the theory proposed by plaintiffs necessarily presupposes that Damar acquired an interest in plaintiffs' real property merely by signing the construction contract. To the contrary, only if the landowner fails to pay for the improvements placed upon his real estate may the builder acquire an interest in the land and improvements and that right is acquired by perfecting a mechanic's lien. * * *

Judgment affirmed.

REAL ESTATE RECOVERY FUNDS— PUBLIC PROTECTION AGAINST BROKER MALPRACTICE

Professionals, whether they be doctors, lawyers, or real estate practitioners, are feeling the increased growth in consumer allegations of malpractice.

The recent push for ceilings on malpractice actions, especially in the medical field, has brought the malpractice issue to the forefront. The issue as it regards medical practitioners has been well examined, though not solved, in recent articles. This column will examine malpractice problems of real estate licensees, focusing on one of the attempted solutions: the real estate recovery fund.

Purpose of the Fund. The real estate recovery fund is not meant to eliminate liability for the licensee who acts improperly. Rather, it is a source of money to pay the claim of an injured member of the public. It is designed to satisfy, or at least indemnify to a degree, an injured party who was damaged as a result of the improper actions of a real estate licensee. It does not remove the need for malpractice actions or errors and omissions insurance. The fund, generally supported by other participant-licensees in the field, merely provides a source for indemnification of the injured party, within certain limits and based upon certain qualifications, where that injured third party cannot collect against the licensee for some reason, such as an inability to locate the licensee or an insolvent licensee.

How Recovery Funds Work. Real estate recovery funds have been enacted by a number of states.[1] The standards for obtaining a judgment and collecting on the fund vary from state to state. Generally, the acts provide some general language that allows an injured party to file a claim notice with the fund representative after meeting certain preliminary requirements—for example, attempting to collect from the wrongdoer-licensee. In some states, however, the grounds for collecting against the fund are quite restricted. For example, many funds require proof that the licensee is guilty of committing fraud, willful misrepresentation, improper intentional actions, such as conversion of funds, or willful misrepresentations of other types, before payout will be authorized. Generally, a negligence suit will not support collection.[2] Most funds also impose time limits, such as a one-year statute of limitations, notice of the pending position, judicious and timely actions, and similar administrative prerequisites. Further, there is usually a dollar limitation on claims. A failure to include a maximum limitation against the fund ($15,000 in some states) may result in a complete depletion of the fund.[3]

---

[1] According to the National Association of Real Estate License Law Officials (NARELLO), twelve states had enacted some type of recovery fund by 1974 to allow compensation to the injured party. 1974 NARELLO Report, p. 25. According to a December 1975 survey made by the author, seventeen states now have such funds, including Alaska, Arizona, California, Colorado, Connecticut, Delaware, Georgia, Illinois, Kansas, Kentucky, Maryland, Minnesota, Nevada, North Dakota, Ohio, Texas, Utah. Several other states are considering or have considered enacting such funds: Florida, Massachusetts, Virginia, New Jersey.

[2] However, see later discussion in the text with regard to the Colorado law.

[3] This point was noted by Keith Koske, director of the Colorado Real Estate Commission, in a letter to the author dated December 16, 1975, with regard to Ari-

To enforce a subrogation position in favor of the fund, most statutes provide that if the fund does make payments to a third party due to the improper actions of a licensee, the commission can refuse to issue a new license (if it would in any event) until repayment is made to the fund by the licensee. Statutes also usually give the commission the right to proceed against the licensee where the fund has made payments on behalf of that licensee to some injured third party.

Licensees Still Need Insurance. Again, the passing of legislation to create a real estate recovery fund will not eliminate the requirement or need for errors and omissions insurance by licensees. Funds help to insure the public, not the broker. It may become a requirement in the near future that errors and omissions insurance be presented by a licensee prior to or a short time after the license is issued. This is a common requirement in many jurisdictions with regard to other licenses, such as the licensing of professional corporation law firms.

Some states attempt to give some support to an injured third party, in addition to a direct action against the licensee, by providing a minimum bond requirement. For example, twenty-one states require a bond in one form or another. The amount of the bond which must be posted for the licensee varies from approximately $1,000 up to $10,000.[4]

Fund Payouts and the Likelihood of Suit. Funding of the various real estate recovery funds is usually by contributions from the licensees. Many states provide that each licensee, upon renewal of the license or at various other times, must contribute a given amount of money, usually $5 to $20, toward the recovery fund. A portion of this money is used for the recovery fund, and other amounts often pass to general educational funds or other uses for support for the real estate industry.[5] Some of the earliest funds allowed easy access to the monies. As a result, many of the funds were depleted substantially before they had a chance to get off the ground.[6]

Possibly because of the very adverse effects of decisions regarding the early no-limit recovery funds, many states became very restrictive as to requirements to qualify for collection from the fund. Colorado's law, for example, initially required a short statute of limitations of one year after the cause of action occurred. After this period, the action would be barred. Also, the law required that action be brought judiciously and only after

---

zona. Since Arizona was apparently the first state to enact a recovery fund, it is understandable why it may have fallen into this trap. Most other states, noting Arizona's experience, have taken the precaution of providing a maximum dollar limitation on any claim against the fund.

[4] 1974 NARELLO Report.

[5] Only Colorado does not allow a transfer of a portion of the recovery funds to aid real estate industry education. Statement made by Mr. Koske, note 3 *supra.*

[6] See note 3 *supra.*

there was a failure to collect the monies directly against the defendant-licensee. Proof had to be shown of the failure to be *able* to collect the judgment against the licensee. This was on a showing of reasonable diligence.

Fund dollar limitations in many states are very restricted. Colorado initially restricted the liability to $15,000. The $15,000 was for one claim, and would be divided among the various claimants if more than one party was injured in the same act. Recently, Colorado amended its recovery fund[7] to provide an increase in the limit from $15,000 to $50,000. Obviously, this makes the fund much more attractive as a source of payment. More important, Colorado, like some other states, now allows[8] an action on negligence against the broker or salesman. Previously, the action required fraud, material intentional misrepresentation, or similar types of activity to allow a claim against the fund. The door has been enlarged substantially by the new provision of negligence.

Colorado, like some other states, also provides for court costs and attorneys' fees to be recoverable from the fund. This, too, will encourage consumer suits.

Whether Pandora's box has been opened by changes like those in Colorado remains to be seen, but there is a good deal of apprehension among real estate commission members.[9] As a source of funds for a client who has been injured, recovery funds may be the golden goose (assuming the plaintiff can sustain his position and allegations as to the improper actions of the licensee). Many cases in the past have resulted in judgments which are worthless, due to an insolvent licensee. Hence, attorneys are reluctant to take a claim unless there is a solvent licensee. But if the recovery fund stands in the shoes of the licensee from the standpoint of monies available, it seems probable claims will proliferate.

If more states follow Colorado, which has deleted the requirement that the creditor exhaust all means to attempt to recover its judgment against the licensee before seeking redress from the fund, claims will surely increase in number. Colorado now merely requires a showing that the judgment debtor will not pay the debt. The plaintiff, having judgment, can then place a claim with the recovery fund and receive its monies, assuming it qualifies. Apparently, in one other state, California, the fund has paid out substantial funds of monies. Possibly, we will see an extension of these payouts by other states as well.

[7] Under Colorado Senate Bill 158.
[8] *Id.*
[9] "It is expected that many more claims will be made against the fund when knowledge of its existence becomes more widespread. There has been very little publicity in legal circles concerning this fund." Statement by Mr. Koske, note 3 *supra.*

REAL ESTATE RECOVERY FUND— CONTINUED

A case is reviewed in the context of a recovery fund in the following pages. This case involved a party who was licensed as a real estate salesperson. The licensee acted improperly with regard to certain funds, and the question on appeal is whether there is a right by the injured party, plaintiff, to recover against the Arizona Real Estate Recovery Fund. The liability is not in question; rather, the issue is whether the actions by the licensee result in a basis for recovery under the Arizona Real Estate Recovery Fund. It is apparent at the review of the case that the actions of the licensee were not within the scope of a real estate salesperson, *at the time of the actions,* and therefore no recovery against the fund is allowed. See the case of *Martin* v. *State of Arizona Real Estate Commission.*

---

26 Ariz. App. 239 (1976)
Harold MARTIN and Fern Martin, husband and wife, Appellants,
v.
STATE of Arizona REAL ESTATE COMMISSION, Appellee.
* * *

* * *

OPINION

KRUCKER, Judge.

Appellants obtained a judgment on November 20, 1973, against John T. Foley in the approximate sum of $51,000.00. Foley was a licensed contractor and a licensed real estate salesman. Appellants sought to recover a part of the judgment out of the Real Estate Recovery Fund. * * * The Arizona Real Estate Commission contested the claim and pursuant to the provisions of A.R.S. § 32-2188(C), a hearing was held to determine whether recovery should be had against the Real Estate Recovery Fund. The lower Court, having heard all of the evidence and arguments, denied appellants' application and judgment was entered May 4, 1974.

The questions presented to us on appeal are whether Foley was acting in the capacity of a licensed real estate salesman at the time of the transactions out of which this claim arose and whether the Real Estate Recovery Fund was liable for the acts of Foley.

The facts necessary to a determination of this appeal are briefly as follows. Appellants had purchased Lot 665 in Arizona City and made payments on it for approximately six years. Foley approached appellants and inquired if they would like to build a home on their lot. As Lot 665 was encumbered, appellants traded it for Lot 384, which was unencumbered. Nothing indicates that Foley had anything to do with the exchange of lots. Appellants obtained a construction loan of $20,000 from Southwest Savings and Loan and Foley began construction of the house. He withdrew approximately $17,000 of the loan funds, but never completed the house. After Foley abandoned the project, some $6,000 in liens were placed against appellants' property. The scanty record before us does not reveal what Foley did with the $17,000.00.

The Real Estate Recovery Fund is to protect the public from acts of real estate licensees which violate the provisions of Ch. 20, Title 32, A.R.S., or the regulations thereunder. A.R.S. § 32-2186(A) provides, in part:

' "The commissioner is authorized and directed to establish and maintain a real estate recovery fund from which any person . . . aggrieved by an act, representation, transaction or conduct of a duly licensed broker or salesman, which is in violation of the provisions of this chapter or the regulations promulgated pursuant thereto, may recover by order of the Superior Court or Justice Court of the county where the violation occurred for only actual or compensatory damages . . ."

A.R.S. § 32-2188(B) provides as follows:

"When any aggrieved person recovers a valid judgment in any Court of competent jurisdiction against any broker or salesman, for any act, representation, transaction, or conduct which is in violation of the provisions of this chapter or the regulations promulgated pursuant thereto . . . the aggrieved person may . . . file a verified claim . . ."

Appellants argue that because of a related agreement concerning the future sale of the property and because of the serious financial distress caused by Foley and the planned future sale of the house being built by Foley, the matter was within the purview of A.R.S. § 32-2188. They concede that there are no Arizona cases in point and cite some cases from other jurisdictions which we do not consider controlling.

There is nothing in the record to show that Foley violated the provisions of Ch. 20, Title 32, A.R.S., or the regulations thereunder. As far as we can discern, all Foley's acts were done as a contractor under his contractor's license. The Trial Court correctly denied recovery from the Real Estate Recovery Fund.

Affirmed.

CHAPTER 12

Ethics

REALTORS' CODE OF ETHICS

The National Association of Realtors, like other professional organizations, has a Code of Ethics covering such factors as fair dealings with the public and fellow practitioners, following standards set by the governing body, changes that affect the field, and not engaging in unauthorized practice of law. Many courts have held that ethics can help determine liability or responsibility. The Association issues opinions and Standards of Ethical Practice to interpret and refine the Code.

FAIR AND EQUITABLE

The following case of *MacDonald* v. *Dormaier* illustrates the importance of a real estate broker acting on a fair and equitable basis in all circumstances, whether acting for another or himself. The court clearly states that the statute dealing with real estate brokers and salespeople extends the duty of licensees to fair dealings, whether for other people or for themselves.

The obvious way to avoid the problem in the MacDonald case was to transact the arrangement with full disclosure and fair dealing.

ADDITIONAL DUTIES IMPOSED ON A REAL ESTATE LICENSEE-PURCHASER

Would you consider that a purchaser, who otherwise acted properly, but was also a licensed real estate broker, would be entitled to specific performance if he contracted, as a purchaser, and not as a real estate licensee, to purchase property in a circumstance in which the purchaser modified the terms of the agreement prepared by the seller's counsel? That is, having the right to modify the terms of the contract proposed to the purchaser, the purchaser modified the contract by eliminating a 10-year provision for the purchaser to pay off the balance of the contract. However, assume that the purchaser did not advise the owner of this change and that the owner did not pick this up. Again, assume that there is no fraud involved but simply that the change was made without specifically indicating that change to the seller. The issue is whether this purchaser would be entitled to specific performance under the contract, again assuming no fraud or deceit, and simply weighing the fact that the purchaser is licensed and therefore, arguably, possesses a greater amount of expertise. This issue was examined by the Supreme Court of Oregon in 1975 under the MacDonald case, which follows.

Joseph F. MacDONALD, Appellant,

v.

Fred DORMAIER and Lillian A. Dormaier, Respondents.
Supreme Court of Oregon,
In Banc.
Argued and Submitted at Pendleton
May 5, 1975.
Decided May 22, 1975.

* * *

HOWELL, Justice.

This is a suit for specific performance of an option to purchase ranch property in eastern Oregon. The Trial Court entered a decree in favor of defendant denying plaintiff's request for specific performance, and plaintiff appeals. We affirm.

As Mrs. Dormaier is only a nominal party defendant, we shall refer to Mr. Dormaier as the defendant. Defendant's wheat ranch in Sherman County was heavily mortgaged and for financial reasons he decided to sell a portion. He contacted Carl Joplin, a realtor who was also a good friend, and Joplin introduced him to the plaintiff. Plaintiff had recently moved to Oregon from Washington and was interested in buying and selling property. In January, 1970 plaintiff and defendant executed an earnest money receipt for the sale of the property to plaintiff for $139,000. However, the mortgagee, Travelers Insurance Company, would not agree to the terms of the earnest money receipt, and the transaction failed. Thereafter, other attempts were made to sell defendant's property but they were all unsuccessful.

In April, 1970 plaintiff loaned defendant $20,000 which was to be repaid at $5,000 per year. The loan was secured by a second mortgage. At the same time, defendant gave plaintiff an option to purchase the ranch for $135,000, with $25,000 down and the balance to be payable at "eight thousand dollars or more per annum including interest at 6¾% per annum. Full balance including interest to be cashed out within ten years from date of first payment." (Emphasis supplied).

In early 1972 defendant had paid plaintiff $10,000 on the April, 1970 note. Defendant desired to refinance the real property mortgage and made arrangements with Equitable Life Assurance Society to borrow $55,000 to pay off plaintiff and release the mortgage to Travelers Insurance Company on the ranch. In June, 1972 defendant's attorney prepared a mortgage satisfaction and a quitclaim deed to be executed by plaintiff, plus another option to purchase the property. The latter option was to be recorded after the Equitable mortgage was filed.

The option, like the previous April, 1970 option, provided that if the option was exercised, the balance, after a down payment of $25,000, was to be paid at $8,000 per year or more at 6¾% interest. It also contained the same provision that the entire unpaid balance should be paid not later than 10 years from the date of the down payment. These documents were sent by defendant to plaintiff with directions that they were to be returned to Wasco Title Oregon Ltd. as the escrow agent.

Approximately a week later plaintiff sent a satisfaction of mortgage, a quitclaim deed, and an option to purchase to Wasco Title, who notified defendant to come to its office to sign the documents. The option sent by plaintiff did not contain the clause that the balance must be paid in full not later than 10 years from the time of the down payment. Defendant, without reading all the documents, signed them and the transaction was completed.

When plaintiff attempted to exercise the option, defendant refused, and this suit was instituted.

Approximately a year prior to the transaction and during the time the plaintiff, Joplin, and defendant were negotiating on the sale of the defendant's ranch, the plaintiff acquired a real estate salesman's license in Oregon. He planned to use it in conjunction with Joplin's real estate office. Joplin was interested in having plaintiff in his office "because he bought a lot of land and he sold a lot of land and to me that meant a lot because I knew if his license were hanging in my office, he would have me to do his work for him."

The plaintiff argues, and we agree, that a principal and agency relationship did not exist between plaintiff and defendant because plaintiff, as the owner of the option, was acting in his own behalf and not for defendant. However, this lack of principal-agency relationship does not excuse the plaintiff in this case from a duty of fair dealing with the defendant.

In 1969 the legislature expanded the duty of fair dealing to include not only transactions by the broker or salesman when he is acting for a principal, but also transactions where the broker or salesman is acting in his own behalf. The statute, ORS 696-020(2), states:

"A person who is licensed as a real estate broker or real estate salesman shall be bound by and subject to the requirements of ORS 696-010 to 696.490, 696.610 to 696.730 and 696.990 in doing any of the acts specified by subsection (8) or (9) of ORS 696.010:

"(a) While acting for another; and

"(b) While acting in his own behalf." (Emphasis added.)

Under the provisions of the above statute, the realtor is required to comply with ORS 696.300(q), which proscribes:

"Any act or conduct, whether of the same or a different character than specified above in this section, which constitutes or demonstrates bad faith, incompetency or untrustworthiness, or dishonest, fraudulent or improper dealings."

We completely disagree with plaintiff that the pertinent statutes in Chapter 696 limit the duty of full and fair disclosure only to situations where the realtor is acting as agent for his principal. While the statutes relating to real estate brokers and salesmen make no attempt to prevent such parties from making private transactions with property owners, the legislative history of the 1969 amendment clearly shows that the legislature intended to extend the code of ethics for realtors to situations where the realtor is engaged in private dealings.

A similar case involving the duties of a broker when he is selling his private property was before the Court of Appeals in Blank v. Black, 14 Or. App. 470, 512 P.2d 1016 (1973). The Court stated:

"By statute he is held to a strict fiduciary standard of good faith and fair dealing. ORS 696.300. The 1969 legislature expanded this statute to cover sales and exchanges of the realtor's own property. ORS 696.020(2)(b). The effect of this statutory change was to raise the standard of business conduct of realtors when engaged in selling their own property to the same high standard applicable when they are functioning in transactions between private parties. Thus the 1969 amendment evidences legislative intent to restrict a realtor's right to engage in an arm's length transaction for his own account. The amendment operated to raise the standard of conduct from that applicable to an arm's length caveat emptor transaction between laymen to that applicable to a fiduciary transaction." * * *

We conclude that plaintiff was obligated to advise defendant that he had changed the terms of the option prepared by defendant's counsel by eliminating the 10-year provision for plaintiff to pay off the balance of the contract. It is true that defendant should have read all the documents sent back to him by plaintiff, but plaintiff had the prior and foremost duty to advise defendant that he had changed the terms of the option. Failing to have done so, plaintiff is not entitled to specific performance.

Affirmed.

CHAPTER 13

Advice—Tax and Other

REAL ESTATE TRANSACTIONS

A tangentially related area to the "Realtors' exposure" is to understand, at least in the tax area affecting real estate, the potential exposure for audits affecting Realtors and real estate transactions. A short summary of this area is included in the following pages.

TAX CONSIDERATION FOR THE REALTOR

Another area which can affect the Realtor, especially those dealing in a commercial field, is the field of taxation. When the Realtor is proposing the sale of a substantial property, there obviously can be enormous tax implications.

One area affecting the tax field in recent years has been the concept of a tax-free exchange. Although the intent herein is not to examine in detail tax issues, reference is made to a discussion of this area in *Real Estate Transactions, Tax Planning,* Levine, Mark Lee (West Publishing Co. 1979, as supplemented). The tax issue of a tax-free (deferred) transaction under Code Section 1031 was raised in the Starker case. In summary, this case allowed a deferred tax-free exchange wherein Party B was allowed to exchange certain property to Party C, with the understanding that C, *some time in the future,* would transfer acceptable exchange property to B. The legal or tax issue raised in the case is whether this transaction qualified for a tax-deferred exchange.

The court in 1975 held that this transaction did qualify for a tax-deferred exchange. Subsequently, many people relied on this decision for a similar type of transaction. In 1977 this same court in Oregon held that the prior Starker case, labeled Starker I, was in error, and Starker II would now prohibit that type of activity.

The legal liability issue for the Realtor in this area is the extent of exposure to a Realtor if he promulgated the decision to prospective sellers and buyers. That is, what if the Realtor proposed this type of activity to a prospective party, based on the 1975 decision? Would he be liable as a result of a subsequent reversal of that posture? The Starker cases follow and illustrate this point.

STARKER v. UNITED STATES OF AMERICA (I)
U.S. District Court, Dist. Ore., Civil No. 74-133, 1975.
75-1 USTC para. 9443

* * *

OPINION

SOLOMON, District Judge.

On April 1, 1967, plaintiffs, Bruce and Elizabeth Starker, entered into a "Real Estate Exchange Agreement" with Longview Fibre Company (Longview Fibre). Under this agreement, the Starkers agreed to convey to Longview Fibre certain timberland in Columbia County, Oregon, and Longview Fibre agreed to transfer similar properties to the Starkers in the future.

The Starkers conveyed the land to Longview Fibre on April 28, 1967. Thereafter, a credit for $105,811.00 was entered in Longview Fibre's books in the Starkers' names. This amount was referred to as the "Exchange Value" and was used to compute the amount of property to be transferred to the Starkers by Longview Fibre. The Starkers did not have control over the cash used by Longview Fibre to purchase like-kind properties selected by the Starkers in exchange for their land. Nor did the Starkers have the right under the contract to demand cash in lieu of property. Each year the remaining "Exchange Value" increased six per cent to reflect the increase in value of the Starkers' land which resulted from growing timber.

Although Longview Fibre agreed to convey "from time to time Oregon timberlands or other real estate acceptable to the (Starkers)," before any conveyance would be made by Longview Fibre the parties had to "agree in writing to the value of any such parcel to be conveyed in this exchange to (plaintiffs)." If there was a credit balance in the Starkers' names on or after April 1, 1972, Longview Fibre would have the right to pay in cash the amount of the remaining credit balance to the Starkers.

Longview Fibre conveyed eight different parcels of land to the Starkers during the period 1968-1972; the first conveyance was on October 7, 1968, and the last on January 17, 1972. At the end of the transactions, there was a zero balance and no money was paid to the Starkers.

Also on April 1, 1967, the Starkers entered into a "Land Exchange Agreement with Crown Zellerbach Corporation (Crown Zellerbach). The Crown Zellerbach agreement contained provisions which were almost identical to those in the Longview Fibre agreement. Under it, the Starkers were required to convey to Crown Zellerbach certain timberland located in Columbia County, Oregon. They conveyed the land on May 31, 1967.

A credit for $73,500.00 was entered in Crown Zellerbach's books for the Starkers. This amount, referred to as the "Exchange Value," was to be reduced by the agreed value of the properties which Crown Zellerbach would later convey to the Starkers. Crown Zellerbach conveyed three parcels of land to the Starkers, all in 1967. Their total value equalled the "Exchange Value," and no cash was paid to the Starkers.

In their income tax returns for the year 1967, the Starkers treated both the Longview Fibre and the Crown Zellerbach transfers as tax-exempt transfers under Section 1031 of the Internal Revenue Code (26 U.S.C. § 1031). The I.R.S. concluded that these transactions were not tax exempt and assessed a tax deficiency of $35,248.41. On June 30, 1969, the Starkers paid the deficiency and filed a claim for refund, which the I.R.S. disallowed. The Starkers timely filed this action.

The sole issue is whether Section 1031 of the Internal Revenue Code covers transactions in which a taxpayer disposes of all his rights in property for a promise from the transferee to convey like-kind properties in the future.

In my view, the transfers qualify for non-recognition treatment under Section 1031 of the Internal Revenue Code.

I find that the plaintiffs held the properties which they conveyed to Longview Fibre and Crown Zellerbach for productive use in their trade or business or for investment.

I further find that they exchanged these properties solely for properties of a like kind to be held by them either for productive use in their trade or business or for investment within the meaning of Section 1031(a) of the Internal Revenue Code.

I further find that the plaintiffs did not intend to sell the properties to Longview Fibre or Crown Zellerbach and would not have conveyed the properties to them without an exchange agreement.

I recognize that neither Longview Fibre nor Crown Zellerbach at the time the exchange agreements were executed owned the specific properties which they transferred or conveyed to the plaintiffs. Nevertheless, I do not believe that this lack of ownership prevents plaintiffs from obtaining non-recognition treatment under Section 1031 of the Internal Revenue Code.

There are no decisions directly in point, but in my view *Alderson* v. *United States* (63-2 USTC II 9499), 317 F.2d 790 (9th Cir. 1963) requires this result.

This opinion shall constitute findings of fact and conclusions of law under F. R. Cov, P.52(a).

STARKER v. UNITED STATES OF AMERICA (II)
U.S. District Court, Dist. Ore.,
77-2 USTC

* * *

OPINION

SOLOMON, Judge.

Plaintiff T. J. Starker (plaintiff) filed this action for a tax refund, claiming that he is entitled to non-recognition treatment under 26 U.S.C. § 1031(a), * * * for property transferred to Crown Zellerbach Corporation (Crown).

On April 1, 1967, plaintiff and plaintiff's son and daughter-in-law, Bruce and Elizabeth Starker (Starkers), entered into a Land Exchange Agreement (Agreement) with Crown. In accordance with this Agreement, plaintiff and the Starkers conveyed 1,843 acres of timberland to Crown and Crown entered an "Exchange Value" balance (exchange balance) on its books of $1,502,500 for plaintiff and $73,500 for the Starkers.

Under the Agreement, plaintiff and the Starkers were to locate acceptable parcels of real property which Crown would then buy and convey to them. As each parcel was purchased, the exchange balance was reduced by the purchase price and the acquisition costs.

Plaintiff and the Starkers received an additional credit for a six per cent annual "growth factor" based on the exchange balance remaining on Crown's books at the end of each month. This growth factor was added to the exchange balance.

The Agreement also provided that if there was an exchange balance in favor of the plaintiff or the Starkers after five years, Crown could pay the balance in cash rather than property.

Between July 1967 and May 1969, twelve parcels of property were located by plaintiff. They were acquired by Crown and conveyed to plaintiff. The total value of the twelve parcels was $1,577,387.91.

During the time the twelve parcels were being located and acquired, a six percent growth factor of $74,887.91 was added to plaintiff's exchange balance. Plaintiff did not receive any cash because the exchange balance, including the growth factor, equalled the cost of the twelve parcels.

In 1967, Crown conveyed three parcels of property to the Starkers. The value of these parcels equalled their exchange balance of $73,500, and the Starkers did not receive any cash.

In their income tax returns for 1967, plaintiff and the Starkers treated the transfers to Crown as non-recognition transactions under Section 1031 of the Internal Revenue Code. The Internal Revenue Service (IRS) ruled that the transactions were not tax exempt and assessed a tax deficiency of $300,930.31 plus interest against the plaintiff and $35,248.41 against the Starkers. They paid the deficiencies and filed claims for refunds, which the IRS disallowed.

The Starkers filed an action for a tax refund. Although no case was directly in point, on May 1, 1975, I held that under *Alderson* v. *United States* (63-2 USTA ¶ 9499), 317 F.2d 790 (9th Cir. 1963), the transfer was entitled to non-recognition treatment. The government appealed, but the appeal was voluntarily dismissed and the Starkers received their refund.

On January 26, 1976, plaintiff filed this action for tax refund of $363,758.79.

Contentions

Plaintiff contends that the transaction here qualifies for non-recognition treatment under Section 1031. He also contends that the government is collaterally estopped from litigating this issue because of my decision in *Starker* v. *United States,* 75-1 USTC ¶ 87,142 (D. Or.) (Civil No. 74-133, April 23, 1975) (Starker I).

In the alternative plaintiff contends that in 1967 the unfulfilled obligations of Crown did not have a fair market value, and therefore gain may be recognized only to the extent that cash or other property received in 1967 exceeded plaintiff's basis. * * *

Conclusions

Section 1031 was enacted to defer recognition of gain or loss when a taxpayer makes a direct exchange of property with another party. * * *

In Starker I, I held that the taxpayers were entitled to non-recognition treatment under § 1031 because I believed that *Alderson* v. *United States* (63-2 USTA ¶ 9499), 317 F.2d 790 (9th Cir. 1963), required this result. I realized that Alderson was not directly in point, but, at the time, I thought that the reasoning of Alderson required that result.

This case raises issues which were not raised in Starker I. Here, unlike Starker I, Crown transferred property to third persons, such as plaintiff's daughter, Jean S. Roth. In Starker I, the government argued that there was no exchange because there was no simultaneous transfer of property between Crown and the Starkers. Here, the government also argues that there is no like-kind exchange because plaintiff transferred his property in return for a promise which is the equivalent of cash.

Nevertheless, I recognize that many of the transfers here are identical to those in Starker I.

Plaintiff contends that the government is estopped from litigating whether his transfer to Crown qualifies for non-recognition treatment under § 1031 because of Starker I.

I have reconsidered my opinion in Starker I. I now conclude that I was mistaken in my holding as well as in my earlier reading of Alderson. Even if Alderson can be interpreted as contended by plaintiff, I think that to do so would be improper. It would merely sanction a tax avoidance scheme and not carry out the purposes of § 1031. * * *

Here, plaintiff did not make either a reciprocal or a simultaneous exchange. He transferred all of his rights in the timberland to Crown in return for a promise, here called an exchange balance. At the time of the transfer, Crown did not own any of the twelve parcels which Crown either transferred or caused to be transferred to plaintiff or to plaintiff's nominees. When plaintiff made the Agreement, he did not know whether he would find acceptable property to exchange for his property or whether he would eventually be paid in cash.

Plaintiff makes much of the fact that the Agreement recites that he would be paid in cash only at Crown's option. I think this provision was not made in good faith and that it was inserted solely to make the transaction appear as an exchange and not a sale.

Plaintiff seeks to expand the definition of "exchange" to include not only reciprocal transfers, but also transactions in which the taxpayer transfers his property in return for a promise that he will receive like-kind property in the future.

When residential property is sold or exchanged for other residential property within one year, the gain is given non-recognition treatment to sales and reinvestment transactions in the limited circumstances specified in §§ 1033 and 1034. * * *

Section 1031 is in marked contrast to §§ 1033 and 1034. If Congress had intended to give non-recognition treatment to a taxpayer who disposed of a business or investment property for later acquired property of a like kind, it would have included sale and reinvestment provisions in § 1031. It would have used "sale or exchange" rather than "exchange" alone. Plaintiff ignores this distinction and reads both a sale and reinvestment provisions into § 1031.

I find that plaintiff exchanged his property for a promise to convey like-kind property in the future, and I hold that Plaintiff's transfer to Crown does not qualify for non-recognition treatment under § 1031. * * *

The Agreement provided that plaintiff would be paid a growth factor of six per cent on the exchange balance and that this growth factor was to be added to the exchange balance "at the time of the last offsetting charge to (the plaintiff)."

In my view, the term "growth factor" was used in the Agreement to conceal the true nature of the transaction. It was really interest and should be taxed as ordinary income.

Crown filed a Form 1099 for 1969 which reported $74,887.91 in interest paid to the plaintiff. Plaintiff argues that even if the growth factor is interest, it is taxable in 1969 because Crown reported it as interest in that year and because the Agreement provides that the growth factor is to be added to the exchange balance at the time of the last offsetting charge. * * *

In spite of this report and the provision in the Agreement, the parties themselves treated these payments as having been received in 1967. The books show that interest was calculated on a daily basis, and $56,182.72 was credited to plaintiff's account in 1967. Crown kept a running total of the growth factor on its books under the heading "interest." When Crown purchased the exchange properties for the plaintiff, the purchase price of each parcel was first subtracted from the accrued interest. The principal was reduced only to the extent that the interest was insufficient to cover the cost of the property. This arrangement was advantageous to plaintiff because it permitted plaintiff to get additional interest.

The government is therefore entitled to a judgment dismissing plaintiff's action. * * *

Here, plaintiff urges me to reconsider my holding on collateral estoppel. He asserts that even if I was wrong, I cannot change my holding and that the Government is collaterally estopped. Plaintiff was not a party to the Starker I action. Even if he was, I do not believe that the authorities require a finding of collateral estopped.

My opinion in Starker I has been given wide publicity. I believe that it is desirable that my opinion in this case be published to prevent the mischief which I believe Starker I has caused. I therefore propose to publish the opinion immediately.

I have prepared and signed a judgment dismissing plaintiff's action.

INSTALLMENT SALES—MORTGAGE IN EXCESS OF BASIS

Your client has recently approached you and asked if it might be possible for him to make a sale of his property on what he has heard is the installment sale basis under Code Section 453. He understands that this section allows the sale of property with the concomitant inclusion of gain in the year, proportionately, as it is received. In the transaction contemplated, the sales price is $100,000. The client tells you his basis or cost as adjusted in the property is $20,000. He also tells you he has a mortgage on the property of $30,000. He tells you that he would like to sell the property and postpone part of the gain as he collects the payments, over time.*

You found a purchaser for the property who was willing to pay $30,000 in cash and assume the existing mortgage. He would also give your client a second mortgage. The legal question that is asked of you is whether this transaction will qualify for an installment sale.

(Keep in mind that the mortgage in the example given is $30,000, but your client's basis is only $20,000.)*

When deciding this case, you might want to note that there have been earlier decisions allowing the type of transaction described to qualify as an installment sale where the purchaser, using the figures given, paid $30,000 in cash and gave the seller a mortgage for $70,000. He did not assume the existing first mortgage nor take subject to the same. See Stonecrest and United Pacific. Advise your client, and afterwards, consider the implications of the following Voight case.

* Note: To qualify for § 453, the Seller cannot receive more than 30% of the sales price in the year of sale. The rule is that a mortgage in excess of basis ($30,000 is $10,000 "in excess" of $20,000) results in the excess treated as a payment in the year of sale.

FLOYD J. VOIGHT
68.10 P-H TC

* * *

Official Tax Court Syllabus

(1) Petitioners sold real property, the mortgages on which exceeded petitioners' adjusted basis, under an installment contract. The purchaser guaranteed payment of the mortgages to the mortgagee but did not expressly assume the mortgages. Pursuant to an option granted in the contract, the purchaser paid the part of the selling price attributable to the mortgage directly to the mortgagee. Held, the purchaser assumed the mortgages within the meaning of section 1.453-4(c), Income Tax Regs., with the result that payments in the year of sale included the excess of the mortgages over the petitioners' adjusted basis. *Stonecrest Corp.* v. *Commissioner,* 24 T.C. 659 (1955), distinguished.

SCOTT, Judge: Respondent determined deficiencies in petitioners' Federal income tax. * * *

FINDINGS OF FACT

Some of the facts have been stipulated and are found accordingly.

Petitioners Floyd J. Voight and Marion C. Voight, husband and wife as of the end of calendar years 1968 and 1969, filed joint Federal income tax returns for those years with either the District Director, Internal Revenue Service, Milwaukee, Wisconsin or the Director, Internal Revenue Service Center, Kansas City, Missouri. Petitioners Floyd J. Voight and C. Lorraine Perk Voight, husband and wife as of the end of calendar years 1970 and 1971, filed joint Federal income tax returns for those years with the Director, Internal Revenue Service Center, Chamblee, Georgia. * * * At the time of filing the petitions in these cases, consolidated here for trial and opinion, all petitioners resided in Palm Beach, Florida.

In 1968, petitioner Floyd J. Voight owned certain real property and leasehold improvements in Madison, Wisconsin. Most of this property was operated as a Holiday Inn motel, and the rest was land adjoining the motel. The leasehold improvements were constructed on land leased from a trust of which Mr. Voight's children were the beneficiaries. Prior to 1968, petitioner's property was owned by a corporation, HIM, Inc., of which petitioner was an officer.

In 1968, Mr. Voight determined to sell the Holiday Inn and the adjoining property (hereinafter referred to as the Holiday Inn property) in anticipation of his retirement and move to Florida. He found a buyer, Madison Motor Inn, Inc., a subsidiary of General Management Corporation. However, he encountered some difficulty in arranging the sale. The property was subject to three mortgages held by First Federal Savings and Loan Association of Wisconsin (hereinafter referred to as First Federal) totaling $1,136,698.72 on October 1, 1968. Petitioner's adjusted basis in the property on October 1, 1968, was $625,696.22. Petitioner wanted to report the gain on the sale of the property under the installment method, and he believed that selling by means of a contract for deed was the only way that would allow him to do so in these circumstances.

On October 1, 1968, petitioners Floyd J. Voight and his then wife Marion C. Voight entered into an agreement with Madison Motor Inn, Inc. (Madison) and its parent, General Management Corporation (General), for sale to Madison of the Holiday Inn property. * * *

OPINION

Petitioners sold real property in 1968 under a contract providing for payment to be made in monthly installments over a period of several years and providing for title to be delivered at the end of that period. Petitioners elected to report the gain realized on this sale under the installment method provided by section 453(b). The controversy here arises from the fact that at the time of the sale the property was encumbered by three mortgages the unpaid balances of which exceeded petitioners' adjusted basis in the property.

Section 453(a) * * * provides that certain sellers of personal property on the installment plan may return as income from the sale of such property in any year the proportion of the payments actually received in that year that the gross profit on the sale bears to the total contract price. This treatment is extended to sale of real property in section 453(b) * * * if any payments in the year of sale do not exceed 30 percent of the selling price. The parties here disagree over whether petitioners received payments in the year of sale exceeding this 30 percent limitation. Petitioners assert that the only payments received were cash payments totaling $35,814.95. Respondent determined that, in addition to these cash payments, petitioners received a payment in the year of sale equal to the excess of the mortgages over the adjusted basis of the property, an amount equal to $511,002.50.

Although section 453 does not expressly provide any special treatment for sales of mortgaged property, respondent's regulations provide in part:

> (c) Determination of "selling price." In the sale of mortgaged property the amount of the mortgage, whether the property is merely taken subject to the mortgage or whether the mortgage is assumed by the purchaser, shall, for the purpose of determining whether a sale is on the installment plan, be included as a part of the "selling price"; and for the purpose of determining the payments and the total contract price as those terms are used in section 453, and section 1.453-1 through 1.453-7, the amount of such mortgage shall be included only to the extent that it exceeds the basis of the property. The terms "payments" does not include amounts received by the vendor in the year of sale from the disposition to a third person of notes given by the vendee as part of the purchase price which are due and payable in subsequent years. Commissions and other selling expenses paid or incurred by the vendor shall not reduce the amount of the payments, the total contract price, or the selling price. (Emphasis added.)

Respondent's regulation is not applicable to all sales of mortgaged property, however. By its terms, it applies only where the mortgage is assumed or where property is taken subject to the mortgage. *Stonecrest Corp.* v. *Commissioner,* 24 T.C. 659.666 (1955). See also *Estate of Lamberth* v. *Commissioner,* 31 T.C. 302, 314 (1958); *United Pacific Corp.* v. *Commissioner,* 39 T.C. 721 (1963).

In *Stonecrest Corp.* v. *Commissioner,* supra, this Court held that the expressions used in the regulation, "property is merely taken subject to the mortgage" and "mortgage is assumed by the purchaser," have the meanings customarily attributed to them in transactions involving transfer of mortgaged property. * * *

In our view, we need not decide whether under state law the provisions of these documents, considered as a whole result in a technical assumption of the mortgages by the purchaser. We have previously held that the absence of a formal promise to assume the mortgage in the documents executed does not negate the existence of an assumption when all the facts and circumstances surrounding the transaction show an intent of the parties that the mortgage be assumed by the purchaser. * * *

While the transaction before this Court was not an assumption in form, we have found that all elements of an assumption, as that term is customarily understood, were present either in the express agreements or implied understandings of the parties. The sellers had a right to receive only the amount of their equity or redemption interest, the buyer was obligated to both the seller and the mortgagee to pay the mortgage payments, and the mortgage payments were in fact made directly to the mortgagee by the buyer. On this basis, Madison assumed the First Federal mortgages within the meaning of respondent's regulation. * * * Therefore, petitioners must include in payments in the year of sale the excess of the mortgage balances over their adjusted basis in the property. Because this amount exceeds 30 percent of the selling price of the property, petitioners are not entitled to use the installment method of reporting their gain under section 453. * * *

See *Real Estate Taxation, Problems and Clauses,* by Mark Lee Levine, published by Professional Publications and Education, Inc. (1979).

CHAPTER 14

Litigation

DISCOVERY

Privilege and Disclosure. The importance of the Realtor's working with a CPA and attorney, along with his client, emphasizes the need to know the protection of records and testimony that may exist if the government seeks these confidential recordings and information which may affect tax matters in which the Realtor was and is involved.

The Realtor must also be cognizant of the rules which allow the government to call the Realtor as a witness. The Realtor generally will not be able to refuse to testify. No privilege will exist. The Realtor's records can be examined by the government. Therefore, the Realtor should be concerned that his records adequately support the position of the client, consistent with the transaction.

Discovery, Privilege, and the Realtor. In the area of tax, there is the problem with the exposure to the taxpayers' records by the government, and the potential acquisition of records affecting the taxpayer-Realtor that may be held by the Realtors' agents, such as a CPA or attorney. There is further concern to the extent that records are held by the Realtor for the client of the Realtor.

In particular, the issue raised at this point is to review the possibility of the Internal Revenue Service, or other arms of the government, acquiring records held by the parties noted. If, for example, the Realtor has discussed a tax position with his agent, the CPA or attorney, and such discussion involves at least a borderline case so far as the current legal position on the deductibility of an item, the treatment of an item as a capital gain, whether it constitutes a tax-deferred exchange, the use of an involuntary conversion

(§ 1033), whether an item will qualify for an installment sale, or similar problems, it is clear the Realtor would prefer not to have these records obtained by the government.

A good example might be the previously discussed Starker decision or that of Voight. The Starker case dealt with the deferred exchange concept, and the Voight case covered the issue of a mortgage in excess of basis where a wrap around would be used to avoid the excess of basis rule, or attempt to do so (see Chapter 13). Once again, the issue raised is whether these records can be obtained by the government and the damage that might follow if the same were obtained.

The following material emphasizes the potential for discovery of these items and the potential of any defenses that might be raised by the taxpayer or other parties involved. For example, there is a review and examination of a concept, such as privilege, which may exist between a taxpayer and his attorney, the rights under the Fourth Amendment as to reasonable search and seizure, the right of due process and related rights under the Fifth and Fourteenth Amendments, the right to counsel under the Sixth Amendment, and so forth. Although the cases may involve CPAs, attorneys, or others who are not Realtors, the principles are generally applicable and important to Realtors.

Privilege. The doctrine of privilege, that is, certain information that cannot be obtained, in this case by the government, arises in many fields. For example, the law has established the importance of a privilege between a doctor and his patient, the clergy and the member of the congregation, and the accountant and his client. Although the concept of privilege does not apply in many situations, as the following cases illustrate, it is clear that no state has passed any statute that allows the Realtor, in that capacity, and not in the capacity as an attorney or otherwise, to assert a privilege or to have the client assert the privilege on behalf of records held by the Realtor. Likewise, there has been no case discovered by this author that allows the client to prohibit the testimony of the Realtor on confidential matters.

The theoretical support for privilege is to allow the *confidential* relations to take place. Without it, the potential criminal would be hesitant to discuss his case with his attorney, and therefore the attorney could not adequately prepare a defense for his client. On the other hand, the general rule in the courts is to allow evidence in so that the courts may weigh the facts available and make the determination, along with the jury who may be present with regard to factual issues. Since the concept of privilege is incongruous with the doctrine of free support of and allowance in of evidence, the privilege concept is often narrowly construed. It is clear that the privilege rule or doctrine has not been extended in many jurisdictions and will not exist in many circumstances, once again as illustrated by the cases.

In particular, you will notice from the cases that the privilege does not exist with a CPA and his client on the federal level. Some states, approximately one third, have a limited privilege concept with a CPA and his client. Following this discussion is an example of one statute that allows for the privilege on a state basis. However, once again the privilege concept is very restricted with the accountant and client, and therefore it is important to recognize limitations of the argument of privilege in a given state and that it does not exist on the federal level.

The importance of this position so far as the Realtor is concerned is to emphasize the reluctance that must exist when disclosing confidential information to an accountant. This is not to say that the accountant does not need to be informed and that the accountant is not capable of giving the best tax advice available. The fact is that if there is damaging information the client would not desire to have come forth in court, the Realtor/client must be aware of this limitation, and the Realtor must be aware of this rule so far as the clients that may be referred by the Realtor to a CPA in the event that the case may come to court.

Most sophisticated accountants are well aware of the limitations on the privilege, and therefore if a criminal issue arises or may arise, a good accountant, properly informed, will take steps to encourage the client to talk with an attorney and to hold confidential disclosures on this issue to the relationship between the attorney and the client.

Incidentally, you will see from the cases that follow that even the privilege between the attorney and the client is becoming more and more limited on the federal level. The cases that follow, Couch, Bellis, Kasmir, Fisher, Miller and Andresen, illustrate many of the concepts that have been discussed above.

RECORDS AND THE FIFTH AMENDMENT

Suppose that recently you performed work for a client. The records and your papers are in your possession. You were served with a *subpoena duces tecum* (a command to appear with certain papers) which ordered you to turn over the client's records to the government. Are you required to turn over these records? Might you assert a privilege between Realtor and his client? The case follows: *Couch* v. *U.S.,* 409 U.S. 322 (1973), dealing with a CPA.

Lillian V. COUCH, Petitioner,
v.
UNITED STATES and Edward F. Jennings, etc.
409 U.S. 322, 34 L.Ed.2d 548
Decided Jan. 9, 1973.
Syllabus*

Petitioners challenge an Internal Revenue Service (IRS) summons directing an accountant, an independent contractor with numerous clients, to produce business records that she had been giving to him for preparation of her tax returns from 1955 to 1968, when the summons was issued. The District Court and the Court of Appeals concluded that the privilege against self-incrimination asserted by petitioners was not available. Held: On the facts of this case, where petitioners had effectively surrendered possession of the records to the accountant, there was no personal compulsion against petitioners to produce the records. The Fifth Amendment therefore constitutes no bar to their production by the accountant, even though the IRS tax investigation may entail possible criminal as well as civil consequences. Nor does petitioner, who was aware that much of the information in the records had to be disclosed in her tax returns, have any legitimate expectation of privacy that would bar production under either the Fourth or Fifth Amendment. Pp. 613-618.
    449 F.2d 141, affirmed.
    John G. Rocovich, Jr., Roanoke, Va., for petitioner.
    Lawrence G. Wallace, Washington, D.C., for respondents.
    Mr. Justice POWELL delivered the opinion of the Court.
    On January 7, 1970, the Government filed a petition in the United States District Court for the Western District of Virginia, pursuant to 26 U.S.C. §§ 7402(b) and 7604(a), seeking enforcement of an Internal Revenue summons in connection with an investigation of petitioner's tax liability from 1964-1968. The summons was directed to petitioner's accountant for the production of:

*** The syllabus constitutes no part of the opinion of the Court but has been prepared by the Reporter of Decisions for the convenience of the reader.

"All books, records, bank statements, cancelled checks, deposit ticket copies, workpapers and all other pertinent documents pertaining to the tax liability of the above taxpayer."

The question is whether the taxpayer may invoke her Fifth Amendment privilege against compulsory self-incrimination to prevent the production of her business and tax records in the possession of her accountant. Both the District Court and the Court of Appeals for the Fourth Circuit held the privilege unavailable. We granted certiorari.

Petitioner is the sole proprietress of a restaurant. Since 1955 she had given bank statements, payroll records, and reports of sales and expenditures to her accountant, Harold Shaffer, for the purpose of preparing her income tax returns. The accountant was not petitioner's personal employee but an independent contractor with his own office and numerous other clients who compensated him on a piecework basis. When petitioner surrendered possession of the records to Shaffer, she, of course, retained title in herself.

During the summer of 1969, Internal Revenue Agent Dennis Grove commenced an investigation of petitioner's tax returns. After examining her books and records in Shaffer's office with his permission, Groves found indications of a substantial understatement of gross income. Groves thereupon reported the case to the Intelligence Division of the Internal Revenue Service.

Special Agent Jennings of the Intelligence Division next commenced a joint investigation with Groves to determine petitioner's correct tax liability, the possibility of income tax fraud and the imposition of tax fraud penalties, and, lastly, the possibility of a recommendation of a criminal tax violation. Jennings first introduced himself to petitioner, gave her Miranda warnings as required by IRS directive, and then issued the summons to Shaffer after the latter refused to let him see, remove, or microfilm petitioner's records.

When Jennings arrived at Shaffer's office on September 2, 1969, the return day of the summons, to view the records, he found that Shaffer, at petitioner's request, had delivered the documents to petitioner's attorney. Jennings thereupon petitioned the District Court for enforcement of the summons, and petitioner intervened, asserting that the ownership of the records warranted a Fifth Amendment privilege to bar their production.

I

It is now undisputed that a special agent is authorized, pursuant to 26 U.S.C. § 7602, to issue an Internal Revenue summons in aid of a tax investigation with civil and possible criminal consequences.

II

The importance of preserving inviolate the privilege against compulsory self-incrimination has often been stated by this Court and need not be elaborated.

It is important to reiterate that the Fifth Amendment privilege is a personal privilege: it adheres basically to the person, not to information that may incriminate him. As Mr. Justice Holmes put it: "A party is privileged from producing the evidence, but not from its production." *Johnson* v. *United States,* 228 U.S. 457, 458, 33 S.Ct. 572, 57 L.Ed. 919 (1913). The Constitution explicitly prohibits compelling an accused to bear witness "against himself": it necessarily does not proscribe incrimi-

nating statements elicited from another. Compulsion upon the person asserting it is an important element of the privilege, and "prohibition of
compelling a man . . . to be witness against himself is a prohibition of
the use of physical or moral compulsion to extort communications from
him."

In the case before us the ingredient of personal compulsion against an
accused is lacking. The summons and the order of the District Court enforcing it are directed against the accountant. He, not the taxpayer, is the
only one compelled to do anything. And the accountant makes no claim
that he may tend to be incriminated by the production. Inquisitorial pressure or coercion against a potentially accused person, compelling her,
against her will, to utter self-condemning words or produce incriminating
documents is absent. In the present case, no "shadow of testimonial compulsion upon or enforced communication by the accused" is involved.

The divulgence of potentially incriminating evidence against petitioner
is naturally unwelcome. But petitioner's distress would be no less if the
divulgence came not from her accountant but from some other third
party with whom she was connected and she possessed substantially equivalent knowledge of her business affairs. The basic complaint of petitioner
stems from the fact of divulgence of the possibly incriminating information, not from the manner in which or the person from whom it was extracted. Yet such divulgence, where it does not result from coercion of
the suspect herself, is a necessary part of the process of law enforcement
and tax investigation.

III

Petitioner argues, nevertheless, that grave prejudice will result from a
denial of her claim to equate ownership and the scope of the privilege.
She alleges that "(i)f the IRS is able to reach her records the instant those
records leave her hands and are deposited in the hands of her retainer
whom she has hired for a special purpose then the meaning of the privilege is lost." That is not, however, the import of today's decision. We do
indeed believe that actual possession of documents bears the most significant relationship to Fifth Amendment protections against governmental
compulsions upon the individual accused of crime. Yet situations may
well arise where constructive possession is so clear or the relinquishment
of posession is so temporary and insignificant as to leave the personal
compulsions upon the accused substantially intact. But this is not the case
before us. Here there was no mere fleeting divestment of possession: the
records had been given to this accountant regularly since 1955 and remained in his continuous possession until the summer of 1969 when the
summons was issued. Moreover, the accountant himself worked neither
in petitioner's office nor as her employee. The length of his possession of
the petitioner's records and his independent status confirm the belief that

petitioner's divestment of possession was of such a character as to disqualify her entirely as an object of any impermissible Fifth Amendment compulsion.

IV

Petitioner further argues that the confidential nature of the accountant-client relationship and her resulting expectation of privacy in delivering the records protect her, under the Fourth and Fifth Amendments, from their production. Although not in itself controlling, we note that no confidential accountant-client privilege exists under federal law, and no state-created privilege has been recognized in federal cases. Nor is there justification for such a privilege where records relevant to income tax returns are involved in a criminal investigation or prosecution. There can be little expectation of privacy where records are handed to an accountant, knowing that mandatory disclosure of much of the information therein is required in an income tax return. What information is not disclosed is largely in the accountant's discretion, not petitioner's. Indeed, the accountant himself risks criminal prosecution if he willfully assists in the preparation of a false return. 26 U.S.C. § 7206(e). His own need for self-protection would often require the right to disclose the information given him. Petitioner seeks extensions of constitutional protections against self-incrimination in the very situation where obligations of disclosure exist and under a system largely dependent upon honest self-reporting even to survive. Accordingly, petitioner here cannot reasonably claim, either for Fourth or Fifth Amendment purposes, an expectation of protected privacy or confidentiality.

V

The criterion for Fifth Amendment immunity remains not the ownership of property but the "physical or moral compulsion exerted." We hold today that no Fourth or Fifth Amendment claim can prevail where, as in this case, there exists no legitimate expectation of privacy and no semblance of governmental compulsion against the person of the accused. It is important, in applying constitutional principles, to interpret them in light of the fundamental interests of personal liberty they were meant to serve. Respect for these principles is eroded when they leap their proper bounds to interfere with the legitimate interest of society in enforcement of its laws and collection of the revenues.

The judgment of the Court of Appeals is affirmed.

Judgment affirmed.

Mr. Justice BRENNAN, concurring.

Mr. Justice MARSHALL, dissenting.

PARTNERSHIP RECORDS

Suppose that recently you and two other members of your partnership agreed to dissolve the firm. The partnership records are now in your office. During the windup, you are served with a summons which orders you to produce the partnership records to a grand jury for a federal investigation. Because of what you consider a privilege for the records you hold for yourself and your partners, you have decided not to produce the records under the support of the Fifth Amendment privilege against self-incrimination.

Would you be successful on this issue? What grounds would support or not support your position? The case follows: *Bellis* v. *U.S.*

BELLIS v. UNITED STATES
Opinion of the Court
BELLIS v. UNITED STATES
CERTIORARI TO THE UNITED STATES COURT OF APPEALS FOR THE THIRD CIRCUIT
Mr. JUSTICE MARSHALL delivered the opinion of the Court.

The question presented in this case is whether a partner in a small law firm may invoke his personal privilege against self-incrimination to justify his refusal to comply with subpoena requiring production of the partnership's financial records.

Opinion of the Court

Until 1969, petitioner Isadore Bellis was the senior partner in Bellis, Kolsby & Wolf, a law firm in Philadelphia. The firm was formed in 1955 or 1956. There were three partners in the firm, the three individuals listed in the firm name. In addition, the firm had six employees: two other attorneys who were associated with the firm, one part-time; three secretaries; and a receptionist. Petitioner's secretary doubled as the partnership's bookkeeper, under the direction of petitioner and the firm's independent accountant. The firm's financial records were therefore maintained in petitioner's office during his tenure at the firm.

Bellis left the firm in late 1969 to join another law firm. The partnership was dissolved, although it is apparently still in the process of winding up its affairs. Kolsby and Wolf continued in practice together as a new partnership, at the same premises. Bellis moved to new offices, leaving the former partnership's financial records with Kolsby and Wolf, where they remained for more than three years. In February or March

1973, however, shortly before issuance of the subpoena in this case, petitioner's secretary, acting at the direction of petitioner or his attorney, removed the records from the old premises and brought them to Bellis' new office.

On May 1, 1973, Bellis was served with a subpoena directing him to appear and testify before a federal grand jury and to bring with him "all partnership records currently in your possession for the partnership of Bellis, Kolsby & Wolf for the years 1968 and 1969." App. 6. Petitioner appeared on May 9, but refused to produce the records, claiming, inter alia, his Fifth Amendment privilege, against compulsory self-incrimination. After a hearing before the District Court on May 9 and 10, the court held that the petitioner's personal privilege did not extend to the partnership's financial books and records, and ordered their production by May 16. When petitioner reappeared before the grand jury on that date and again refused to produce the subpoenaed records, the District Court held him in civil contempt, and released him on his own recognizance pending an expedited appeal.

On July 9, 1973, the Court of Appeals affirmed in a per curiam opinion, stated that "the privilege has always been regarded as personal in the sense that it applies only to an individual's words or personal papers" and thus held that the privilege against self-incrimination did not apply to "records of an entity such as a partnership which has a recognizable juridical existence apart from its members." 483 F.2d, at 962. After MR. JUSTICE WHITE had stayed the mandate of the Court of Appeals on August 1, we granted certiorari, 414 U.S. 907 (1973), to consider this interpretation of the Fifth Amendment privilege and the applicability of our White decision in the circumstances of this case. We affirm.

It has long been established, of course, that the Fifth Amendment privilege against compulsory self-incrimination protects an individual from compelled production of his personal papers and effects as well as compelled oral testimony. In Boyd v. United States, 116 U.S. 616 (1886), we held that "any forcible and compulsory extortion of a man's own testimony or of his private papers to be used as evidence to convict him of crime" would violate the Fifth Amendment privilege. The privilege applies to the business records of the sole proprietor or sole practitioner as well as to personal documents containing more intimate information about the individual's private life. As the Court explained in *United States* v. *White,* "(t)he constitutional privilege against self-incrimination . . . is designed to prevent the use of legal process to force from the lips of the accused individual the evidence necessary to convict him or to force him to produce and authenticate any personal documents or effects that might incriminate him."

On the other hand, an equally long line of cases has established that an individual cannot rely upon the privilege to avoid producing the records of a collective entity which are in his possession in a representative capacity, even if these records might incriminate him personally.

To some extent, these decisions were based upon the particular incidents of the corporate firm, the Court observing that a corporation has limited powers granted to it by the State in its charter, and is subject to the retained "visitorial power" of the State to investigate its activities. See, e.g., *Wilson* v. *United States,* supra, at 382-385. But any thought that the principle formulated in these decisions was limited to corporate records was put to rest in *United States* v. *White,* supra.

These decisions reflect the Court's consistent view that the privilege against compulsory self-incrimination should be "limited to its history function of protecting only the natural individual from compulsory incrimination through his own testimony or personal records."

Since no artificial organization may utilize the personal privilege against compulsory self-incrimination, the Court found that it follows that an individual acting in his official capacity on behalf of the organization may likewise not take advantage of his personal privilege.

The Court's decisions holding the privilege inapplicable to the records of a collective entity also reflect a second, though obviously interrelated policy underlying the privilege, the protection of an individual's right to a " 'private enclave where he may lead a private life.' "

Partnerships may and frequently do represent organized institutional activity so as to preclude any claim of Fifth Amendment privilege with respect to the partnership's financial records.

Despite the force of these arguments, we conclude that the lower courts properly applied the White rule in the circumstances of this case. While small, the partnership here did have an established institutional identity independent of its individual partners. This was not an informal association or a temporary arrangement for the undertaking of a few projects of short-lived duration.

Equally important, we believe it is fair to say that petitioner is holding the subpoenaed partnership records in a representative capacity. The documents which petitioner has been ordered to produce are merely the financial books and records of the partnership.

This might be a different case if it involved a small family partnership, if there were some other pre-existing relationship of confidentiality among the partners. But in the circumstances of this case, petitioner's possession of the partnership's financial records in what can be fairly said to be a representative capacity compels our holding that his personal privilege against compulsory self-incrimination is inapplicable.

Affirmed.

MR. JUSTICE DOUGLAS, dissenting.

SUBPOENA DUCES TECUM

Suppose you have received a *subpoena duces tecum* for a deposition you must give regarding a client. Can you be forced to reveal your work papers at this deposition (under Ohio law)? See *Ex Parte* Frye, 98 N.E.2d 798, 155 Ohio St. 345 (1951), which follows:

Ex Parte FRYE.
Supreme Court of Ohio
1955 Ohio St. 345
May 2, 1951

In November 1948 Raymond J. Saile instituted an action against Meridian Plastics, Inc., hereinafter called Meridian, in the Common Pleas Court of Guernsey County, which action is still pending, Saile was a sales agent employed by the defendant. In the first cause of action set out in his petition he alleges that a certain amount of money is due him as commissions earned under a contract with Meridian to be computed on a percentage basis on all sales of merchandise made by Meridian to distributors established by him and on all sales made by him directly to retail outlets. In the second case of action he alleges there is due him from Meridian on a quantum meruit basis a certain amount of money.

Saile in the prosecution of that action served a subpoena duces tecum on Marion A. Frye, a resident of Lorain county, a certified public accountant and auditor for Meridian, to appear before a notary public in Cuyahoga county for the purpose of giving testimony. She is not a party to that action.

The material part of the subpoena reads as follows: "Please bring with you all records or copies of records in your possession relating to the financial condition or operation of Meridian Plastics, Inc., from the date of its organization to the present day; including copies of all * * * tax returns, state or federal * * *."

Upon receiving notice of the taking of Frye's deposition and before it was taken, counsel for Meridian filed a motion for an injunction, as follows: "Now comes the defendant and moves the court that the plaintiff or his attorneys be enjoined from taking the deposition of Marion A. Frye which deposition is scheduled for hearing on the 16th day of December, 1948, at 10 a.m. * * *."

That motion was overruled, whereupon Meridian perfected an appeal to the Court of Appeals for Guernsey County, and that court, in January 1949, affirmed the judgment of the Common Pleas Court.

In a written opinion, that court, in part, said: "It would be impossible for this court in advance to know what questions would be asked or what answers might be given by said witness. We do not know whether they would be incompetent or irrelevant. This court cannot speculate on these matters, and in the final analysis the competency or relevancy of the testimony must be determined by the trial judge."

No appeal was taken from the judgment of the Court of Appeals, and the time for such appeal has expired.

On February 7, 1949, Saile, pursuant to the subpoena theretofore served, proceeded to take the deposition of Frye, he and Meridian each being represented by counsel. Frye was not represented generally by counsel. She testified, without objection, that she had been Meridian's auditor since its organization; and that she had present the papers called for by the subpoena and had her work sheets covering the account of Saile as to the commissions owing to him from Meridian for the years 1946, 1947. She submitted them to be marked as exhibits in connection with her testimony. In all, 30 exhibits, consisting of examination reports on the books of the company, financial statements and commission statements, were identified by the witness.

The taking of the deposition was adjourned until February 14, 1949, for the purpose of having photostats made, when Frye appears with her own counsel who objected to the introduction in evidence as a part of the deposition Frye's personal work sheets or photostatic replicas thereof.

On that date, on examination of Frye by her own counsel, she testified that she was not an officer or employee of Meridian, but did work for it as an independent contractor in the capacity of auditor; that she had no records which belonged to Meridian; that the records which she had previously identified were her own personal records; and that when she made up the tax returns for the company she gave it the originals and copies for its files and the company did the filing.

Counsel for Frye then stated that he refused to permit either the original work sheets or the photostatic copies to be made a part of the deposition. Upon Frye's refusal to surrender the exhibits which had previously been identified by her, she was placed under technical arrest and technically committed to jail by the sheriff of Cuyahoga county.

A petition for a writ of habeas corpus for the release of Frye was filed in the Common Pleas Court of Cuyahoga County. The issues were made up by the submission of an agreed statement of facts by counsel for Saile and Frye.

The stipulation covered a copy of the petition in the Saile action, a copy of a motion for injunction, the appeal proceedings in the Court of Appeals for Guernsey County, a copy of the opinion of the Court of Appeals, a copy of the journal entry of the Court of Appeals affirming the judgment of the Common Pleas Court, a copy of the transcript of the deposition, in which Frye substantiated the fact that plaintiff's exhibits

1 through 30 were her work sheets and copies of her reports made as auditor of Meridian, a copy of the articles of commitment of Frye by the notary public and a statement that the taking of the deposition, the subpoena of the witness, the attendance of the witness and the taking of her testimony were all in conformance to law.

Frye was discharged from custody by the Common Pleas Court of Cuyahoga County.

Upon appeal to the Court of Appeals, the judgment of the Common Pleas Court was affirmed without opinion, one judge dissenting.

HART, Judge.

The general rule is that a witness, especially when not a party to the controversy, may be required to testify upon any subject concerning which judicial inquiry is made and upon which he possesses specific personal information. To this general rule, there are certain well recognized exceptions. Witness may always claim as privileged that which tends to incriminate him. Article V, Amendments, U.S. Constitution, and Section 10, Article 1, Constitution of Ohio.

Frye seeks to broaden the area of these privileges. In the first place, she claims that the papers and documents sought to be introduced in evidence through her are her own personal property—work sheets and memoranda made by her, not as an employee but as an independent contractor in her private and confidential employment as a public accountant, from the private books and papers of her employer made at large expense to the latter; and that she should not be required to disclose this confidential information and to part with her property for attachment to an official court document.

In the absence of a privilege created by constitution of statute not to disclose available information, a witness may not refuse to testity to pertinent facts in a judicial proceeding merely because such testimony comprehends a communication or report from himself as agent to his principal or as independent contractor to his employer, no matter how confidential may be the character of the communication itself or the relationship between the parties thereto. And where one possesses knowledge of facts which are pertinent to a judicial inquiry, he may be required to testify or to produce papers and documents as to such facts.

It must be recognized that this is cumbersome procedure with which to determine the rights and privileges of a witness whose deposition is being taken before a commissioner appointed by a court or before a notary public. In cases where the nature and subject matter of the testimony sought by deposition can be anticipated in advance of the taking of the deposition, a witness may protect himself from the enforced disclosure of privileged or harmful subject matter by an appeal to a court of equity where equitable principles may be applied in determining the specific rights of a witness.

An attempt to follow this method of procedure was made in the Saile action, so far as the rights of Meridian were concerned, but the court denied the remedy because the injunctive relief sought was either too broad or lacked merit, or both.

The judgment of the Court of Appeals is reversed and the cause is remanded to the Common Pleas Court for proceedings according to law, consistent with this opinion.

Judgment reversed.

STATUTES

The following statute illustrates the Colorado position in CRS 1973, 13-90-107, on various privileged positions with regard to testimony. Consider the benefits and limits of this statute and compare them with your own state's statute, if different.

13-90-107. WHO MAY NOT TESTIFY WITHOUT CONSENT. (1) There are particular relations in which it is the policy of the law to encourage confidence and to preserve it inviolate; therefore, a person shall not be examined as a witness in the following cases:

(a) A husband shall not be examined for or against his wife without her consent, nor a wife for or against her husband without his consent; nor during the marriage or afterward shall either be examined without the consent of the other as to any communications made by one to the other during the marriage; but this exception does not apply to a civil action or proceeding by one against the other nor to a criminal action or proceeding for a crime committed by one against the other.

(b) An attorney shall not be examined without the consent of his client as to any communication made by the client to him or his advice given thereon in the course of professional employment; nor shall an attorney's secretary, stenographer, or clerk be examined without the consent of his employer concerning any fact, the knowledge of which he has acquired in such capacity.

(c) A clergyman or priest shall not be examined without the consent of the person making the confession as to any confession made to him in his professional character in the course of discipline enjoined by the church to which he belongs.

(d) A physician or surgeon duly authorized to practice his profession under the laws of this state, or any other state, shall not be examined without the consent of his patient as to any information acquired in attending the patient, which was necessary to enable him to prescribe or act for the patient; except this section shall not apply to a physician or surgeon who is sued by or on behalf of a patient or by or on behalf of the heirs, executors, or administrators of a patient on any cause of action arising out of or connected with the physician's care or treatment of such patient, or to physician or surgeon so sued on the case out of which said suit arises.

(e) A public officer shall not be examined as to communications made to him in official confidence, when the public interests, in the judgment of the court, would suffer by the disclosure.

(f) A certified public accountant shall not be examined without the consent of his client as to any communication made by the client to him in person or through the media of books of account and financial records, or his advice, reports, or working papers given or made thereon in the course of professional employment; nor shall a secretary, stenographer, clerk, or assistant of a certified public accountant be examined without the consent of the client concerned concerning any fact, the knowledge of which he has acquired in such capacity.

(g) A certified psychologist shall not be examined without the consent of his client as to any communication made by the client to him, or his advice given thereon in the course of professional employment; nor shall a certified psychologist's secretary, stenographer, or clerk be examined without the consent of his employer concerning any fact, the knowledge of which he has acquired in such capacity; nor shall any person who has participated in any psychological therapy, conducted under the supervision of a person authorized by law to conduct such therapy, including but not limited to group therapy sessions, be examined concerning any knowledge gained during the course of such therapy without the consent of the person to whom the testimony sought relates.

SUMMONS AND THE 1976 TAX REFORM ACT

There has been a great deal of controversy over disclosure requirements by third parties who are issued a summons to testify or otherwise produce documents. The 1976 Tax Reform Act has made certain changes in this area.

A new section has been added, Code Section 7609, which provides that if a summons names a specific taxpayer, any summons which is served on any party who is a third party bookkeeper and the summons requires a production of records contained in the summons, the notice of the summons must be given to any person (the taxpayer in general, so identified within three days of the date on which the service is made, but in no event later than 14 days before the date fixed in the summons as the date on which such records are to be examined.)

There are exceptions to the rule: Code Section 7609 (a) (4) provides that it will not apply to determine whether records of the business transaction of some identified person are fair, have been made, or kept. Further, there are other exceptions, such as the possibility of the loss of the records if notice is given. See also Code Section 7609 (f).

In the event the notice provisions apply, the taxpayer's agent will have the right to intervene in the case as to the enforcement of the summons. There are also stay orders provided to prevent the enforcement of the summons, with certain procedures to be followed. There are other special exceptions to the new rules. However, it does provide at least some notice provisions, contrary to what previously existed as a formal code section.

TAX RETURNS

Your client, Mr. Taxpayer, was recently paid an informal visit by Internal Revenue Service agents. They interviewed him on a possible criminal and civil matter relative to income tax due.

Subsequent to this contact, your client obtained from you certain documents relating to your preparation of tax projections. After the client obtained these documents he took them to Mr. Attorney, whom your cilent retained with regard to the tax issue and the investigation under hand.

Subsequently, the Internal Revenue Service served the attorney with a summons directing him to produce various documents under a *subpoena duces tecum*. (You come, with documents!)

Is the summons enforceable? And therefore, is there a privilege?

See Fisher, 500 F.2d 683 (3rd Cir. 1974) and Kasmir, 499 F.2d 444 (5th Cir. 1974); see also Tiltzer, Ira, "Supreme Court Narrows Fifth Amendment Privilege for Records Held by Third Party," 2 *Journal of Taxation* (July 1976).

UNITED STATES of America and James S. Mabrey,
Special Agent of the Internal Revenue Service,
Plaintiffs-Appellees.
v.
C. D. KASMIR and Jerry A. Candy,
Defendants-Appellants.
United States Court of Appeals, Fifth Circuit.
Aug. 21, 1974.
Before BELL, THORNBERRY and DYER, Circuit Judges.

In United States v. White, 5th Cir. 1973, 477 F.2d 757, aff's en banc, 487 F.2d 1335, we phrased the issue presented thusly:

... whether the constitutional privilege against compulsory self-incrimination may be invoked in behalf of a taxpayer by his attorney to prevent the production of income tax workpapers in his attorney's possession. . . .

That same issue is before us again, this time with a different factual background.

On January 3, 1973, the taxpayer, Dr. Mason, was visited in his office in Dallas, Texas, by two Special Agents of the Internal Revenue Service who informed Mr. Mason that his tax returns for the years 1969, 1970, and 1971 were under investigation and gave him Miranda warnings. During the visit, one of the Special Agents asked to see Dr. Mason's personal books and records. Dr. Mason complied with the request, but at the same time, he called his accountant, Candy, who advised him not to show any of his records to the Agents. The doctor followed Candy's advice, withdrew the records and the desk, and concluded the interview.

Following Dr. Mason's call to Candy, Candy called Kasmir and informed him of the visit. At Candy's request, Kasmir called Dr. Mason that afternoon and was retained by the doctor as his attorney. Early the next morning, at the direction of his employer, Candy delivered an assortment of records and documents to Dr. Mason at the doctor's office, and simultaneously relinquished to the taxpayer "the rightful, indefinite and legitimate possession of" the materials. Within minutes of receiving the materials, the taxpayer turned them over to appellant Kasmir as his attorney.

The next day summonses were served on Candy and Kasmir, ordering the latter to give up the documents and the former to give testimony concerning them. When neither appellant agreed to comply with the summonses, the government sought enforcement. In a pre-*White* and pre-*Couch* v. *United States* hearing and order, the district court granted the government's petition on the grounds that the records were owned by the accounting firm and that at the time the summonses were served, the records were in Kasmir's possession. The district court stayed its order pending this appeal.

Appellants contend that in the circumstances of this case, (1) the taxpayer's attorney has standing to raise the taxpayer's constitutional right to be free from self-incrimination, (2) enforcement of the summons for the production of records violates the taxpayer's Self-Incrimination Privilege, and (3) enforcement of the summons for production of records should be denied because IRS agents materially misrepresented themselves before the taxpayer.

Following the procedure employed in White, we begin with appellants' second contention, for recognition of standing in the attorney would be of little comfort to appellants unless the attorney's client does have Fifth Amendment rights in the summoned materials. Appellants contend here, as the appellant did in White, that enforcement of the summons violates the taxpayer's privilege because possession of the records by the taxpayer's attorney constitutes constructive possession by the taxpayer. Initially faced with our en banc decision in White as a formidable wall to scale, appellants have launched a methodical effort in order to dissuade us from the notion that White compels their defeat. They argue that the taxpayer doctor's actual possession of the summoned documents is a crucial factual distinction between this case and White. They see further significance in the fact that here the taxpayer turned the papers over to his attorney pursuant to their attorney-client relationship while in White the transfer of the documents was not from the client to the attorney but from the taxpayer's accountant to the attorney. Both parties agree that the question before this court is whether those factual differences warrant a result different from that reached in White.

The government attacks the appellants' position from two sides. First, the government argues that an accused may not object to summons of records owned by third parties even if in the accused's possession. The government's theory is that an accused cannot invoke the Fifth Amendment privilege against self-incrimination unless he both owns and possesses the documents in question. Second, the government contends that the taxpayer never had "rightful possession" of the papers because this enterprise by the appellants and the taxpayer was "a frantic last minute effort to put the requested records beyond the reach of a legitimate tax investigation" by "winning a footrace with agents of the government."

In the theatre of criminal tax investigations, few issues have been more hotly contested than the determination of the scope of the Fifth Amendment privilege against self-incrimination. Drawing heavily upon the historical evolution of the privilege, the Supreme Court in *Couch* v. *United States,* 1973, 409 U.S. 322, 93 S.Ct. 611, 34 L.Ed.2d 548, has now spoken on the subject before us in a manner that guides our journey far down the road to judgment, but not to the very end. Lillian Couch was the sole proprietress of a restaurant who, since 1955, had given all of her financial records to an independent accountant for the purpose of preparing her income tax returns, although she retained title to the records. After a summons had been issued and served upon the accountant, the taxpayer instructed the accountant to deliver all of the sought-after documents directly to her attorney. In upholding enforcement of the summons against the accountant, the Supreme Court held that the taxpayer had no Fifth Amendment privilege in documents which she merely owned, which had been in the continuous possession of an independent accountant for over a decade, and with respect to which she could show no legitimate expectation of privacy.

The Court began its inquiry by quoting from *Murphy* v. *Waterfront Comm'n of New York Harbor,* 1964, 378 U.S. 52, 84 A.Ct. 1594, 12 L.Ed.2d 678, on the nature of the Self-Incrimination Privilege and the interests it was designed to protect. Writing for the Court in Murphy, Justice Goldberg offered this statement:

> . . . It (the privileges) reflects many of our fundamental values and most noble aspirations: our unwillingness to subject those suspected of crime to the cruel trilemma of self-accusation, perjury or contempt; our preference for an accusatorial rather than an inquisitorial system of criminal justice; our fear that self-incriminating statements will be elicited by inhumane treatment and abuses; our sense of fair play which dictates "a fair state-individual balance by requiring the government to leave the individual alone until good cause is shown for disturbing him and by requiring the government in its contest with the individual to shoulder the entire loan," 8 Wigmore, Evidence (McNaughton rev., 1961), 317; our respect for the inviolability of the human personality and of the right of each individual "to a private enclave where he may lead a private life," *United States* v. *Grunerwald,* 2 Cir., 233 F.2d 556, 581-582 (Frank J., dissenting), rev'd 353 U.S. 391, 77 S.Ct. 63, 1 L.Ed.2d 931; our distrust of self-deprecatory statements; and our realization that the privilege, while sometimes "a shelter to the guilty," is often "a protection to the innocent." *Quinn* v. *United States,* 349 U.S. 155, 162, 75 S.Ct. 668, 673, 99 L.Ed. 964. . . .

Id. 378 U.S. at 55, 84 S.Ct. at 1596-1597.

The Couch Court held that actual possession, rather than ownership, "bears the most significant relationship in Fifth Amendment protections against state compulsions upon the individual accused of crime." *Couch* v. *United States,* supra, 409 U.S. at 333, 93 S.Ct. at 618. But the Court was careful to note that "actual possession" is not necessarily the sine qua non for successful assertion of the Fifth Amendment privilege:

> . . . Yet situations may well arise where constructive possession is so clear or the relinquishment of possession is so temporary and insignificant as to leave the personal compulsions upon the accused substantially intact . . .

Id. The Court explained further:

> . . . We do indeed attach constitutional importance to possession, but only because of its close relationship to those personal compulsions and intrusions which the Fifth Amendment forbids . . . (W)e do not adopt any per se rule. We also decline to conjecture broadly on the significance of possession in cases and circumstances not before this Court . . .

Id. 409 U.S. at 336, 93 S.Ct. at 620 N. 20.

As a positive indication that lack of physical possession is not necessarily determinative, the Court did not stop with its conclusion that the papers were in the possession of the accountant, not the taxpayer, at the time the summons was served, but inquired further into the nature of the records sought by the summons and concluded that the taxpayer could show no legitimate expectation of privacy with regard to them because

> . . . there can be little expectation of privacy where records are handed to an accountant, knowing that mandatory disclosure of much of the information therein is required in an income tax return. What information is not disclosed is largely in the accountant's discretion, not petitioner's. Indeed, the accountant himself risks criminal prosecution if he knowingly assists in the preparation of a false return. . . . His own need for self-protection would often require the right to disclose the information given him. Petitioner seeks extensions of constitutional protections against self-incrimination in the very situation where obligations of disclosure exist and under a system largely dependent upon honest self-reporting even to survive. Accordingly, petitioner here cannot reasonably claim, . . . and expectation of protected privacy or confidentiality.

Id., 409 S.Ct. at 335, 93 S.Ct. at 619, 34 L.Ed.2d at 558. Thus the method adopted by the Court focuses the inquiry on two factors: (1) the party in possession of the evidence and (2) where the actual possessor is not the taxpayer, the taxpayer's legitimate expectation of privacy with regard to the evidence. By considering not only the question of physical, personal compulsion upon the accused, but also any expectation of privacy which might reasonably attach to the summoned materials, the Court was weighing the extent to which any of the variety of policies enumerated in Murphy would be furthered by application of the privilege. Indeed, in Murphy, the Court noted that "it will not do . . . to assign one isolated policy to the privilege," and on that basis to decide whether applying the privilege is in furtherance of "the" policy. *Murphy* v. *Waterfront Comm'n of New York Harbor,* supra, 378 U.S. at 56 n.5, 84 S.Ct. at 1597 n.5.

We had our first opportunity to apply the lesson of Couch only recently in *United States* v. *White,* supra, 477 F.2d 575, aff'd en banc, 487 F.2d 1335. After an IRS investigation had commenced but prior to the issuance of a summons, the taxpayers' accountant had turned over workpapers and other documents directly to the taxpayers' attorney White. A year later, a summons was served upon the attorney who resisted enforcement by asserting his client taxpayers' Fifth Amendment privilege. Since the taxpayers were obviously not in actual possession of the requested material, their only hope lay in the contention that they were in constructive possession through their attorney. Although the high court did not attempt to define that term in Couch, in writing for this court in White, Judge Gewin attempted to explicate the Supreme Court's thinking:

. . . As possible examples of such a case the Court cited *Schwimmer* v. *United States* and *United States* v. *Guterma*. In both of these cases a claim of privilege was successfully asserted to prevent the government from obtaining documents the parties had temporarily stored on the premises of corporations. The reference to these cases in Couch indicates that a claim of privilege might be valid on the constructive possession theory if the taxpayer has placed papers in the hands of another person or entity for custodial safekeeping, thereby retaining the right to immediate possession though not having actual possession . . .

The following two cases cover Kasmir and Fisher. The USSC decided the issue which split the lower Circuit Courts.

Solomon Fisher et al.,
    Petitioners,   On Writ of Certiorari to the
74-18   v.   United States Court of Appeals
United States et al.   for the Third Circuit.
United States et al.,
    Petitioners,   On Writ of Certiorari to the
74-611   v.   United States Court of Appeals
C. D. Kasmir and Jerry A. Candy   for the Fifth Circuit.
(April 21, 1976).

WHITE, J., delivered the opinion of the Court, in which BURGER, C. J., and STEWART, BLACKMUN, POWELL, and REHNQUIST, JJ., joined. BRENNAN and MARSHALL, JJ., filed opinions concurring in the judgment. STEVENS, J., took no part in the consideration or decision of the cases.

Mr. JUSTICE WHITE delivered the opinion of the Court.

In these two cases were we called upon to decide whether a summons directing an attorney to produce documents delivered to him by his client in connection with the attorney-client relationship is enforceable over claims that the documents were constitutionally immune from summons in the hands of the clients and retained that immunity in the hands of the attorneys.

I

In each case, an Internal Revenue agent visited the taxpayer or taxpayers and interviewed them in connection with an investigation of possible civil or criminal liability under the federal income tax laws. Shortly after the interviews—one day later in No. 74-611 and a week or two later in No. 74-18—the taxpayers obtained from their respective accountants certain documents relating to the preparation by the accountant of their tax returns. Shortly after obtaining the documents—later the same day in No. 74-611 and a few weeks later in No. 74-18—the taxpayers transferred the documents to their lawyers—respondent Kasmir and petitioner Fisher, respectively—each of whom was retained to assist the taxpayer in connection with the investigation. Upon learning of the whereabouts of the documents, the Internal Revenue Service served summonses on the attorneys directing them to produce documents listed therein. In No. 74-611, the documents were described as "the following records of Tannebaum Bindler & Lewis (the accounting firm):

"1. Accountant's workpapers pertaining to Dr. E. J. Mason's books and records of 1969, 1970 and 1971.
"2. Retained copies of E. J. Mason's income tax returns for 1969, 1970 and 1971.
"3. Retained copies of reports and other correspondence between Tannebaum Bindler and Lewis and Dr. E. J. Mason during 1969, 1970 and 1971."

In No. 74-18, the documents demanded were analyses by the accountant of the taxpayers' income and expenses which had been copied by the accountant from the taxpayers' cancelled checks and deposit receipts. In No. 74-611, a summons was also served on the accountant directing him to appear and testify concerning the documents to be produced by the lawyer. In each case, the lawyer declined to comply with the summons directing production of the documents, and enforcement actions were commenced by the Government under 26 U.S.C. §§ 7402(b) and 7604 (a). In No. 74-611, the attorney raised in defense of the enforcement action the taxpayers' accountant-client privilege, his attorney-client privilege, and his Fourth and Fifth Amendment rights. In No. 74-18, the attorney claimed that enforcement would involve compulsory self-incrimination of the taxpayers in violation of their Fifth Amendment privilege, would involve a seizure of the papers without necessary compliance with the Fourth Amendment, and would violate the taxpayers' right to communicate in confidence with their attorney. In No. 74-18 the taxpayers intervened and made similar claims.

In each case the summons was ordered enforced by the District Court and its order was stayed pending appeal. In No. 74-18, *Fisher* v. *United States,*—F.2d—(1974), petitioners' appeal raised, in terms, only their Fifth Amendment claim, but they argued in connection with that claim that enforcement of the summons would involve a violation of the taxpayers' reasonable expectation of privacy and particularly so in light of the confidential relationship of attorney to client. The Court of Appeals for the Third Circuit after reargument en banc affirmed the enforcement order, holding that the taxpayers had never acquired a possessory interest in the documents and that the papers were not immune in the hands of the attorney. In No. 74-622, a divided panel of the Court of Appeals for the Fifth Circuit reversed the enforcement order. *Kasmir* v. *United States,* —F.2d—(1974). The court reasoned that by virtue of the Fifth Amendment the documents would have been privileged from production pursuant to summons directed to the taxpayer had he retained possession and, in light of the confidential nature of the attorney-client relationship, the taxpayer retained, after the transfer to his attorney "a legitimate expectation of privacy with regard to the materials he placed in his attorney's custody, that he retained constructive possession of the evidence and thus retained Fifth Amendment protection." We granted certiorari to resolve the conflict created.—U.S.—.Because in our view the documents were not privileged either in the hands of the lawyers or of their clients, we affirm the judgment of the Third Circuit in No. 74-18 and reverse the judgment of the Fifth Circuit in No. 74-611.

II

All of the parties in this case and the Court of Appeals for the Fifth Circuit have concurred in the proposition that if the Fifth Amendment would have excused a taxpayer from turning over the accountant's papers had he possessed them, the attorney to whom they are delivered for the purpose of obtaining legal advice should also be immune from subpoena. Although we agree with this proposition for the reasons set forth in Part III, infra, we are convinced that, under our decision in *Couch* v. *United States,* 409 U.S. 322 (1973), it is not the taxpayer's Fifth Amendment privilege that would excuse the attorney from production.

The relevant part of that Amendment provides:

> "No person . . . shall be *compelled* in any criminal case to be a *witness* against himself." (Emphasis added.)

The taxpayer's privilege under this Amendment is not violated by enforcement of the summonses involved in these cases because enforcement against a taxpayer's lawyer would not "compel" the taxpayer to do anything—and certainly would not compel him to be a "witness" against himself. The Court has held repeatedly that the Fifth Amendment is limited to prohibiting the use of "physical or moral compulsion" exerted on the person asserting the privilege. In *Couch* v. *United States,* supra, we recently ruled that the Fifth Amendment rights of a taxpayer were not violated by the enforcement of a documentary summons directed to her accountant and requiring production of the taxpayer's own records in the possession of the accountant. We did so on the ground that in such a case "the ingredient of personal compulsion against an accused is lacking."

Here, the taxpayers are compelled to do no more than was the taxpayer in Couch. The taxpayers' Fifth Amendment privilege is therefore not violated by enforcement of the summonses directed toward their attorneys. This is true whether or not the Amendment would have barred a subpoena directing the taxpayer to produce the documents while they were in his hands.

The fact that the attorneys are agents of the taxpayers does not change this result. Couch held as much, since the accountant there was also the taxpayer's agent, and in this respect reflected a long-standing view. In *Hale* v. *Henkel,* 201 U.S. 43, 69-70 (1906), the Court said that the privilege "was never intended to permit (a person) to plead the fact that some third person might be incriminated by his testimony, even though he were the agent of such person . . . the amendment is limited to a person who shall be compelled in any criminal case to be a witness against himself." (Emphasis in original.) "It is extortion of information from the accused which offends our sense of justice." Agent or no, the lawyer is not the taxpayer. The taxpayer is the "accused," and nothing is being extorted from him.

Nor is this one of those situations, which Couch suggested might exist, where constructive possession is so clear or relinquishment of possession so temporary and insignificant as to leave the personal compulsion upon the taxpayer substantially intact. In this respect we see no difference between the delivery to the attorneys in these cases and delivery to the accountant in the Couch case. As was true in Couch, the documents sought were obtainable without personal compulsion on the accused.

Respondents argue, and the Fifth Circuit Court of Appeals apparently agreed, that if the summons was enforced, the taxpayers' Fifth Amendment privilege would be, but should not be, lost solely because they gave their documents to their lawyers in order to obtain legal advice, but this misconceives the nature of the constitutional privilege. The amendment protects a person from being compelled to be a witness against himself. Here, the taxpayers retained any privilege they ever had not to be compelled themselves to produce private papers in their possession. This personal privilege was in no way decreased by the transfer. It is simply that by reason of the transfer of the documents to the attorneys, those papers may be subpoenaed without compulsion on the taxpayer. The protection of the Fifth Amendment is therefore not available. "A party is privileged from producing evidence but not from its production."

The Court has never suggested that every invasion of privacy violates the privilege. Within the limits imposed by the language of the Fifth Amendment, which we necessarily observe, the privilege truly serves privacy interests; but the Court has never on any ground, personal privacy included, applied the Fifth Amendment to prevent the otherwise proper acquisition or use of evidence which, in the Court's view, did not involve compelled testimonial self-incrimination of some sort.

The proposition that the Fifth Amendment protects private information obtained without compelling self-incriminating testimony is contrary to the clear statements of this Court that under appropriate safeguards private incriminating statements of an accused may be overheard and used in evidence, if they are not compelled at the time they were uttered, and that disclosure of private information may be compelled if immunity removes the risk of incrimination. If the Fifth Amendment protected generally against the obtaining of private information from a man's mouth or pen or house, its protections would presumably not be lifted by probable cause and a warrant or by immunity. The privacy invasion is not mitigated by immunity; and the Fifth Amendment's strictures, unlike the Fourth's, are not removed by showing reasonableness. The Framers addressed the subject of personal privacy directly in the Fourth Amendment. They struck a balance so that when the State's reason to believe incriminating evidence will be found becomes sufficiently great, the invasion of privacy becomes justified and a warrant to search and seize will issue. They did not seek in still another Amendment—the Fifth—to achieve a general protection of privacy but to deal with the more specific issue of compelled self-incrimination.

We cannot cut the Amendment completely loose from the moorings of its language, and make it serve as a general protector of privacy—a word not mentioned in its text and a concept directly addressed in the Fourth Amendment. We adhere to the view that the Fifth Amendment protects against "compelled testimony not the disclosure of private information."

III

Our above holding is that compelled production of documents from an attorney does not implicate whatever Fifth Amendment privilege the taxpayer might have enjoyed from being himself compelled to produce them. The taxpayers in these cases, however, have from the outset consistently urged that they should not be forced to expose otherwise protected documents to summons simply because they have sought legal advice and turned the papers over to their attorneys. The government appears to agree unqualifiedly. The difficulty is that taxpayers have erroneously relied on the Fifth Amendment without urging the attorney-client privilege in so many words. They have nevertheless invoked the relevant body of law and policies and govern the attorney-client privilege. In this posture of the case, we feel obliged to inquire whether the attorney-client privilege applies to documents in the hands of an attorney which would have been privileged in the hands of the client by reason of the Fifth Amendment.

Confidential disclosures by a client to an attorney made in order to obtain legal assistance are privileged. However, since the privilege has the effect of withholding relevant information from the fact-finder, it applies only where necessary to achieve its purpose. Accordingly it protects only those disclosures—necessary to obtain informed legal advice—which might not have been made absent the privilege.

Since each taxpayer transferred possession of the documents in question from himself to his attorney, in order to obtain legal assistance in the tax investigations in question, the papers, if unobtainable by summons from the client, are unobtainable by summons directed to the attorney by reason of the attorney-client privilege. We accordingly proceed to the question whether the documents could have been obtained by summons addressed to the taxpayer while the documents were in his possession. The only bar to enforcement of such summons asserted by the parties or the courts below is the Fifth Amendment's privilege against self-incrimination. On this question the Court of Appeals for the Fifth Circuit in this case is at odds with the Court of Appeals for the Second Circuit, *United States* v. *Beattie,* ___ F.2d ___ (1975).

IV

The proposition that the Fifth Amendment prevents compelled production of documents over objection that such production might incriminate stems from *Boyd* v. *United States,* 116 U.S. 616 (1886).

Among its several pronouncements, Boyd was understood to declare that the seizure, under warrant or otherwise, of any purely evidentiary materials violated the Fourth Amendment and that the Fifth Amendment rendered these seized materials inadmissible.

It is also clear that the Fifth Amendment does not independently proscribe the compelled production of every sort of incriminating evidence but applies only when the accused is compelled to make a testimonial communication that is incriminating. We have, accordingly, declined to extend the protection of the privilege to the giving of blood samples, Schmerber, supra, at 763-764; to the giving of handwriting exemplars, *Gilbert* v. *California,* 388 U.S. 263, 265-267 (1967); voice exemplars, *United States* v. *Wade,* 388 U.S. 263, 265-267 (1967), or the donning of a blouse worn by the perpetrator, *Holt* v. *United States,* 218 218 U.S. 245 (1910). Furthermore, despite Boyd, neither a partnership nor the individual partners are shielded from compelled production of partnership records on self-incrimination grounds. *Bellis* v. *United States,* 417 U.S. 85 (1974). It would appear that under that case the precise claim sustained in Boyd would now be rejected for reasons not there considered.

The pronouncement in Boyd that a person may not be forced to produce his private papers has nonetheless often appears as dictum in later opinions of this Court. To the extent, however, that the rule against compelling production of private papers rested on the proposition that seizures of or subpoenas for "mere evidence," including documents, violated the Fourth Amendment and therefore also transgressed the Fifth, *Gouled* v. *United States,* supra, the foundations for the rule have been washed away.

A subpoena served on a taxpayer requiring him to produce an accountant's work papers in his possession without doubt involves substantial compulsion. But it does not compel oral testimony; nor would it ordinarily compel the taxpayer to restate, repeat or affirm the truth of the contents of the documents sought. Therefore, the Fifth Amendment would not be violated by the fact alone that the papers on their face might incriminate the taxpayer, for the privilege protects a person only against being incriminated by his own compelled testimonial communications. The accountants' work papers are not the taxpayer's. They were not prepared by him and they contain no testimonial declarations by him. Furthermore, as far as this record demonstrates, the preparation of all of the papers sought in these cases was wholly voluntary, and they cannot be said to contain compelled testimonial evidence, either of the taxpayer or of anyone else. The taxpayer cannot avoid compliance with the subpoena merely by asserting that the item of evidence which he is required to produce contains incriminating writing, whether his own or that of someone else.

The act of producing evidence in response to a subpoena nevertheless has communicative aspects of its own, wholly aside from the contents of the papers produced. Compliance with the subpoena tacitly concedes the existence of the papers demanded with their possession or control by the taxpayer. It also would indicate the taxpayer's belief that the papers are those described in the subpoena. Curcio United States, 354 U.S. 118, 125 (1957). The elements of compulsion are clearly present, but the more difficult issues are whether the tacit averments of the taxpayer are both "testimonial" and "incriminating" for purposes of applying the Fifth Amendment. These questions perhaps do not lend themselves to categorical answer; their resolution may instead depend on the facts and circumstances of particular cases or classes thereof. In light of the records now before us, we are confident that however incriminating the contents of the accountant's work papers might be, the act of producing them—the only thing which the taxpayer is compelled to do—would not itself involve testimonial self-incrimination.

Whether the Fifth Amendment would shield the taxpayer from producing his own tax records in his possession is a question not involved here; for the papers demanded here are not his "private papers," see *Boyd* v *United States,* supra, at ___. We do hold that compliance with a summons directing the taxpayer to produce the accountant's documents involved in this case would involve no incriminating testimony within the protection of the Fifth Amendment.

The judgment of the Court of Appeals for the Fifth Circuit in No. 74-611 is reversed. The judgment of the Court of Appeals for the Third Circuit in No. 74-18 is affirmed.

MR. JUSTICE STEVENS took no part in the consideration or disposition of these cases.

MR. JUSTICE BRENNAN, concurring in the judgment.

DISCOVERY AND THE PRIVILEGE QUESTION

In addition to the cases discussed, the crux of the issue of discovery—obtaining records—has been brought to the forefront, along with that of the attorney-client privilege, in two very recent cases subsequent to Couch and the other cases discussed earlier. These cases include the Miller decision, dealing with the bank records of the taxpayer, and the Andresen case, dealing with discovery of the taxpayer's records by use of a search warrant, which arguably did not violate the Fourth Amendment but may have violated the Fifth.

As the Miller case indicates, the bank records were not determined to be private in nature, and there is no property interest in the same. This decision resulted in discovery against the taxpayer and therefore effectively incriminating evidence against him. The distinction made by the court in the Miller case and in Andresen illustrates the privilege is personal and also there is a requirement of an intent for privileged information as opposed to an intent to show that it was public, or certainly in the hands of a third party, and therefore not privileged. There is also the very careful distinction made by the court, although highly questioned by many constitutional attorneys, as to use of the Fourth Amendment as opposed to the Fifth and therefore allowing the information into evidence.

Both these cases raise the question as to what privilege if any may exist for records in the attorney's hands and in a Realtor's hands. It should further raise the personal question as to whether there is an infringement on the constitutional protection of the Fifth Amendment of the right to not testify. It is clear that the taxpayer can and may be testifying against himself via the records that he has made with regard to bank purposes and via the records that the taxpayer personally holds.

The question is what is the next step: That is, might not the Internal Revenue Service be coming into the Realtor's office even though the Realtor passed the records back to the taxpayer before the Realtor had a proprietary interest or a possessory interest? What if these records were subsequently passed to the attorney? Although some questions are still unanswered, these cases severely dilute the attorney-client privilege. There clearly is no Realtor-client privilege. (See this point for the CPA as per the United States Supreme Court in the Couch case already decided.)

United States, Petitioner,
v.
Mitchell Miller.
On Writ of Certiorari to the
United States Court of
Appeals for the Fifth Circuit.
(April 21, 1976)
Syllabus

MR. JUSTICE POWELL delivered the opinion of the Court.

Respondent was convicted of possessing an unregistered still, carrying on the business of a distiller without giving bond and with intent to defraud the Government of whiskey tax, possessing 175 gallons of whiskey upon which no taxes had been paid, and conspiring to defraud the United States of tax revenues. Prior to trial respondent moved to suppress copies of checks and other bank records obtained by means of allegedly defective subpoenas duces tecum served upon two banks at which he had accounts. The records had been maintained by the banks in compliance with the requirements of the Bank Secrecy Act of 1970.

The District Court overruled respondent's motion to suppress and the evidence was admitted. The Court of Appeals for the Fifth Circuit reversed on the ground that a depositor's Fourth Amendment rights are violated when bank records maintained pursuant to the Bank Secrecy Act are obtained by means of a defective subpoena. It held that any evidence so obtained must be suppressed. Since we find that respondent had no protectable Fourth Amendment interest in the subpoenaed documents, we reverse the decision below.

I

On December 18, 1972, in response to an informant's tip, a deputy sheriff from Houston County, Ga., stopped a van-type truck occupied by two of respondent's alleged co-conspirators. The truck contained distillery apparatus and raw material. On January 9, 1973, a fire broke out in a Kathleen, Ga., warehouse rented to respondent. During the blaze firemen and sheriff department officials discovered a 7,500 gallon-capacity distillery, 175 gallons of nontax-paid whiskey, and related paraphernalia.

Two weeks later agents from the Treasury Department's Alcohol, Tobacco & Firearms Unit presented grand jury subpoenas issued in blank by the clerk of the District Court, and completed by the United States Attorney's office, to the presidents of the Citizens & Southern National Bank of Warner Robins and the Bank of Byron, where respondent maintained accounts. The subpoenas required the two presidents to appear on January 24, 1973, and to produce

"all records of accounts, i.e., savings, checking, loan or otherwise, in the name of Mr. Mitch Miller (respondent), 3859 Mathis Street, Macon, Ga. and/or Mitch Miller Associates, 100 Executive Terrace, Warner Robins, Ga., from October 1, 1972, through the present date (January 22, 1973, in the case of the Bank of Byron, and January 23, 1973, in the case of the Citizens & Southern National Bank of Warner Robins)."

The banks did not advise respondent that the subpoenas had been served but ordered their employees to make the records available and to provide copies of any documents the agents desired. At the Bank of Byron, an agent was shown microfilm records of the relevant account and provided with copies of one deposit slip and one or two checks. At the Citizens & Southern National Bank microfilm records also were shown to the agent, and he was given copies of the records of respondent's account during the applicable period. These included all checks, deposit slips, two financial statements and three monthly statements. The bank presidents were then told that it would not be necessary to appear in person before the grand jury.

The grand jury met on February 12, 1973, 19 days after the return date on the subpoenas. Respondent and four others were indicted. The overt acts alleged to have been committed in furtherance of the conspiracy included three financial transactions—the rental by respondent of the van-type truck, the purchase by respondent of radio equipment, and the purchase by respondent of a quantity of sheet metal and metal pipe. The record does not indicate whether any of the bank records were in fact presented to the grand jury. They were used in the investigation and provided "one or two" investigatory leads. Copies of the checks were also introduced at trial to establish the overt acts described above.

The Government contends that the Court of Appeals erred in three respects: (i) in finding that respondent had the Fourth Amendment interest necessary to entitle him to challenge the validity of the subpoenas duces tecum through his motion to suppress; (ii) in holding that the subpoenas were defective; and (iii) in determining that suppression of the evidence obtained was the appropriate remedy if a constitutional violation did take place.

We find that there was no intrusion into any area in which respondent had a protected Fourth Amendment interest and that the District Court therefore correctly denied respondent's motion to suppress. Because we reverse the decision of the Court of Appeals on that ground alone, we do not reach the Government's latter two contentions.

II

In *Hoffa* v. *United States*, 385 U.S. 293, 301-302 (1966), the Court said that "no interest legitimately protected by the Fourth Amendment" is implicated by governmental investigative activities unless there is an intrusion into a zone of privacy, into "the security a man relies upon when he places himself or his property within a constitutionally protected area." The Court of Appeals, as noted above, assumed that respondent had the necessary Fourth Amendment interest, pointing to the language in *Boyd* v. *United States,* 116 U.S., at 622, which describes that Amendment's protection against the "compulsory production of a man's private papers." We think that the Court of Appeals erred in finding the subpoenaed documents to fall within a protected zone of privacy.

On their face, the documents subpoenaed here are not respondent's "private papers." Unlike the claimant in Boyd, respondent can assert neither ownership nor possession. Instead, these are the business records of the banks.

Respondent argues, however, that the Bank Secrecy Act introduces a factor that makes the subpoena in this case the functional equivalent of a search and seizure of the depositor's "prviate papers." We have held, in *California Bankers Assn.* v. *Schultz,* supra, at 54, that the mere maintenance of records pursuant to the requirements of the Act "invade(s) no Fourth Amendment right to any depositor." But respondent contends that the combination of the recordkeeping requirements of the Act and the issuance of a subpoena to obtain those records permits the Government to circumvent the requirements of the Fourth Amendment by allowing to obtain a depositor's private records without complying with the legal requirements that would be applicable had it proceeded against him directly. Therefore, we must address the question whether the compulsion embodied in the Bank Secrecy Act as exercised in this case creates a Fourth Amendment interest in the depositor where none existed before.

Respondent urges that he has a Fourth Amendment interest in the records kept by the banks because they are merely copies of personal records that were made available to the banks for a limited purpose and in which he has a reasonable expectation of privacy. We must examine the nature of the particular documents sought to be protected in order to determine whether there is a legitimate "expectation of privacy" concerning their contents.

Even if we direct our attention to the original checks and deposit slips, rather than to the microfilm copies actually viewed and obtained by means of the subpoena, we perceive no legitimate "expectation of privacy" in their contents. The checks are not confidential communications but negotiable instruments to be used in commercial transactions. All of the documents obtained, including financial statements and deposit slips, contain only information voluntarily conveyed to the banks and exposed to their employees in the ordinary course of business. The lack of any legitimate expectation of privacy concerning the information kept in bank records was assumed by Congress in enacting the Bank Secrecy Act, the expressed purpose of which is to require records to be maintained because they "have a high degree of usefulness in criminal, tax, and regulatory investigations and proceedings."

The depositor takes the risk, in revealing his affairs to another, that the information will be conveyed by that person to the government. *United States* v. *White,* 401 U.S. 745, 751-752 (1971).

This analysis is not changed by the mandate of the Bank Secrecy Act that records of depositors' transactions be maintained by banks. In *California Bankers Assn.* v. *Schultz,* we rejected the contention that banks, when keeping records of their depositors' transactions pursuant to the Act, are acting solely as agents of the government. But, even if the banks could be said to have been acting solely as government agents in transcribing the necessary information and complying without protest with the requirements of the subpoenas, there would be no intrusion upon the depositors' Fourth Amendment rights.

III

Since no Fourth Amendment interests of the depositor are implicated here, this case is governed by the general rule that the issuance of a subpoena to a third party to obtain the records of that party does not violate the rights of a defendant, even if a criminal prosecution is contemplated at the time the subpoena is issued.

Many banks traditionally kept permanent records of their depositors' accounts, although not all banks did so and the practice was declining in recent years. By requiring that such records be kept by all banks, the Bank Secrecy Act is not a novel means designed to circumvent established Fourth Amendment rights. It is merely an attempt to facilitate the use of a proper and longstanding law enforcement technique by insuring that records are available when they are needed.

We hold that the District Court correctly denied respondent's motion to suppress, since he possessed no Fourth Amendment interest that could be vindicated by a challenge to the subpoenas.

IV

Respondent contends not only that the subpoenas duces tecum directed against the banks infringed his Fourth Amendment rights, but that a subpoena issued to a bank to obtain records maintained pursuant to the Act is subject to more stringent Fourth Amendment requirements than is the ordinary subpoena. In making this assertion, he relies on our statement in California Bankers Assn., supra, at 52, that access to the records maintained by banks under the Act is to be controlled by "existing legal process."

In any event, for the reasons stated above, we hold that respondent lacks the requisite Fourth Amendment interest to challenge the validity of the subpoenas.

V

The judgment of the Court of Appeals is reversed. The court deferred decision on whether the trial court had improperly overruled respondent's motion to suppress distillery apparatus and raw material seized from a rented truck. We remand for disposition of that issue.

So ordered.

MR. JUSTICE BRENNAN, dissenting.

No. 74-2646

Peter C. Andresen, Petitioner,

v.

State of Maryland.

on Writ of Certiorari to the Court of Special Appeals of Maryland.

(June 29, 1976)

Syllabus

MR. JUSTICE BLACKMUN delivered the opinion of the Court.

This case presents the issue whether the introduction into evidence of a person's business records, seized during a search of his offices, violates the Fifth Amendment's command that "(n)o person . . . shall be compelled in any criminal case to be a witness against himself." We also must determine whether the particular searches and seizures here were "unreasonable" and thus violated the prohibition of the Fourth Amendment.

I

In early 1972, a Bi-County Fraud Unit, acting under the joint auspices of the State's Attorney's Offices of Montgomery and Prince George's Counties, Md., began an investigation of real estate settlement activities in the Washington, D.C., area. At the time, petitioner Andresen was an attorney who, as a sole practitioner, specialized in real estate settlements in Montgomery County. During the Fraud Unit's investigation, his activities came under scrutiny, particularly in connection with a transaction involving Lot 13T in the Potomac Woods subdivision of Montgomery County. The investigation, which included interviews with the purchaser, the mortgage holder, and other lienholders of Lot 13T, as well as an examination of county land records, disclosed that petitioner, acting as settlement attorney, had defrauded Standard-Young Associates, the purchaser of Lot 13T. Petitioner had represented that the property was free of liens and that, accordingly, no title insurance was necessary, when in fact, he knew that there were two outstanding liens on the property. In addition, investigators learned that the lienholders, by threatening to foreclose their liens, had forced a halt to the purchaser's construction on the property. When Standard-Young had confronted petitioner with this information, he responded by issuing, as an agent of a title insurance company, a title policy guaranteeing clear title to the property. By this action, petitioner also defrauded that insurance company by requiring it to pay the outstanding liens.

The investigators, concluding that there was probable cause to believe that petitioner had committed the state crime of false pretenses, against Standard-Young, applied for warrants to search petitioner's law office and the separate office of Mount Vernon Development Corporation, of which petitioner was incorporator, sole shareholder, resident agent, and director. The application sought permission to search for specified documents pertinent to the sale and conveyance of Lot 13T. A judge of the Sixth Judicial Circuit of Montgomery County concluded that there was probable cause and issued the warrants.

The searches of the two offices were conducted simultaneously during daylight hours on October 31, 1972. Petitioner was present during the search of his law office and was free to move about. Counsel for him was present during the latter half of the search. Between 2% and 3% of the files in the office were seized. A single investigator, in the presence of a police officer, conducted the search of Mount Vernon Development Corporation. This search, taking about four hours, resulted in the seizure of less than 5% of the corporation's files.

Petitioner eventually was charged, partly by information and partly by indictment, with the crime of false pretenses, based on his misrepresentation to Standard-Young concerning Lot 13T, and with fraudulent misappropriation by a fiduciary, based on similar false claims made to three home purchasers. Before trial began, petitioner moved to suppress the seized documents. The trial court held a full suppression hearing. At the hearing, the State returned to petitioner 45 of the 52 items taken from the offices of the corporation. The trial court suppressed six other corporation items on the ground that there was no connection between them and the crimes charged. The net result was that the only item seized from the corporation's offices that was not returned by the State or suppressed was a single file labelled "Potomac Woods General." In addition, the State returned to petitioner seven of the 28 items seized from his law office, and the trial court suppressed four other law office items based on its determination that there was no connection between them and the crime charged.

With respect to all the items not suppressed or returned, the trial court ruled that admitting them into evidence would not violate the Fifth and Fourth Amendments. It reasoned that the searches and seizures did not force petitioner to be a witness against himself because he had not been required to produce the seized documents, nor would he be compelled to authenticate them. Moreover, the search warrants were based on probable cause, and the documents not returned or suppressed were either directly related to Lot 13T, and therefore within the express language of the warrants, or properly seized and otherwise admissible to show a pattern of criminal conduct relevant to the charge concerning Lot 13T.

At trial, the State proved its case primarily by public land records and by records provided by the complaining purchasers, lienholders, and the title insurance company. It did introduce into evidence, however, a number of the seized items. Three documents from the "Potomac Woods General" file, seized during the search of petitioner's corporation, were admitted. These were notes in the handwriting of an employee who used them to prepare abstracts in the course of his duties as a title searcher and law clerk. The notes concerned deeds of trust affecting the Potomac Woods subdivision and related to the transaction involving Lot 13T. Five items seized from petitioner's law office were also admitted. One contained information relating to the transactions with one of the defrauded home buyers. The second was a file partially devoted to the Lot 13T transaction; among the documents were settlements, the deed conveying the property to Standard-Young Associates, and the original and a copy of a notice to the buyer about releases of liens. The third item was a file devoted exclusively to Lot 13T. The fourth item consisted of a copy of a deed to trust, dated March 27, 1972, from the seller of certain lots in the Potomac Woods subdivision to a lienholder. The fifth item contained drafts of documents and memoranda written in petitioner's handwriting.

After a trial by jury, petitioner was found guilty upon five counts of false pretenses and three counts of fraudulent misappropriation by a fiduciary. He was sentenced to eight concurrent two-year prison terms.

On appeal to the Court of Special Appeals of Maryland, four of the five false pretenses counts were reversed because the indictment had failed to allege intent to defraud, a necessary element of the state offense. Only the count pertaining to Standard-Young's purchase of Lot 13T remained. With respect to this count of false pretenses and the three counts of misappropriation by a fiduciary, the Court of Special Appeals rejected petitioner's Fourth and Fifth Amendment Claims. Specifically, it held that the warrants were supported by probable cause, that they did not authorize a general search in violation of the Fourth Amendment, and that the items admitted into evidence against petitioner at trial were within the scope of the warrants or were otherwise properly seized. It agreed with the trial court that the search had not violated petitioner's Fifth Amendment rights because petitioner had not been compelled to do anything. 24 Md. App. 128, 331 A.2d 78 (1975).

We granted certiorari limited to the Fourth and Fifth Amendment issues.

II

The Fifth Amendment, made applicable to the States by the Fourteenth Amendment, *Malloy* v. *Hogan,* 378 U.S. 1, 8 (1964), provides that "(n)o person . . . shall be compelled in any criminal case to be a witness against himself." As the Court often has noted, the development of this protection was in part a response to certain historical practices, such as ecclesiastical inquisitions and the proceedings of the Star Chamber, "which placed a premium on compelling subjects of the investigation to admit guilt from their own lips." The "historic function" of the privilege has been to protect a "natural individual from compulsory incrimination through his own testimony or personal records."

There is no question that the records seized from petitioner's offices and introduced against him were incriminating. Moreover, it is undisputed that some of these business records contain statements made by petitioner.

Petitioner contends that "the Fifth Amendment prohibition against compulsory self-incrimination applies as well to personal business papers seized from his offices as it does to the same papers being required to be produced under a subpoena." He bases his argument, naturally, on dicta in a number of cases which imply, or state, that the search for and seizure of a person's private papers violate the privilege against self-incrimination. Thus, in *Boyd* v. *United States,* the Court said: "(W)e have been unable to perceive that the seizure of a man's private books and papers to be used in evidence against him is substantially different from compelling him to be a witness against himself." And in *Hale* v. *Henkel,* it was observed that "the substance of the offense is the compulsory production of private papers, whether under a search warrant or a subpoena duces tecum, against which the person . . . is entitled to protection."

We do not agree, however, that these broad statements compel suppression of this petitioner's business records as a violation of the Fifth Amendment. In the very recent case of *Fisher* v. *United States,*–U.S.– (1976), the Court held that an attorney's production, pursuant to a lawful summons, of his client's tax records in his hands did not violate the Fifth Amendment privilege of the taxpayer "because enforcement against a taxpayer's lawyer would not 'compel' the taxpayer to do anything—and certainly would not compel him to be a 'witness' against himself." Id., at–(slip op. 5). We recognized that the continued validity of the broad statements contained in some of the Court's earlier cases had been discredited by later opinions. In those earlier cases, the legal predicate for the inadmissibility of the evidence seized was a violation of the Fourth Amendment; the unlawfulness of the search and seizure was thought to supply the compulsion of the accused necessary to invoke the Fifth Amendment. Compulsion of the accused was also absent in *Couch* v. *United States,* where the Court held that a summons served on a taxpayer's accountant requiring him to produce the taxpayer's personal business records in his possession did not violate the taxpayer's Fifth Amendment rights.

Similarly, in this case, petitioner was not asked to say or to do anything. The records seized contained statements that petitioner had voluntarily committed to writing. The search for and seizure of these records were conducted by law enforcement personnel. Finally, when these records were introduced at trial, they were authenticated by a handwriting expert, not by petitioner. Any compulsion of petitioner to speak, other than the inherent psychological pressure to respond at trial to unfavorable evidence, was not present.

This case thus falls within the principle stated by Mr. Justice Holmes: "A party is privileged from producing the evidence but not from its production." *Johnson* v. *United States,* 228 U.S. 457, 458 (1913). This principle recognizes that the protection afforded by the self-incrimination clause of the Fifth Amendment "adheres basically to the person, not to information that may incriminate him." *Couch* v. *United States,* 409 U.S., at 328. Thus, although the Fifth Amendment may protect an individual from complying with a subpoena for the production of his personal records in his possession because the very act of production may constitute a compulsory authentication of incriminating information, see *Fisher* v. *United States,* supra, a seizure of the same materials by law enforcement officers differs in a crucial respect—the individual against whom the search is directed is not required to aid in the discovery, production, or authentication of incriminating evidence.

A contrary determination that the seizure of a person's business records and their introduction into evidence at a criminal trial violates the Fifth Amendment, would undermine the principles announced in earlier cases.

Moreover, a contrary determination would prohibit the admission of evidence traditionally used in criminal cases and traditionally admissible despite the Fifth Amendment. For example, it would bar the admission of an accused's gambling records in a prosecution for gambling; a note given temporarily to a bank teller during a robbery and subsequently seized in the accused's automobile or home in a prosecution for bank robbery; and incriminating notes prepared, but not sent, by an accused in a kidnapping or blackmail prosecution.

We find a useful analogy to the Fifth Amendment question in those cases that deal with the "seizure" of oral communications. As the Court has explained, " '(t)he constitutional privilege against self-incrimination . . . is designed to prevent the use of legal process to force from the lips of the accused individual the evidence necessary to convict him or to force him to produce and authenticate any personal documents or effects that might incriminate him.' " *Bellis* v. *United States,* 417 U.S., at 88, quoting *United States* v. *White,* 322 U.S., at 698. The significant aspect of this principle was apparent and applied in *Hoffa* v. *United States,* 385 U.S. 293 (1966), where the Court rejected the contention than an informant's "seizure" of the accused's conversation with him, and his subsequent testimony at trial concerning that conversation, violated the Fifth Amendment. The rationale was that, although the accused's statements may have been elicited by the informant for the purpose of gathering evidence against him, they were made voluntarily. We see no reasoned distinction to be made between the compulsion upon the accused in that case and the compulsion in this one. In each, the communication, whether oral or written, was made voluntarily. The fact that seizure was contemporaneous with the communication in Hoffa but subsequent to the communication here does not affect the question whether the accused was compelled to speak.

Finally we do not believe that permitting the introduction into evidence of a person's business records seized during an otherwise lawful search would offend or undermine any of the policies undergirding the privilege. *Murphy* v. *Waterfront Comm'n,* 378 U.S. 52, 55 (1964).

In this case, petitioner, at the time he recorded his communication, at the time of the search, and at the time the records were admitted at trial, was not subjected to "the cruel trilemma of self-accusation, perjury or contempt." Ibid. Indeed, he was never required to say or to do anything under penalty of sanction. Similarly, permitting the admission of the records in question does not convert our accusatorial system of justice into an inquisitorial system. "The requirement of specific charges, their proof beyond a reasonable doubt, the protection of the accused from confessions extorted through whatever form of police pressures, the right to a prompt hearing before a magistrate, the right to assistance of counsel, to be supplied by government when circumstances make it necessary, the duty to advise the accused of his constitutional rights—these are all characteristics of the accusatorial system and manifestations of its demands." *Watts* v. *Indiana,* 338 U.S. 49, 54 (1949). None of these attributes is endangered by the introduction of business records "independently secured through skillful investigation." Further, the search for a seizure of business records poses no danger greater than that inherent in every search that evidence will be "elicited by inhumane treatment and abuses." In this case, the statements seized were voluntarily committed to paper before the police arrived to search for them, and petitioner was not treated discourteously during the search. Also, the "good cause" to "disturb," ibid., petitioner was independently determined by the judge who issued the warrants; and the State bore the burden of executing them. Finally, there is no chance, in this case, of petitioner's statements being self-deprecatory and untrustworthy because they were extracted from him —they were already in existence and had been made voluntarily.

We recognize, of course, that the Fifth Amendment protects privacy to some extent. However, "the Court has never suggested that every invasion of privacy violates the privilege." Here, as we have already noted, petitioner was not compelled to testify in any manner.

Accordingly, we hold that the search of an individual's office for business records, their seizure, and subsequent introduction into evidence does not offend the Fifth Amendment's prescription that "(n)o person . . . shall be compelled in any criminal case to be a witness against himself."

III

We turn next to petitioner's contention that rights guaranteed him by the Fourth Amendment were violated because the descriptive terms of the search warrants were so broad as to make them impermissible "general" warrants, and because certain items were seized in violation of the principles of Warden v. Hayden, supra.

The specificity of the search warrants.

In the present case, when the special investigators secured the search warrants, they had been informed of a number of similar charges against petitioner arising out of Potomac Woods transactions, And, by reading numerous documents and records supplied by the Lot 13T and other complainants, and by interviewing witnesses, they had become familiar with petitioner's method of operation. Accordingly, the relevance of documents pertaining specifically to a lot other than Lot 13T, and their admissibility to show the Lot 13T offense, would have been apparent. Lot 13T and the other lot had numerous features in common. Both were in the same section of the Potomac Woods subdivision; both had been owned by the same person; and transactions concerning both had been handled extensively by petitioner. Most important was the fact that there were two deeds of trust in which both lots were listed as collateral. Unreleased liens respecting both lots were evidenced by these deeds of trusts. Petitioner's transactions relating to the other lot, subject to the same liens as Lot 13T, therefore were highly relevant to the question whether his failure to deliver title to Lot 13T free of all encumbrances was mere inadvertance. Although these records subsequently were used to secure additional charges against petitioner, suppression of this evidence in this case was not required. The fact that the records could be used to show intent to defraud with respect to Lot 13T permitted the seizure and satisfied the requirements of *Warden* v. *Hayden.*

The judgment of the Court of Special Appeals of Maryland is affirmed.

It is so ordered.

MR. JUSTICE BRENNAN, dissenting.

CONSIDERATIONS IN LITIGATION*

There are many ways to summarize the area of liability. Maybe one of the best is what might be read into the statement by Dame Elizabeth Words-

* Reprinted with permission from *A CPAs Liability, the Local Practice,* Levine, Mark Lee, Colorado Society of CPAs (1977).

worth, *St. Christopher and Other Poems:*

> *"If all good people were clever,*
> *And all clever people were good,*
> *The world would be nicer than ever*
> *We thought that it possibly could.*
>
> *"But somehow, 'tis seldom or never*
> *That two hit it off as they should;*
> *The good are so harsh to the clever,*
> *The clever so rude to the good."*

CHAPTER 15

Insurance

ERRORS AND OMISSIONS INSURANCE

Because anyone can make an error, even though it may not involve absconding of funds or any intentional act, professional liability insurance is an important part to any practice. The National Association of Real Estate Boards has issued a pamphlet designed for members of the National Association of Realtors relative to an errors and omissions insurance policy. This particular pamphlet emphasizes the vulnerable position of the Realtor. It asks the question of whether the Realtor can afford a lawsuit of one million dollars. Analogies are given to the American Medical Association with regard to the frightening and staggering liability situations with regard to physicians.

PROFESSIONAL LIABILITY COVERAGE
FOR THE PRACTITIONER

Once the practitioner realizes his exposure as a result of the profession, and the possibility that one will commit negligence at some phase within the practice, it becomes apparent that professional liability insurance of some sort is necessary. This type of insurance may be labeled as errors and omissions, general professional coverage, or under some other label.

The following material examines in a very cursory form the potential problem areas when construing and reviewing professional liability policies. The reader should keep in mind that professional liability policies vary in content from insurance company to insurance company, jurisdiction to jurisdiction. Interpretations by various cases may create other variables.

241

Various types of professional liability policies have different clauses and construction. For example, professional liability policies for attorneys vary somewhat from those of doctors, accountants, real estate salespeople, and so forth.

In most circumstances, subject to a great number of exceptions and exclusions, the professional liability policy will cover the liability from acts by the professional, along with the defense and expenses incident to any defense with regard to claims arising from or relative to the professional practice.

GENERAL TYPES OF COVERAGE IN POLICIES

There may be a "claims made" policy or coverage clause in some professional liability policies. A "claims made" policy will only cover the insured for claims *made or brought* during the existence of the policy. That is, the coverage is controlled by the date on which the claim is made and whether the policy exists. This type of policy can be contrasted with an "occurrence" policy, which allows for coverage based on the claim falling within the time frame on which the insurance was carried. As an example, a "claims made" policy that runs from January 1, 1979 through December 31, 1979 would only cover a claim where the *assertion* of that claim or coverage is made in the year 1979. In contrast, an occurrence policy would cover the transaction even if the claim was made in 1980, so long as the policy existed for the calendar year, 1979.

Although we generalize the coverage clauses into a "claims made" or "occurrence" policy, it should be emphasized that there are various forms of policies which may result in a blending of the "claims made" or "occurrence coverage" or some other variables.

Even with a "claims made" policy, it is clear that one cannot have knowledge of a pre-existing area of liability, undertake a "claims made" policy, and have the claim made or asserted within the correct time frame and still have coverage. There would obviously be an exclusion on a "claims made" policy, or for that matter an "occurrence" policy, where the insured had knowledge or should have known of the issue in question which would give rise to the claim.

On an "occurrence" policy, there would be no coverage with regard to a claim or matter that existed previous to taking out the coverage under an "occurrence" policy. There may be various hybrid forms of policies which will not cover any claims before the occurrence policy was undertaken, cover only certain types of claims, or cover other variables.

Since a "claims made" policy will only cover the transaction if the claim is made during the coverage time, there can be some after risk once the policy has been terminated. Thus there is a development of a type of coverage sometimes referred to as "risk tail." This is an attempt to have a policy cover a claim that is made after the "claims made" policy has ended. There is potential exposure because a statute of limitation might not have run on the "tail" of the exposure.

There may be other variables within the types of policies, such as coverage even with a "claims made" policy if notice is held by the insured during the term of the insurance that a possible claim may exist.

Along these same lines, considering the possibility of terminating coverage and having an issue arise subsequently, there can be special retirement type policies to cover exposure subsequent to the termination of practice. In such circumstance the premiums, where this policy is allowed, would be substantially less, because it is an attempt to cover the potential claims which arose during the practice period.

Another general demarcation between insurance policies is between an *indemnification* policy and *legal liability coverage*. The indemnification clause should be less favored by the professional. It means that the liability insurer will not have a duty of payment until the insured has actual loss, which is covered under the terms of the policy. The legal liability provision would allow for coverage previous to the actual showing of damage, although there must be a showing of liability against the insured for the insurer to be responsible.

There can be demarcations in policies to provide for very broad coverage or for specific coverage. Some policies provide a broad statement of coverage and then specifically itemize additional items as part of the broad coverage, to distinguish the finite areas within the broad coverage rule.

PROFESSIONAL CAPACITY

Most insurance policies restrict the coverage of the insured to his actions within his *professional capacity*. If this professional is an attorney, CPA, Realtor, doctor, or whatever, the coverage is for the professional in *that* capacity. This point becomes very important if there is an argument that the professional is not covered because he was not acting in that professional capacity. This issue has arisen in a number of cases, such as an insurance company denying coverage for an accountant where he gave tax advice. The argument by the insurance company is that this was unauthorized practice of *law*, as opposed to accounting practice. Although most insurance companies have lost in this type of case, it illustrates the point mentioned.

There may be many circumstances in which the professional is not rendering professional advice at the given time. Again, this may be illustrated by an attorney who is acting as a Realtor in a transaction. The insurance company may deny coverage because he is acting as a Realtor, as opposed to an attorney. It may also involve an attorney-Realtor, where the coverage is on the real estate side. The insurance company may deny coverage because, they argue, the Realtor was not acting as a Realtor. He was rather acting as an attorney. The examples are manifold. It illustrates the argument by the insurance company as to *exclusion* of coverage because the person is not acting in a professional capacity. The same point can be illustrated in circumstances where the professional acts only in a part-time capacity or works for other entities, such as corporations, management companies, a professor, or the like.

COVERAGE AS TO DOLLAR LIMITS

Another point that must be reviewed very carefully by the insurance company and the insured is the *amount* of coverage. If the coverage is in the *aggregate,* such as $500,000 coverage, there must be clear language to determine if this will apply on any one claim or whether one claim might be limited, for example, to $200,000, with a total or aggregate coverage of $500,000. Most policies are written in a single limit per claim coverage, such as the $200,000, with an aggregate overall limit in a given transaction. This might be illustrated by a claim made by a group against the professional, where there are five people in the group who have suffered $500,000 in damages. The aggregate and per claim limitations would then possibly come into play.

The amount of coverage a professional should have depends on the *nature* of practice by the professional and his exposure. If the transactions generally handled by the practitioner are small in nature and the exposure is small, this would dictate the limits. On the other hand, activities dealing with securities, whether by a CPA, Realtor, or attorney, generally connote a larger exposure.

On this latter point, many policies exclude certain types of coverage without a *special endorsement*. Securities is one area in which some insurance companies either exclude coverage all together or require a separate endorsement, and therefore a separate premium for this coverage.

EXCLUSIONS

There can be a great number of areas in which the professional liability policy might *appear* to give coverage, but in fact there may be holes in the "bulletproof jacket." Coverage may not exist. There are specific exclusions in which there may be no question as to the lack of coverage. The only interpretive problem in many circumstances is to determine if the transaction falls within that category. For example, most policies exclude "fraudulent acts" by the insured. They further exclude "criminal acts" by the insured and anything having a taint of either one of these areas, such as a "dishonest act" which may be construed to be criminal or fraudulent. Some policies are more specific about their exclusions, such as *intentional* fraud as opposed to a *constructive* fraud, the latter type of fraud being one the courts deem to exist, but there may be a lack of "evil" intent.

Another area of potential problems as to excluded coverage deals with the professional's staff. That is, one must carefully review the policy to see what acts are excluded from coverage when undertaken by the professional or by his staff. Once again, dishonest acts by the professional's employees, such as a secretary, may also be excluded from coverage.

OTHER EXCLUSIONS

As mentioned, there can be a number of exclusions in the policy. Keep in mind that the policy must be reviewed in great detail to determine the exact scope of coverage, conditions that exist, areas that are specifically excluded, potential ambiguities. The time frame covered under the policy, parties covered, professional capacity in which coverage exists, and much more.

DEDUCTIBLE CLAUSES

An additional consideration by the professional is the *amount* of deductible. Should the professional have no deductible, $5,000, $10,000, or what deductible? Once again, this seems to be a function of the nature of the professional's practice. However, generally speaking, the insured is concerned with the larger claims and not with the smaller claims. Therefore, a deductible to therefore allow a "self-insurance level" of say $5,000 to $10,000 may make sense.

The premiums saved by a higher deductible may be worthwhile in and of itself. It may encourage a higher deductible amount. The major concern by most professionals is normally on the amount of coverage as opposed to the deductible. Most professionals can withstand a claim of $10,000 against their business. Few professionals could stand a claim of $500,000 if they only had insurance up to $500,000 and the claim, which might be successful, is for $1,000,000.

THE DEFENSE

In addition to the general coverage under the policy, the policy should also consider covering defense of the issues. What claims will the insurer insurance company cover or defend against on behalf of the professional? Along with this same issue, there should be a statement in the policy as to *when* the defense amounts will not be covered, what defense amounts are clearly covered under the policy, and what duties exist on the professional to cooperate with the insurance company.

There can be related issues to the defense question, such as whether the expenses for the defense *reduce* the amount of coverage. Thus if the coverage is $100,000 and the insurance company pays $20,000 in fees for defense of the case, is the insurance company liable for an additional $100,000 or only for $80,000? This is subject to the given type of policy.

Other issues with regard to the defense question will be the *amount* of cooperation that is imposed on the insured, the right to determine the legal counsel used in the case, and other determinations necessary to the defense. What amount of input will the professional have as to the defense of the case involving his reputation and his liability?

CONDITIONAL CLAUSES IN THE CONTRACT

One of the major conditions in the insurance coverage is to make sure the insured *notifies* the insurance company as to any claim or possible claim. A failure to so notify the company may result in prejudicial damage to the insurance company. As such, this has proved to be an out for the insurance company.

If the insured had noticed of a claim against the insured and failed to notify the insurance company, some statutes shift the burden to the insured, and away from the insurer, to show that there was *not* damage to the insurer as to the defense of the case as a result of the insured failing to give notice to the insurer of the claim or potential claim. This often proves to be a very fruitful out for the insurance company. Therefore, all professionals are encouraged to review their policies for *notice* requirements.

There are other conditions and requirements within the policy, such as the duty of cooperation, and the duty to give evidence. These can be conditions of the policy. Therefore, the insured must comply with these to protect his coverage.

OTHER POLICIES

Most insurance policies provide for an exclusion of coverage if another policy covers the claim. If multiple policies cover the same point, there may be a sharing of the liability. In any event, it is important for the insured to recognize this potential exclusion.

Many professionals are purchasing "excess policies" which will cover them on additional liability, once the *primary* policy or primary coverage has been consumed. One must make certain that there is coordination in coverage and proper coverage on the primary policy, versus the excess policy, to ensure that the excess will accomplish the purpose intended. The excess policy usually results in a lower premium cost to the insured as to the excess amount.

CHAPTER 16

Preventive Medicine, Updating Your Knowledge, Steps to Protect the Realtor

UPDATING YOUR KNOWLEDGE

Professional Knowledge. The requirement of a real estate broker to be properly informed and trained under the circumstances has been illustrated time and time again. One older case, *Smith* v. *Fidelity and Columbia Trust Co.,* 12 S.W.2d 276 (1928), supports this proposition. Although this is an older case, it illustrates the importance of a real estate broker being properly trained and nonnegligent in conducting transactions.

In the particular case in question, the issue is one of proper evaluation of the property, where the real estate broker gave an opinion on the same. An important quote from the case reads: "It is the duty of a broker to exert his best efforts and to exercise his best judgment for the benefit of his principal. Like any other agent for pay, it is the broker's duty to advise his principal fully of all of the facts within his knowledge affecting the matter in hand reasonably calculated to influence his judgment, and to make an honest and diligent effort to accomplish the purpose of the agency. The broker is likewise under a duty to possess and employ that degree of skill in a business that is usually possessed and exercised by persons professing that particular calling."

This particular case held that although a house was listed for $30,000 and a subsequent offer was received for $27,000, the failure to seek a higher offer from the person who had previously offered $26,000 was not negligence. Nevertheless, the case does illustrate the potential of keeping the principal-owner informed and the importance of this point.

Would Realtors be Held Liable for Failing to Take Update Courses? An interesting question which may be posed, but cannot be answered by this author, is whether the courts might, in a given case, hold a Realtor liable if he has failed to undertake sufficient *post*-licensing courses or programs to keep a professional status or knowledge level to sustain his position. Obviously, the action could arise in context of a case wherein a Realtor was held to have been negligent or otherwise failed to undertake certain alleged duties. For example, if a Realtor fails to be aware of a major real estate decision that affected his field, such as a tax case which held that a given item was not deductible or that a given type of exchange in real estate was not permitted, it might be argued that the Realtor should have undertaken some sort of professional post-licensing training to allow him to keep current. The requirement to be current and knowledgeable in the field is well established by case law.

STEPS TO PROTECT THE REALTOR

Guidelines to Avoid/Limit Exposure—Protective Steps. List at least 15 items which may cause a suit against you relative to professional conduct as a Realtor and use the cases discussed.

Planning and Protecting—You. Exactly what can the Realtor do to avoid exposure?

The Realtor must realize that he is in no different position from the standpoint of suits than many other professionals. With this in mind, lessons learned and precautions taken by other professionals can be applied to the Realtor.

Considerations might include:

1. *Errors and Omissions Insurance:* This method is not a preventive measure, but it does indicate some support for the symptom and remedial action. As to what types of insurance to maintain, the protection under the insurance, the amount of insurance, and related issues, see Chapter 15.

2. *Professional Care:* The best protection is the exercise of due care (nonnegligent). This does not ensure that one will not be sued. It is clear from many of the cases that injured parties tend to look for possible sources of indemnification.

3. *Documentation:* Spell it out! Documentation in support of your posi-

tion is crucial. If your position is clearly delineated, this should reduce exposure and accusations.

4. *Professional Standards:* Again, the points noted earlier under negligence and due care are stressed by complying with proper standards and the Code of Professional Ethics of the NAR.

5. *Investigation:* The concept of investigation is important. Litigation may be apparent from the inception. If your client is in trouble from the beginning and has a history of bad faith, "tricky deals," and questionable tactics, ask questions about their current activities. You are "requesting" trouble by dealing with this type.

6. *Know Your Field:* Do not try to sell (at least, alone) commercial property (or whatever) if you are not yet qualified.

Insurance. Review errors and omissions insurance in light of the Realtor liability field.

Summary. List at least five areas where you feel you and/or your firm might have exposure and what you might do to reduce this exposure.

Bibliography

Adler, M. F., "Are Real Estate Agencies Entitled to Practice a Little Law" 4
  Arizona L. Rev. 1 (Spring, 1963).
"Anti-trust Law: An Emerging Problem for Florida Realtors," 24 *Univ. of
  Florida L. Rev.* 266 (Winter, 1972).
"Anti-trust Violations in Real Estate Transactions," 60 Ill. L. J. 856 (Jan.,
  1972).
Baier, L. E., "Developing Principles in the Law of Unauthorized Practice Re-
  garding Real Estate Brokers," 9 *St. Louis Univ. L. J.* 127 (Fall, 1964).
Barasch, C. S., "Anti-trust Actions and Commissions," 3 *R.E.L.J.* 227 (Winter,
  1975).
"Blockbusting: Judicial and Legislative Responses to Real Estate Dealers Ex-
  cesses," 22 *DePaul L. Rev.* 818 (Summer, 1973).
Davenport, Gary, "The Colorado Real Estate Recovery Fund Act," *The Colo-
  rado Lawyer,* 1507 (Sept., 1977).
"Duties to Prospective Purchasers," *Brigham Young L. Rev.* 513 (1976).
"Fair Housing Laws and Brokers Defamation Suits," The New York Experience,
  64 *Mich. L. Rev.* 919 (March, 1966).
"Federal Courts-Standing-Concurrent Solicitation Activities of Realtors Confers
  on Attorney Generals Standing to Sue Pursuant to Anti-blockbusting Pro-
  vision of Fair Housing Act of 1968," 2 *Florida State Univ. L. Rev.* 382
  (Spring, 1974).
Graybeal, G. F., "Anti-trust Violations and Real Estate Transactions," 60 *Ill.
  B. J.* 856 (July, 1972).
Jacobson, L. H., "Liability for Sale of Defective Home." 52 *LABJ* 346 (Jan.,
  1977).
"Kickbacks, Rebates and Tying Arrangements and Real Estate Transactions:
  The Federal Real Estate Settlement Act of 1974, Anti-trust and Unfair
  Practices," 2 *Pepperdine L. Rev.* 309 (1975).
"Knight, W. H., "Liability of the Vendor for Misrepresentations by Real Estate
  Agents," 4 *UBC L. Rev.* 195 (Dec., 1969).

"Let the Seller Beware-Unconscionability and The Real Estate Broker's Employment Contract." 5 *Memphis State Univ. L. Rev.* 59 (Fall, 1974).

"Liability for Sale of Defective Homes," 52 *LABJ* 346 (Jan., 1977).

"Liability in Tort for Negligent Misstatement," 7 *Sydney L. Rev.* 293 (Summer, 1974).

"Monopolies-Restraint of Trade-Associations and Clubs," 18 *Western Reserve L. Rev.* 321 (1966).

"New Anti-trust Actions Have Affected Real Estate Brokers' Commissions," 3 *Real Estate L.J.* 227 (Winter, 1975).

"Racial Steering Title VIII," 85 *Yale L. J.* 808 (May, 1976).

"Racial Steering: The Real Estate Brokers Title VIII," 85 *Yale L. J.* 808 (March, 1976).

Reynolds, F. M., "Real Estate Agents and Deposits Again," 88 *Rev.* 184 (April, 1972).

"Sherman Applicability to Real Estate Boards," 10 *American Business L. J.* 139 (Fall, 1972).

Smith, V. E., "Professionalization of Real Estate Brokers-A Realistic Goal," 43 *Lav. Bulletin* 499 (Oct., 1968).

Spellman, H., "Sunshine," 64 *Ill. L. J.* 42 (1975).

Sprig, "Fair Housing-Standing to Sue," 2 *Florida State Univ. L. Rev.* 382 (Spring, 1974).

"Standard for Determining Unauthorized Practice of Law by Real Estate Brokers in Ohio," 40 *Univ. of Cincinnati L. Rev.* 319 (Summer, 1971).

Tuobey, C. G., "Kickbacks, Anti-trust," 2 *Pepperdine L. Rev.* 309 (1975).

"Unauthorized Practice of Law: Attorney v. Real Estate Broker," 7 *Santa Clara Law* 132 (Fall, 1966).

"Unauthorized Practice of Law by Real Estate Brokers in New Jersey. A Call for Compromise," 2 *Rutgers L. J.* 322 (Fall, 1970).

Appendix

Checklists are helpful reminders in any field. With this in mind, the following checklists illustrate certain key items to be considered when offering to purchase a property and at a closing. A reminder, notwithstanding the number of times one has closed a transaction, is of utmost importance, especially when the parties are handling multiple items at a closing. The following are reprinted from the author's texts with Professional Publications and Education, Inc.

CONSIDERATIONS WHEN PURCHASING REAL ESTATE

1. Adjustments
   (a) Taxes.
   (b) Special assessments.
   (c) Personal property tax.
   (d) Insurance.
   (e) Water.
   (f) Utilities.
   (g) Rents and deposits.

2. Other loans.

3. Leases and tenancies.
   (a) Type—oral—written.
   (b) Assignment.
   (c) Estoppel letters.

4. Contingent and/or representations:
   (a) Mortgage assumable.
   (b) No notice for correction.
   (c) Good repair.

    (d)   Loan costs (amount, who pays).
    (e)   Purchase of other property.
    (f)   Possession (rent?).
    (g)   Repairs.
    (h)   Subdivision.
    (i)   Building restrictions.
    (j)   Prepayment penalty.
    (k)   Title.
    (l)   Assumption fee (amount, who pays)
    (m)   Sale of other property
    (n)   Estate court approval.
    (o)   Utilities.
    (p)   Bankruptcy-court approval.
    (q)   Mineral interests (confirmed).
    (r)   Escrow.
    (s)   Assignable.
    (t)   No violation of building or other codes.
    (u)   Broker?
    (v)   Survey.
    (w)   Lease review.
    (x)   Assumption fee? (who pays?).
    (y)   Title policy.
    (z)   Others.
    (aa) Soil.
    (bb) Zoning.
    (cc) Use restrictions.
    (dd) Time to accept—in land.
    (ee) Corporate papers in order (resolutions, resignations, etc.).

5.   Balloon payment.

6.   Acceleration.

    (a)   Interest.
    (b)   Principal.

7.   Corporate Resolutions, etc.

8.   Personal property.

    (1)   Inventory list.
    (2)   Bill of sale.
    (3)   Liens—security check.
    (4)   Allocation of price.

9.   Options.

    (a)   Prior to purchase.
    (b)   After purchase.

10. Recording contract for deed or option.

11. Closing costs.
    - (a) Who pays?
    - (b) Date.

12. As-Is.

13. Assumption.

14. Purchase price—allocate.
    - (a) Where to make payments.
    - (b) Prepayment penalty; Rule of 78's.

15. Description of property.

16. Destruction or damage prior to closing.
    - (a) Risk of loss on whom.
    - (b) Insurance.

17. Remedies.
    - (a) Damages.
    - (b) Specific performance.
    - (c) Other.
    - (d) Combination.

18. Assignment of warranties.

19. Contract shall survive closing unless specific language (written) negates and signed by all.

20. Acknowledgment.

21. Zoning changes during interim.

22. Repairs.

23. Farm lease.

24. Pests (termites clause).

25. Title problems:
    - (a) Time to correct.
    - (b) Effect of violation.

26. Right to assign.

27. Time to accept offer. Signed copy delivered in land by set date.

28. Title—how take.

29. Earnest money.

30. Down payment.

31. Right to sublet.

32. Destruction.

33. Signatures.

34. Prorations.

35. Adjustments.

36. Vacancy and rentals during interim.

37. New financing.
    - (a) By owner.
    - (b) Separate source.
    - (c) Purchase—money loan.
    - (d) Security:
        - (a) Trust deed.
        - (b) Mortgage.
        - (c) Collateral security.
        - (d) Security agreement.
        - (e) Rent assignment.

38. Personal property; schedule?

39. Parties (assignee?)

40. Restrictions.

41. Reservations.

42. Easements.

43. Covenants.

LEASE CHECK SHEET

1. Type of lease.
2. Identify landlord and tenant.
3. Spell out definitions.
4. Address of landlord and tenant.
5. Address of property being rented—legal and common number.
6. Any trade names used on tenant and landlord.
7. Attach description and chart of premises.
8. Commencement date of lease if different than date of lease agreement.
9. Provide for pro rata lease for short month.
10. Provide for completion date if not constructed.
11. Provide for minimum guaranteed rental and percentage rental over minimum.

12. Security deposit.

13. Use of security deposit—interest, and segregation.

14. Permitted use of leased premises.

15. Granting clause of the premises.

16. Construction limitations on new premises; provide for occupancy date and determination of construction.

17. Provide for when rent commences.

18. Provide for memorandum of lease—short form.

19. Provide for joint opening of shopping center.

20. Allow exculpatory language if financing and other approvals is not obtained.

21. Exculpatory for commitments.

22. Minimum percentage of lease up to bind the landlord.

23. Rent: where paid; minimum guaranteed rent; percentage rent; dates of payment; termination of rent for any reason; failure to pay rent; penalty; late charges; termination and interim postponement of rent.

24. Definition of gross sales or other method to compute percentage rent; certification regarding rent; CPA, changes if error in rent.

25. Utilities, private streets, change of use, parking spaces, dimensions, employee use, customer use, subtenant use, parking, storage, and others.

26. Construction: what to construct and where; exhibits.

27. Use and care of premises: duty of landlord and tenant regarding repairs, hours to occupy and not to occupy; late charges and additional charges regarding occupancy, written consent, additional rent, restrictions on use of premises, and restrictions with regard to type of sales and outside of leased premises; seasonal sales.

28. Repair and care: duty of landlord and tenant regarding repairs; exterior and interior premises, modifications of the premises, trash pick up and clean up; inspection of premises; delivery of merchandise and timing on same; displaying of merchandise, signs, canopies, and the like.

28. Advertisements, common promotions, licenses, compliance with ordinances and the laws.

29. Maintenance and repair: grass, exterior and interior, subletting, landlord right to correct and charge; condition and repair of premises at expiration of lease; restoration of premises at whose expense.

30. Alterations: A written approval required; restore premises at end of lease at option of landlord; fixtures and improvements to remain property of?

31. Indemnity and insurance: Who maintains, indemnity clauses, proof of insurance, right to secure insurance, no partnership?

32. Right of access: right to inspect, to repair, approve and review; use of roof for landlord.

33. Rules and regulations: signs, decoration, merchant's group, lighting, condition of premises, type of customers, and the like.

34. Utilities and other costs: who pays, when paid, how billed, late charge, interest, in name of tenant, duty to supply; effect of impossibility or impracticability.

35. Interruption of services: no liability of landlord.

36. Insurance: liability, property, and personal; other types of insurance.

37. Casualty loss: no liability of landlord's; termination of rent? Percentage of destruction? Duty to repair? Application of Tenant's insurance to landlord to repair.

38. Eminent domain: responsibility for; when determined; right to proceeds; percentage of area taken; duty to continue rent; when determined to cut off; compensation; common areas.

39. Assignment and subletting: requirements for; written approval; remaining liable; transfer of corporate or other entity interest causes same; restriction on mortgages, and like types of arrangements.

40. Property taxes, personal and real, other types of taxes, when determined, when billed, penalty for non-payment; other types of taxes, income, excise, gift, and new taxes; tenant not pay by law; revise minimum rental.

41. Default: rights of tenant and lessor; terminate lease, terminate part, damages, injunction, written notice; transfer and fraud creditors; lien on property, bankruptcy, receivership, vacating premises; failure to complete work; mechanic's liens assume abandon; liability for possession; nonwaiver; security deposit; attorney fees and costs.

42. Landlord's lien: does exist? on? security interest, local law, fixtures, inventory, foreclosure.

43. Holding over.

44. Subordination clause.

45. Merchant's association; duty to join and cost, charge to whom, obligations of.

46. Notices: in writing, address of each, failure to give.

47. Miscellaneous: not partnership or other relationship; reasonable construction; captions; waiver and covenants; other waivers, statute of limitations; construed by law; attorn; estoppel letters; peaceable and quiet enjoinment; covenant not to compete; entire agreement; oral representation; no broker; duty to pay commission; inure to; options to

renew and terms of options; net lease or general intent; use of security deposit;
48. Liabilities of parties: personally or entity?
49. Signatures.
50. Money, keys, miscellaneous.
51. Exhibits.
52. Addendum noted as part of lease in the lease.
53. Maximum rent, minimum rent.
54. Options: term, conditions, etc.
55. Competing leases.
56. Financing condition; other conditions?

CLOSING CHECKLIST

	Ordered	Received	Notes

1. Inventory lists.
2. Possession date (rent? FED?).
3. Water stock.
4. Warranty.
5. Well registration, certificates of approval.
6. Regulation Z. (Disclosure and right to rescind).
7. Property report, signature on.
8. Zoning and use letter.
9. Abstract.
10. Survey—run to purchaser.
11. a. Personal property tax certificate.
    b. Search certificate—security.
12. Certificate of taxes due.
    Amortization schedule.
13. Assumption statement.
    a. Assumption form.
    b. Escrow funds assigned.
14. Water and sewer.

15. Gas and electric.

16. Contingencies.

17. Ditch and storage rights.

18. Bulk sales notice/w affidavits.

19. Security deposit disclosure statement.

20. Special items.

21. Service contracts—assign?

22. Lease assignments; tenant notice.

23. Estoppel letters from tenants, etc.

24. Rent schedule and deposits.

25. Insurance (assign).
    a. Title
    b. Fire and MP

26. S & L pay off form.

27. Certificate of municipality re
    specials on personal property.

38. Boundary fence (who owns).

29. Title opinion.

30. Title commitment.
    a. Conditions.
    b. Endorsements.

31. Title for mobile homes.

32. FHA: appraisal statement.
    Firm commitment.
    Certificates.
    Antidiscrimination forms.
    Certificate on covenants.
    Final FHA affidavit.

33. Allocation agreement.

34. Copy of listing sheet.

35. Contract to purchase.

36. Mechanic lien waivers.

37. Key.

38. Money.
39. Bill of sale.
40. Warranties, assigned.
41. Other assignments.
42. Assignment of rents. (UCC)
43. Note.
44. Deed.
45. Deed of trust.
46. Receipts.
47. Closing statements.
48. Title company called.
49. Abstract and opinion.
50. Copy of assumed deed of trust.
51. UCCC.

INDEX

263